NINTH EDITION

THE COLLECTOR'S ENCYCLOPEDIA OF
DEPRESSION GLASS

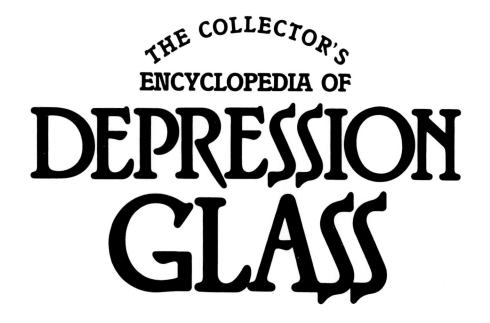

BY GENE FLORENCE

COLLECTOR BOOKS
A Division of Schroeder Publishing Co., Inc.

The current values in this book should be used only as a guide. They are not intended to set prices, which vary from one section of the country to another. Auction prices as well as dealer prices vary greatly and are affected by condition as well as demand. Neither the Author nor the Publisher assumes responsibility for any losses that might be incurred as a result of consulting this guide.

ACKNOWLEDGMENTS

Writing this ninth book has been more of a problem than I could have imagined. Last year when we looked into computers to buy, I was told that getting the Macintosh II would save me tons of work. My current books could be "scanned" and all the listings information sent to me on disks. All I would have to do is write the headings for each pattern and reprice the book. That should cut my time in half! As I sit at my desk in early June, I am three weeks behind where I should be. All that baloney about scanning did not work and everything in the book had to be re-entered in the new system. That is supposed to be great for next time! On top of everything else, my forty-five year old eyes suddenly "went"; and after several days of "blinding" headaches with little or no work accomplished, I had to adjust to bifocal glasses on top of all the other hassles. I even had "special" glasses designed for work at my computer four weeks ago today! As I finish this book, they still haven't arrived from the lab!

There have been over two hundred measurements corrected in this book. These corrections have occurred due to original catalogue mistakes, typing mistakes and errors in measurement in the past. Realize, too, that the same plate or tumbler can vary in each pattern, especially if it were made for a long time. Be sure to read about measurements on page 4.

Amazingly, even after all these years, there have also been approximately **one hundred newly discovered pieces added to the listings!** By the same token, there have been twenty-one deletions from the book of pieces that have never been found that were listed in catalogues or had mysteriously appeared in my listings. Computer people explain it as the "cosmic ray" theory. If you can not find out why it happened, place the blame on something else! Those of you who feel that nothing new is ever found had better look closely at your favorite pattern!

Thanks to all you readers and people at shows who kept me inspired with your letters, cards and reports of new information! Thanks for the measurements and the photographs confirming new discoveries! Those photographs are invaluable when confirming a new piece. If you have trouble photographing glass, take it outside in natural light, place the glass on a neutral surface and forget the camera has a flash attachment. A cloudy bright day works best. Please enclose **SASE** (self addressed stamped envelope) that is **large** enough to send back your pictures, if you wish them returned!

A special thanks to all the clubs and show promoters who invited me to attend their shows. I have enjoyed them, attained knowledge from them, and I hope, contributed to them. Today, more and more shows are conducting seminars to increase collecting knowledge. This is a valuable trend if not overly done at the expense of dealer sales. Now, it has increased attendance at shows - and hopefully, collector's knowledge of glassware!

Cathy, my wife, has become chief editor, critic and non-typist. This is the first book that she has not typed a word for me. (My five words a minute typing is one of the reasons I am three weeks behind). She dutifully tries to make sense out of my run-on or "non" sentences. (I know what I mean!)

A special thanks to "Grannie Bear," my Mom, who spent hours wrapping and packing glass for the numerous photography sessions we had for this book. She, also, has kept records since the last book of prices, measurements and new listings which help me when I write.

Thanks, too, to Cathy's Mom, Sibyl, who helped Cathy sort and pack glass for days and days! My gratitude to Dad, Charles, Sibyl and Marie who kept everything under control at home while we travelled. Thanks to Chad and Marc for keeping the house in one piece - even during the February basement flood!

Glass and information for this book were furnished by Earl and Beverly Hines, Byron Canine, Dot and Jim Kimball, George and Veronica Sionakides, Gladys Florence and numerous readers from across the U.S.A., Canada, England, New Zealand and Australia!

Photographs for this book were made at Curtis and Mays Studio in Paducah by Tom Clouser. Glass arranging, unpacking, sorting, carting and repacking for six photography sessions over two years was accomplished by Steve Quertermous, Jane White, Teri Hatch and Cathy Florence. There is no way anyone could believe what we have to do to get you these photographs short of being there. One helper remarked that she still didn't believe it after four days of working!

Thanks to the special people in the Editing Department at Collector Books: Steve Quertermous, Gail Ashburn, Sherry Kraus and Lisa Chappell who caught some mistakes that Cathy and I missed!

As we go to press with the Ninth Edition, I wish to thank my readers for making this the best selling glass book in America; and I wish you much success in your collecting!

FOREWORD

Depression Glass as defined in this book is the colored glassware made primarily during the Depression years in the colors of amber, blue, black, crystal, green, pink, red, yellow and white. There are other colors and some glass made before, as well as after, this time period; but primarily, the glass within this book was made from the 1920's through the 1930's. This book is mostly concerned with the inexpensively made dinnerware turned out by machine in quantity and sold through the smaller stores or given away as promotional or premium items for other products of that time. Depression glass was often packed in cereal boxes, flour bags or given as gifts at the local movie theaters.

There have been changes in the collecting of Depression Glass since my first book was sold in 1972. Since then over a million of my books have been sold! Prices have soared; seemingly plentiful patterns have been gathered into vast collections and removed from the market. Smaller Depression patterns and previously ignored crystal colors have picked up buyers; in fact, ANYTHING that is Depression Glass, whether it is a known pattern or not, suddenly has added value and collectability. Collectors have become more knowledgeable and sophisticated in their collecting. Many collectors are enhancing their collections of "A to W" (Adam to Windsor) with patterns of hand-made glassware made during the same time period. This broadening interest of collectors prompted me to research and write three more books in the field of Depression Glass, one on ELEGANT glassware of the time, one on the glass KITCHENWARE items of Depression times and another on the VERY RARE glassware of the Depression era.

I am including some later patterns in this edition that are being sought by collectors. These patterns encompass the 1950's and even the early 1960's. This book provides what the collector wants and I am having to change my thinking on the later made glassware to keep up with demand.

Information for this book comes via research, experience, fellow dealers, collectors and over 750,000 miles of travel pursuant to glassware. Too, some of the interesting information has come from readers who were kind enough to share catalogues, magazines, photographs of glass and their special knowledge with me. These gestures I particularly treasure.

PRICING

ALL PRICES IN THIS BOOK ARE RETAIL PRICES FOR MINT CONDITION GLASSWARE. THIS BOOK IS INTENDED TO BE ONLY A GUIDE TO PRICES AS THERE ARE SOME REGIONAL PRICE DIFFERENCES WHICH CANNOT REASONABLY BE DEALT WITH HEREIN.

You may expect dealers to pay from thirty to fifty percent less than the prices quoted. Glass that is in less than mint condition, i. e. chipped, cracked, scratched or poorly molded, will bring only a small percentage of the price of glass that is in mint condition.

Prices have become pretty well nationally standardized due to national advertising carried on by dealers and due to the Depression Glass Shows which are held from coast to coast. However, **there are still some regional differences in prices due** partly **to glass being more readily available in some areas than in others.** Too, companies distributed certain pieces in some areas that they did not in others. Generally speaking, however, prices are about the same among dealers from coast to coast.

Prices tend to increase dramatically on rare items and, in general, they have increased as a whole due to more and more collectors entering the field and people becoming more aware of the worth of Depression Glass.

One of the more important aspects of this book is the attempt made to illustrate as well as realistically price those items which are in demand. The desire was to give you the most accurate guide to collectible patterns of Depression Glass available.

MEASUREMENTS

To illustrate why there are discrepancies in measurements, I offer the following sample from just two years of Hocking's catalogue references:

Year		Ounces		Ounces		Ounces
1935	Pitcher	37,58,80	Flat Tumbler	5,9,13½	Footed Tumbler	10,13
1935	Pitcher	37,60,80	Flat Tumbler	5,9,10,15	Footed Tumbler	10,13
1936	Pitcher	37,65,90	Flat Tumbler	5,9,13½	Footed Tumbler	10,15
1935	Pitcher	37,60,90	Flat Tumbler	5,9,13½	Footed Tumbler	10,15

All measurements in this book are exact as to some manufacturer's listing or to actual measurement. You may expect variance of up to ½ inch or 1-5 ounces. This may be due to mold variation or changes made by the manufacturer.

INDEX

ADAM JEANNETTE GLASS COMPANY, 1932-1934

Colors: Pink, green, crystal, yellow, some Delphite blue. (*See Reproduction Section*)

The Adam/Sierra butter dish is shown on the left in the picture. If you look closely you can see the Sierra design on the top along with the Adam design. The top has both designs. Adam is on the outside of the top and Sierra is on the inside of the top only. You can find these tops on either the Adam or Sierra butter bottoms. The bottoms contain only one pattern. To be this combination butter it has to have BOTH patterns and not one piece of each pattern as I have seen priced as the rare butter. An explanation of how this could happen has been in earlier books.

Although a fair number of Floral lamps have been found, most notably on the Northwest coast, very few of the Adam lamps have been found. You can see Floral lamps which are designed the same as in Adam under that pattern. A sherbet is frosted to hide the wiring and a notch is cut in the top edge to accommodate a switch. A metal cover is applied to the top of the frosted sherbet with a tall bulb connected to a switch which goes through the notch. The prices below are for working lamps. It is the bulb that is hard to find. Notched, frosted sherbets can be found.

There are many pink vases that sit very lopsided. Many collectors are not willing to pay the high price for these. You have to decide if you want a "leaner" or not.

As with several other Jeannette patterns, the sugar and candy lids are interchangeable. Candy dishes have not been reproduced! I had to referee an argument on that point in Nashville recently. Keep up with the reproductions by subscribing to a monthly paper. See back of the book (page 222) for information.

Green Adam is much harder to find than the pink. There are more pieces shown on the right than I have ever shown before! Prices have been rather steady in green for quite a while. They seem ripe for a surge. The butter dish, candy, candlesticks and shakers have all but disappeared. If you start collecting green Adam, buy those pieces first!

Do not use the information given in the Reproduction Section in the back of the book for any other **pieces** in a pattern. You can not apply the directions of the arrows on the butter to any other pieces in Adam. It only applies to the butter. No other pieces in Adam have been reproduced. This goes for all reproductions I have listed in the back. Only apply the yardsticks I have listed for the piece I am describing. Transferring information to some other item will not work.

Inner rims of cereal bowls and other Adam pieces need to be checked carefully. They experienced damage from stacking over the years. It is fine to purchase these as long as you do not pay "mint" prices. Damaged glass is becoming more and more of a problem in collecting. You will have to decide if you are willing to "settle" for less than perfect glass. If it comes time to resale, you will be happier with the price obtained if you purchased mint glassware. Prices in this book are for "mint" condition glass. Some damaged glass can be repaired by competent workmen, but repaired glass should be so labeled.

	Pink	Green			Pink	Green
Ash Tray, ¾"	24.00	18.00	** Cup		19.00	17.00
Bowl, 4¾" Dessert	10.00	10.00	Lamp		225.00	235.00
Bowl, 5¾" Cereal	32.50	30.00	Pitcher, 8", 32 oz.		27.50	35.00
Bowl, 7¾"	16.00	15.00	Pitcher, 32 oz. Round Base		40.00	
Bowl, 9", No Cover	22.00	35.00	Plate, 6" Sherbet		4.00	4.50
Bowl, Cover, 9"	18.00	25.00	*** Plate, 7¾" Square Salad		8.50	9.00
Bowl, 9" Covered	45.00	65.00	Plate, 9" Square Dinner		18.00	17.00
Bowl, 10" Oval	16.00	18.00	Plate, 9" Grill		14.00	13.00
Butter Dish Bottom	15.00	60.00	Platter, 11¾"		15.00	17.00
Butter Dish Top	45.00	195.00	Relish Dish, 8" Divided		10.00	13.00
Butter Dish & Cover	60.00	255.00	Salt & Pepper, 4" Footed		42.50	85.00
Butter Dish Combination			**** Saucer, 6" Square		4.00	5.00
with Sierra Pattern	550.00		Sherbet, 3"		19.00	32.00
Cake Plate, 10" Footed	15.00	18.00	Sugar		12.00	15.00
* Candlesticks, 4" Pr.	60.00	80.00	Sugar/Candy Cover		17.50	32.50
Candy Jar & Cover, 2½"	62.50	80.00	Tumbler, 4½"		20.00	18.00
Coaster,3¼"	16.00	13.50	Tumbler, 5½" Iced Tea		45.00	35.00
Creamer	13.00	15.00	Vase, 7½"		185.00	37.50

* Delphite	$175.00		
** Yellow	$85.00		
*** Round Pink	$50.00	Yellow $85.00	
**** Round Pink	$50.00	Yellow $65.00	

Please refer to Foreword for pricing information

AMERICAN PIONEER LIBERTY WORKS, 1931-1934

Colors: Pink, green, amber and crystal.

American Pioneer has been collected in green more than any other color; but, at present, there appears to be enough pink available to supply those who wish to collect it. Be aware that there are several shades of green. You can see two distinct shades in the lower picture; color variances do not seem to bother collectors as much as in some other Depression glass patterns. American Pioneer collectors are just happy to acquire any new piece.

The dresser set has become the most valuable item in the set; to date, it has only been found in green. This set has become a hot property due, in part, to the many perfume and cologne bottle collectors searching for those collectibles. Many times an item in a Depression glass set becomes more valuable because of collectors from another collecting field. It makes for heated competition, and some frustration, if you are looking for such an item for your collection.

A new listing for this book is the lamp shown in the lower picture in green. The base is similar to a candle holder in some other patterns, but there has never been a candle found in American Pioneer like this. These were discovered in New England. The base is only 1¾" tall and the lamp stands a total of 9½" to top. One recently sold for $45.00. The 8½" glass lamp can be seen in some of my earlier editions. I have been unable to find one to photograph lately. That may give you a hint as to its scarcity!

The few collectors for amber pieces have told me that there is little being found except basic luncheon pieces. To date, the only amber covered pitchers ever found are shown in the top picture. The liners for the pitchers (urns) are the regular 6" and 8" plates. That ought to make finding liners easy except for the 6" pink plate, which is rare.

At a recent show, it was pointed out to me that all cups In American Pioneer aren't the same. Some have more rim flair than others. We measured one cup with a 4" diameter being 2¼" tall while another had 3⅝" diameter and was 2⅜" tall.

There may be additional items in American Pioneer which I do not have listed; so if you find a new piece, be sure to let me know. I do appreciate the information that you readers take time to share with me; and I'm making a point to pass the information along to the readers of my books.

	Crystal, Pink	Green		Crystal, Pink	Green
*Bowl, 5" Handled	12.50	15.00	Lamp, 5½" Round, Ball		
Bowl, 8¾" Covered	80.00	100.00	Shape (Amber $80.00)	60.00	
Bowl, 9" Handled	15.00	20.00	Lamp, 8½" Tall	75.00	95.00
Bowl, 9¼" Covered	80.00	100.00	Mayonnaise, 4¼"	50.00	75.00
Bowl, 10¾" Console	40.00	50.00	**Pitcher, 5" Covered Urn	115.00	145.00
Candlesticks, 6½" Pr.	55.00	75.00	***Pitcher, 7" Covered Urn	135.00	175.00
Candy Jar and Cover, 1 lb	65.00	85.00	Plate, 6"	10.00	12.00
Candy Jar and Cover, 1½ lb.	75.00	100.00	*Plate, 6" Handled	10.00	12.00
Cheese and Cracker Set (In-			*Plate, 8"	6.00	8.00
dented Platter and Comport)	40.00	50.00	*Plate, 11½" Handled	12.00	15.00
Coaster, 3½"	20.00	22.00	*Saucer	3.00	4.00
Creamer, 2¾"	15.00	18.00	Sherbet, 3½"	12.00	16.00
*Creamer, 3½"	16.00	19.00	Sherbet, 4¾"	22.00	25.00
*Cup	8.00	10.00	Sugar, 2¾"	15.00	18.00
Dresser Set (2 Cologne,			*Sugar, 3½"	16.00	19.00
Powder Jar, on Indented 7½" Tray)		275.00	Tumbler, 5 oz. Juice	20.00	25.00
Goblet, 4", 3 oz. Wine	30.00	40.00	Tumbler, 4", 8 oz.	20.00	27.50
Goblet, 6", 8 oz. Water	30.00	35.00	Tumbler, 5", 12 oz.	30.00	40.00
Ice Bucket, 6"	35.00	45.00	Vase, 7", 4 Styles	65.00	85.00
Lamp, 1¾", w/metal pole 9½"		45.00	Vase, 9", round		175.00
			Whiskey, 2¼", 2 oz.	35.00	

*Amber - Triple the price of pink unless noted

**Amber $250.00

***Amber $300.00

Please refer to Foreword for pricing information.

8

AMERICAN SWEETHEART MacBETH-EVANS GLASS COMPANY, 1930-1936

Colors: Pink, Monax, red, blue; some Cremax and color trimmed Monax.

American Sweetheart continues to attract new collectors. There are many reasons for this, but availability is a major asset for this pattern. It comes in numerous colors; it has many easily found items (as well as rarer ones); and it has not been reproduced. An abundant supply of Monax (white color) still prevails. New collectors can still find basic pieces such as cups, saucers, plates, sugar and creamers at reasonable prices. The additional rare pieces offer a challenge to the newer collector as well as those advanced collectors who have already bought all the basic pieces.

Pitchers, tumblers and shakers continue to be the nemesis of collectors of the pink. Many collectors settle for the water sized tumbler without adding juice and iced tea tumblers to their set. The smaller pitcher, shown on the right, is not as plentiful as its larger counter part; however, not all collectors try to find two pitchers to go with their set. Please note that there are pitchers shaped like American Sweetheart that do not have the design of American Sweetheart. These are **not** American Sweetheart (**or** Dogwood), but are blanks made by MacBeth-Evans to go with the plain, no design tumblers they made.

Monax soups, both cream and flat, have become difficult to find. For the novice, a cream soup is two handled and was used for consomme or creamed soups. A pink cream soup can be seen in the lower right hand corner of the top picture . The soups were never a part of basic sets. Today, that means that there are fewer of these to be found. The sugar lid and shakers in monax are finally beginning to move up in price. The sugar lid price has been stuck on the $150.00 mark for several years, but the addition of new collectors has finally caused this price to creep upward. Shakers have just begun to be in short supply for the same reasons, but their price rise seems to be slower. I can remember the early days when $15.00 for a pair of Depression shakers seemed like robbery! Now, $100.00 each, seems like a fair price for many shakers.

Sets of pink and Monax are readily garnered with patience and money. Both colors have tid-bit sets, with a two tier set being shown in Monax. The origin of many of these sets has been questioned over the years. Although many were made at the factory, others were newly made by someone in the St. Louis area in the early 1970's. If you wish to buy a tid-bit, remember that it is almost impossible to tell newly made from old. Because of this, I do not list a price for tid-bits unless they are made up of hard to find plate sizes. Most original tid-bits sell in the $50.00 range.

In the top picture note the two sizes of sherbets on the left. Although the sherbet in front looks much larger than the one on the plate, there is only ½" difference in diameter. The smaller, 3¾", is more difficult to find than the larger; but many collectors only buy one size sherbet, making the prices closer together than rarity indicates. Many times an item is rare, but if few collectors desire it, then the price remains reasonable.

	Pink	Monax
Bowl, 3¾" Flat Berry	27.50	
Bowl, 4½" Cream Soup	32.50	42.50
Bowl, 6" Cereal	10.00	8.50
Bowl, 9" Round Berry	22.50	42.50
Bowl, 9½" Flat Soup	30.00	42.50
Bowl, 11" Oval Vegetable	32.50	47.50
Bowl, 18" Console		285.00
Creamer, Footed	8.00	7.50
Cup	10.00	7.00
Lamp shade		400.00
Plate, 6" or 6½" Bread & Butter	2.50	2.00
Plate, 8" Salad	7.00	6.00
Plate, 9" Luncheon		8.00
Plate, 9¾" Dinner	16.00	13.00
Plate, 10¼" Dinner		14.00
Plate, 11" Chop Plate		9.00
Plate, 12" Salver	9.00	9.00
Plate, 15½" Server		160.00

	Pink	Monax
Platter, 13" Oval	20.00	42.00
Pitcher, 7½", 60 oz.	400.00	
Pitcher, 8", 80 oz.	375.00	
Salt and Pepper, Footed	285.00	210.00
Saucer	2.50	1.50
Sherbet, 3¾" Footed	13.00	
Sherbet, 4¼" Footed (Design Inside or Outside)	10.00	13.00
Sherbet in Metal Holder (Crystal Only)	3.00	
Sugar, Open, Footed	7.50	5.00
* Sugar Lid		165.00
Tid-bit, 2 Tier, 8" & 12"	50.00	50.00
Tid-bit, 3 Tier, 8", 12" & 15½"		175.00
Tumbler, 3½", 5 oz.	47.50	
Tumbler, 4¼", 9 oz.	45.00	
Tumbler, 4¾", 10 oz.	60.00	

*Two style knobs.

Please refer to Foreword for pricing information

AMERICAN SWEETHEART (Cont.)

Blue American Sweetheart still commands more attention than red. Two reasons for that are the abundance of red in comparison to the blue and that there are more people who prefer blue glass to red in any glassware. Mostly, red and blue American Sweetheart was sold in fifteen piece settings consisting of four each cups, saucers and 8" plates with a creamer, sugar and 12" salver.

Note the red sherbet shown on the left in the top picture. This sherbet was made from the mould shape of American Sweetheart, but does not carry the design as we know it. As with the pink pitchers discussed on page 10, these are not American Sweetheart but are only shaped like American sweetheart. You can also find 8" plates and 6" cereal bowls without the design in both red and blue.

For those who are not familiar with terminology, Cremax is the beige-like color illustrated by the 8" bowl turned upside down on the left in the top picture. Compare that color to the Monax 15½" server next to the bowl. That server is missing the handle and is on a lazy susan (ball bearing) base.

The 8" Monax plate with the "Indian Trail" advertisement is the only one I have owned, but I have heard of other ads on these plates. The pattern shot below is of a green trimmed shade found on a floor lamp belonging to a California collector.

Color trimmed Monax (shown in previous books) turns up infrequently. Many collectors try to find a piece or two, but there is not enough found for many collectors to have sets of the colored trims. You will find pieces trimmed in pink, green, yellow or black. The black trimmed has a bluish/gray panel extending to the black edge and is called "Smoke" by collectors. Much of Monax American Sweetheart has a bluish cast to it, but to be "Smoke" it will always have a black trim at the edge. Real 22K gold is also found as a trim on Monax. There is no premium for the gold trim; in fact, many dealers have difficulty selling it because it is difficult to find a full set with gold that is not worn. The gold, and only the gold, can be removed by using a pencil eraser on it. Don't try to use a scouring pad since you may damage the glass!

	Red	Blue	Cremax	Smoke & Other Trims
Bowl, 6" Cereal			8.00	30.00
Bowl, 9" Round Berry			30.00	75.00
Bowl, 18" Console	650.00	750.00		
Creamer, Footed	75.00	85.00		65.00
Cup	65.00	85.00		55.00
Lamp shade			400.00	
Lamp (Floor with Brass Base)			600.00	
Plate, 6" Bread and Butter				15.00
Plate, 8" Salad	40.00	65.00		25.00
Plate, 9" Luncheon				30.00
Plate, 9¾" Dinner				50.00
Plate, 12" Salver	115.00	135.00		75.00
Plate, 15½" Server	225.00	285.00		
Platter, 13" Oval				95.00
Saucer	18.00	22.50		15.00
Sherbet, 4¼" Footed (Design Inside or Outside)				30.00
Sugar, Open Footed	65.00	75.00		60.00
Tid-bit, 2 Tier, 8" & 12"	165.00	200.00		
Tid-bit, 3 Tier, 8", 12" & 15½"	425.00	525.00		

Please refer to Foreword for pricing information

ANNIVERSARY JEANNETTE GLASS COMPANY, 1947-1949

Colors: Pink, recently crystal and iridescent.

Anniversary is purchased by Depression Glass collectors, but it was made much later than the Depression era. Jeannette continued production of this pattern well into the 1970's. The pink was only listed in catalogues from 1947 until 1949, but crystal and the iridized color could be bought in boxed sets in "dish barn" outlets as late as 1975. I am seeing more and more iridized Anniversary at flea markets and other outlets now. It is often priced and marked as if it were Carnival glass, but it is actually selling at prices more comparable to pink than that of crystal now.

While there is a steady demand for pink, prices for crystal Anniversary have remained stagnant for quite a while. If a few more buyers start looking for the crystal, they will discover that it is not very plentiful and the price on the harder to find pieces might begin to rise again. Those items that are hardest to find include the butter dish, pin up vase, candy dish, wine glass and sandwich plate. I might add that the bottom to the butter is harder to find than the top. This seems to hold true for many of the Depression patterns which have heavy lids and smaller bottoms. Evidently, dropping a heavy lid on smaller butter bottoms destroyed many of those over the years.

I still get letters about the word comport after all these years. The Jeannette catalog from 1947 lists the open, three-legged candy as a comport and not a compote. They mean the same thing, but terminology does change.

	Crystal	Pink		Crystal	Pink
Bowl, 4⅞" Berry	1.50	3.00	Pickle Dish, 9"	3.00	7.00
Bowl, 7⅜" Soup	4.00	8.50	Plate, 6¼" Sherbet	1.25	2.00
Bowl, 9" Fruit	7.00	14.00	Plate, 9" Dinner	3.50	6.00
Butter Dish Bottom	10.00	20.00	Plate, 12½" Sandwich Server	4.00	8.00
Butter Dish Top	12.50	22.00	Relish Dish, 8"	4.50	7.50
Butter Dish and Cover	22.50	45.00	Saucer	1.00	1.50
Candy Jar and Cover	17.50	30.00	Sherbet, Footed	2.50	5.00
Cake Plate, 12½"	5.50	8.50	Sugar	2.00	5.00
Cake Plate w/Metal Cover	12.00	15.00	Sugar Cover	4.00	7.50
Candlestick, 4⅞" Pr.	12.50		Vase, 6½"	9.00	20.00
Comport, Open, 3 Legged	3.50	8.00	Vase, Wall Pin-up	10.00	17.50
Creamer, Footed	3.50	7.50	Wine Glass, 2½ oz.	5.00	11.00
Cup	2.50	4.50			

AUNT POLLY U.S. GLASS COMPANY, Late 1920's

Colors: Blue, green, iridescent.

Aunt Polly collectors are finding several pieces extremely difficult to find. The oval vegetable, sugar lid, shakers and vase have always been a problem, but several collectors are having trouble finding sherbet plates. I had not noticed this until it was pointed out to me; and now, I have to agree after searching for a year without finding a mint condition plate. This pattern is very prone to mould imperfections. It has very roughly made seams on most pieces. For collectors who are adamant about mint condition, I suggest you look for some other pattern. Aunt Polly would drive you to distraction.

Blue is still the number one color collected, but there are a few collectors of the iridized and green. The major difficulty in collecting green is the varying shades of green. Some green is almost yellow in appearance as you can see in the photograph on the next page. Note the two handled candy in the foreground. The lid for that candy is the same as the sugar, but for some reason the candy has never been found in blue.

Unfortunately, there are no cups or saucers in Aunt Polly. The popularity of this pattern would soar if any were ever found. That malady affects the other U. S. Glass patterns such as Strawberry and Cherryberry.

	Green, Iridescent	Blue		Green, Iridescent	Blue
Bowl, 4¾" Berry	6.00	10.00	Creamer	22.00	35.00
Bowl, 4¾", 2" High	8.50	15.00	Pitcher, 8" 48 oz.		135.00
Bowl, 5½" One Handle	12.50	17.00	Plate, 6" Sherbet	4.00	9.00
Bowl, 7¼" Oval, Handled Pickle	9.00	20.00	Plate, 8" Luncheon		15.00
Bowl, 7⅞" Large Berry	15.00	22.00	Salt and Pepper		175.00
Bowl, 8⅜" Oval	25.00	55.00	Sherbet	7.50	9.00
Butter Dish and Cover	200.00	175.00	Sugar	20.00	25.00
Butter Dish Bottom	65.00	75.00	Sugar Cover	40.00	85.00
Butter Dish Top	135.00	100.00	Tumbler, 3⅝", 8 oz.		20.00
Candy, Cover, 2-Handled	55.00		Vase, 6½" Footed	20.00	32.50

Please refer to Foreword for pricing information

"AURORA" HAZEL ATLAS GLASS COMPANY, Late 1930's

Colors: Cobalt blue, pink, green and crystal.

Aurora is a small pattern that makes a nice addition to any collection. Cobalt blue attracts collectors in a way no other color seems to do. It will not completely drain your budget because they are so few different pieces (seven) in the set. An eight place setting would not involve thousands of dollars as other cobalt blue will; so, if this is the color you like, here is one pattern to check out! Several readers have suggested patterns which have a tall creamer and no sugar should list the creamer as a milk pitcher. I guess that goes back to some of the earlier glass collecting fields in which milk pitchers were listed.

The smaller 4½" bowl is the prize of this set. No matter how many I have found, not one has lasted in my booth for the whole show! Not all pieces have been found in pink, but those found fetch as high a price as the blue due to scarcity of the pink. I have never seen a pink tumbler.

Note two new colors have been added to the listing. Bowls have been discovered in green and crystal. These colors may be rare or maybe they have been overlooked. Only time will tell; if you find other Aurora pieces in green or crystal, let me know.

	Cobalt, Pink
Bowl, 4½" Deep	20.00
* Bowl, 5⅜" Cereal	8.00
Creamer, 4½"	12.00
Cup	5.00
Plate, 6½"	6.00
Saucer	2.50
Tumbler, 4¾", 10 oz.	14.50

* green $7.00 or crystal $5.00

AVOCADO, NO. 601 INDIANA GLASS COMPANY, 1923-1933

Colors: Pink, green, crystal, white. (See Reproduction Section)

Avocado is one of those patterns that dealers have trouble keeping in stock. Although expensive, it usually sells in large size lots rather than a piece here and a piece there. Green is still the predominant color collected, but pink has almost recovered from those reproduced pitchers and tumblers that were introduced in 1974. I have preached since that time about the reproductions and how to tell the differences so that you will not be taken in by a fake. (On the positive side are reports that that particular glass selling scheme is finally collapsing).

Notice some big price jumps in green; pitchers and tumblers as well as some bowls have just about disappeared from the market. Reproduced green items are much darker than the original green shown here. Pink reproduced items have an orange cast to the color, but this does vary. Buyer beware! Know your dealer and his reputation for integrity.

There are beginning to be a few collectors of crystal, but not all pieces are found in this color. I have reports that crystal is being sold for higher prices than I have listed. That is entirely possible since any price is higher than I have listed. The only pieces I have seen sell in crystal are the deep bowl at $25.00 and the two-handled bowl for $8.50. I will work on as complete a price listing for crystal as I can find for the next book. Help me if you will.

	Pink	Green		Pink	Green
Bowl, 5¼" 2-handled	20.00	25.00	*Pitcher, 64 oz.	525.00	725.00
Bowl, 6" Footed Relish	15.00	20.00	***Plate, 6⅜" Sherbet	10.00	12.50
Bowl, 7" 1 Handle Preserve	14.00	17.00	**Plate, 8¼" Luncheon	13.00	15.00
Bowl, 7½" Salad	27.50	42.50	Plate, 10¼" 2-Handled Cake	27.50	37.50
Bowl, 8" 2-Handled Oval	17.00	22.00	Saucer, 6⅜"	18.00	20.00
Bowl, 9½", 3¼" Deep	75.00	95.00	***Sherbet	42.50	47.50
***Creamer, Footed	25.00	27.50	***Sugar, Footed	25.00	27.50
Cup, Footed	25.00	27.50	*Tumbler	100.00	150.00

*Caution on pink. The orange-pink is new!

**Apple Design $10.00. Amber has been newly made.

***Remade in dark shade of green.

Please refer to Foreword for pricing information

BEADED BLOCK IMPERIAL GLASS COMPANY, 1927-1930's

Colors: Pink, green, crystal, ice blue, vaseline, iridescent, amber, red, opalescent and milk white.

Beaded Block is a pattern that is also purchased by collectors of other patterns who wish an additional serving or display piece of Depression glass. The array of colors found in Beaded Block is not matched by any other pattern in this book. It is one pattern that gets priced by unknowledgeable antique dealers as "Carnival", "Vaseline" or "Pattern" glass. It was originally made in the late 1920's and early 1930's. I say "originally" because Imperial had a reissue of the pink and pink iridized in the late 1970's and early 1980's. This is easily spotted since it is marked **IG** in the bottom. The only other piece that I know is marked is the white lily bowl shown in the back on the right. When I visited the factory in 1981, I was told that the white was made in the early 1950's and the **IG** mark was first used about that time.

There are an abundance of square plates, but most of the round plates must have been turned into bowls. That is how bowls were made in Beaded Block. The edges of plates were turned up to make a bowl. That makes the size variances in this pattern a major headache for collectors. Sizes listed in the Imperial catalogues vary greatly as to actual sizes found today. The sizes listed here were all obtained from actual measurements and not the catalogue. You may find some differences in your measurements, so don't get too alarmed. Read the section on measurements on page 4 in the front of the book.

There are a few more of those white pitchers being found, but the last two found were both damaged to some degree. Damaged glass, unless rare, has little value. Even rare glass has a limited market if damaged. The red lily bowls are still being found in the central Ohio area and that seems to be the only place they were distributed. In fact, no other pieces in red are available except the 4½" lily bowl.

The 6" vases shown in cobalt and pink are not Beaded Block, but are often sold as such. Note that they have no beading and no scalloped edge as do all the other pieces except the white lily bowl previously discussed. Imperial called these tall pieces "footed jellies." These were attained at groceries with a product inside. One found with the original label still attached read "Good Taste Mustard Seed, 3½ oz., Frank Tea & Spice Co., Cin., O." I imagine the edge had to be smooth to take a lid and the sides were changed to a "zipper-like" design. These are a "go-with" piece and not true Beaded Block.

	*Crystal, Pink, Green, Amber	Other Colors		* Crystal, Pink, Green, Amber	Other Colors
Bowl, 4½" 2-Handled Jelly	6.00	14.00	Bowl, 7½" Round, Plain Edge	17.50	20.00
**Bowl, 4½" Round Lily	8.50	17.00	Bowl, 8¼" Celery	11.00	16.00
Bowl, 5½" Square	6.00	8.50	Creamer	14.00	22.00
Bowl, 5½" 1 Handle	6.50	8.50	***Pitcher, 5¼", Pint Jug	85.00	
Bowl, 6" Deep Round	8.50	15.00	Plate, 7¾" Square	5.00	8.00
Bowl, 6¼" Round	6.50	14.00	Plate, 8¾" Round	12.00	17.00
Bowl, 6½" Round	6.50	14.00	Stemmed Jelly, 4½"	8.00	15.00
Bowl, 6½" 2-Handled Pickle	10.00	15.00	Stemmed Jelly, 4½", Flared Top	9.00	16.00
Bowl, 6¾" Round, Unflaired	10.00	14.00	Sugar	12.50	20.00
Bowl, 7¼" Round, Flared	10.00	16.00	Vase, 6" Bouquet	10.00	18.00
Bowl, 7½" Round, Fluted Edges	17.50	20.00			

*All pieces 25% to 40% lower.

**Red $85.00

***White $160.00

"BOWKNOT" MANUFACTURER UNKNOWN, Probably late 1920's

Color: Green

Bowknot still remains a mystery pattern. The mystery is the manufacturer and the exact dates it was made. Add to that a cup with no saucer and two different style tumblers with no pitcher and you have a real "who-done-it?"

I still get letters from novice collectors who feel that they have found the first creamer and sugar. The Fostoria pattern "June" has a bow also but does not come in green. If you find a green Bowknot creamer or sugar, run, don't walk to the nearest phone and give me a call.

My darlin' Cathy thinks this is a neat pattern. Evidently, she is not the only one. It is beginning to sell to other collectors besides her.

	Green		Green
Bowl, 4½" Berry	9.00	Sherbet, Low Footed	9.00
Bowl, 5½" Cereal	13.00	Tumbler, 5", 10 oz.	12.00
Cup	5.00	Tumbler, 5", 10 oz. Footed	12.00
Plate, 7" Salad	7.50		

Please refer to Foreword for pricing information

BLOCK OPTIC, "BLOCK" HOCKING GLASS COMPANY, 1929-1933

Colors: Green, pink, yellow, crystal and some blue.

Block Optic is the pattern that I used to recommend to new collectors because it was economically priced and a beginner could afford to start with it. However, the price is no longer as economical as it once was. Of course, groceries, transportation and rent are not as easily paid for either! As far as collectability goes, Block remains high on the list of collector demand. There is an abundant supply of most of the basic pieces, and the rarely found items are not priced out of sight as is the case of many of the most desirable patterns in green.

Dinner plates received heavy usage and mint ones are premium items today. There are two size saucers which are shown in the pictures on the right. These saucers are the ones with an indented cup ring. In the top picture the pink cup is the style that fits on the 6⅛" saucer; in the bottom picture, the second cup from the right is the proper cup style for the 5¾" saucer.

Add to the four styles of cups shown the fact that there are three different shapes of creamer and sugars. There are variations in handles and slight differences in style to make a total of five different creamers and sugars that can be collected in this set. In yellow, only the fancy handled, rounded type shown in the top picture has been found. There are two types of bases as shown on the pink pair. The pink sugar base is plain whereas the creamer has a rayed base. This is true of many of Hocking's patterns. Some tumblers or stems will show these variations also.

There has been quite a jump in some of the prices of pink. Collectors of this color are finding that the supply is well short of that of the green. The stemware has turned out to be almost non existent in pink.

A comment on the frosted green creamer and sugar shown in the lower picture needs to be made. Hocking, as well as other companies, **satinized** (frosted) many of their dinnerware lines. Evidently, these were special orders or special promotions since many were hand decorated with flowers or fruit. Today, many collectors shy away from these pieces for some reason. Frosted items only bring a fraction of the price of their unfrosted counterparts. Even though these pieces are much more rare, there is so little demand that the price is lessened. That is one of the lessons beginners need to learn as soon as possible about collectibles. Rarity does not determine price! Demand is the major determining factor of price! (I will say that one of the nicest table arrangements I've seen recently at a show involved satinized hand painted Mayfair pieces.)

You will find some green Block with a black foot or stem. There is not enough of this available to collect a set unless you find it all at one time. Popularity of this is limited. Few pieces of crystal block can be found. Only the butter dish has a premium value. Other pieces in crystal sell for about half the prices of green if a buyer can be found.

A reader in California sent some interesting information about the green butter dish top. In the twenty years I have been buying Depression glass, I have seen 15 to 20 green Block butter tops for every bottom. I had assumed that the heavy top had destroyed many of the bottoms over the years since it is difficult to grasp when trying to pick it up. It seems that the tops were also sold as a butter holder for ice boxes. This top slid into a **metal holder** eliminating the need for a glass bottom!

	Green	Yellow	Pink		Green	Yellow	Pink
Bowl, 4¼" diam., 1⅜" tall	6.00		5.00	Plate, 6" Sherbet	1.50	2.00	1.00
Bowl, 4½" diam., 1½" tall	22.50			Plate, 8" Luncheon	3.00	3.75	2.50
Bowl, 5¼" Cereal	8.50		6.00	Plate, 9" Dinner	13.50	30.00	20.00
Bowl, 7" Salad	17.00			Plate, 9" Grill	9.50	30.00	12.00
Bowl, 8½" Large Berry	18.00		15.00	Plate, 10¼" Sandwich	17.50		15.00
Butter Dish and Cover, 3" x 5"	37.50			Salt and Pepper, Footed	25.00	60.00	55.00
Butter Dish Bottom	22.50			Salt and Pepper, Squatty	60.00		
Butter Dish Top	15.00			Sandwich Server, Ctr. Handle	45.00		40.00
Candlesticks, 1¾" Pr.	85.00		60.00	Saucer, 5¾", With Cup Ring	8.00		5.00
Candy Jar & Cover, 2¼" Tall	35.00	45.00	35.00	Saucer, 6⅛", With Cup Ring	7.00		4.50
Candy Jar & Cover, 6¼" Tall	40.00		95.00	Sherbet, Non-Stemmed (Cone)	3.00		
Comport, 4" Wide Mayonnaise	22.00		50.00	Sherbet, 3¼", 5½ oz.	4.50	7.50	6.00
Creamer, 3 Styles: Cone				Sherbet, 4¾", 6 oz.	11.00	13.00	11.00
Shaped, Round, Rayed-Foot and				Sugar, 3 Styles: As Creamer	9.00	9.50	8.00
Flat (5 Kinds)	10.00	10.00	9.50	Tumbler, 3" & 3½", 5 oz. Flat	14.00		13.00
Cup, Four Styles	5.00	7.00	5.00	Tumbler, 9 oz. Flat	10.00		10.00
Goblet, 3½" Short Wine			125.00	Tumbler, 10 oz. Flat	13.00		11.00
Goblet, 4" Cocktail	28.00		25.00	Tumbler, 15 oz., Flat, 5¼",	25.00		25.00
Goblet, 4½" Wine	28.00		25.00	Tumbler, 3¼", 3 oz. Footed	17.00		15.00
Goblet, 5¾", 9 oz.	17.00		20.00	Tumbler, 9 oz. Footed	13.50	18.00	11.00
Goblet, 7¼", 9 oz. Thin		27.50		Tumbler, 6", 10 oz. Footed	19.50		20.00
Ice Bucket	27.50		25.00	Tumble-up Night Set	47.50		
Ice Tub or Butter Tub, Open	30.00		75.00	Tumbler, 3" only	35.00		
Mug	27.50			Bottle only	12.50		
Pitcher, 7⅝", 68 oz., Bulbous	60.00		55.00	Tumbler, 6" High	47.50		
Pitcher, 8½", 54 oz.	25.00		27.50	Vase, 5¾" Blown	175.00		
Pitcher, 8", 80 oz.	42.50		50.00	Whiskey, 1⅝", 1 oz.			30.00
				Whiskey, 2¼", 2 oz.	17.50		17.50

*Green Clambroth $150.00 -Blue $375.00 - Crystal $85.00

Please refer to Foreword for pricing information

"BUBBLE", "BULLSEYE", "PROVINCIAL"

ANCHOR HOCKING GLASS COMPANY, 1934-1965

Colors: Pink, light blue, dark green, red, crystal and any other Hocking color.

Bubble continues to attract new collectors. There are enough cups, saucers and dinner plates available in blue to satisfy all demands for years to come. All the other pieces in blue are in shorter supply with the creamer and sugar reaching the scarce category. For some reason there are are still fewer creamers than sugars found.

Pink is hard to find in any thing other than the 8⅜" bowl. In fact, the cup and saucer in pink are quite rare!

That 8⅜" berry bowl can be found in almost any color that Anchor Hocking made since WWII. There are so many pink bowls available that their $3.00 price has held for over ten years. I mentioned in one of my earlier books how this bowl was stacked to the ceiling at the factory on my first visit in 1972. I haven't been in that part of the storage facility for several years, but there were still plenty of these bowls there the last time I visited. Maybe these were the Edsel of the glass world.

Both Forest Green (dark) and Royal Ruby (red) continue to sell. Years ago, Christmas was the one time of the year that these two colors sold well. Now, they are constant sellers and the only problem is keeping enough stock to keep up with the demand. Note the iridized green sugar in the top picture. I have never found a creamer to go with this piece. Previously, we have shown other iridized pieces such as the 4" berry bowl, but these are more of a novelty than they are collectible.

The 9" blue bowl shown in the center of the top picture still remains the "find" in this pattern. I have only owned two. I received a letter from a collector who found another.

Of note to world travelers, I have recently received a couple of interesting photographs of a pale transparent green Bubble-like pattern. One, from New Zealand, showed a 7" green plate and the other, from British Columbia, a 7" bowl . Maybe there is an English made pattern that is similar to Bubble. All you Canadian and English readers let me know what you discover!

The labels on the crystal Bubble read "Heat Proof." In fact, a 1942 ad guaranteed this "Fire-King" tableware to be "heat-proof", indeed a "tableware that can be used in the oven, on the table, in the refrigerator." Presumably since this ad is dated 1942, they're referring to the light blue color. This added dimension is unique to "Fire-King" as most Depression glass patterns will not hold up to sudden changes in temperature.

	Dark Green	Light Blue	Ruby Red		Dark Green	Light Blue	Ruby Red
Bowl, 4" Berry		10.00		Plate, 6¾" Bread and			
Bowl, 4½" Fruit	5.50	7.00	5.00	Butter	1.50	2.00	
Bowl, 5¼" Cereal	7.50	8.00		Plate, 9⅜" Grill		12.00	
Bowl, 7¾" Flat Soup		10.00		Plate, 9⅜" Dinner	5.00	5.00	5.50
Bowl, 8⅜" Large Berry				Platter, 12" Oval		12.00	
(Pink-$3.00)	8.00	10.00		*** Saucer	1.00	1.00	1.50
Bowl, 9" Flanged		125.00		Sugar	7.00	14.00	
Candlesticks (Crystal -				Tidbit (2 Tier)			25.00
$10.00 Pr.)	17.50			Tumbler, 6 oz. Juice			6.50
Creamer	7.50	25.00		Tumbler, 9 oz. Water			6.00
* Cup	3.00	2.50	4.00	Tumbler, 12 oz. Iced Tea			9.00
Lamp, 3 Styles, Crystal Only - $35.00				Tumbler, 16 oz.			
** Pitcher, 64 oz. Ice Lip			40.00	Lemonade			15.00

*Pink - $75.00
**Crystal - $45.00
***Pink - $20.00

CAMEO, "BALLERINA" or "DANCING GIRL" HOCKING GLASS COMPANY, 1930-1934

Colors: Green, yellow, pink and crystal w/platinum rim. (*See Reproduction Section*)

Cameo remains one of Depression glass's shining stars. It is one of the most sought after patterns in green. There are enough easily found pieces to obtain a set without having all the rare accessory items. However, if you want an eight or twelve place setting with all the serving pieces, then be prepared to dig deep into your savings or equity account. Forgetting the center handled sandwich server, it will take close to $10,000.00 to complete a service for twelve - if you can find it for sale. Many collectors can not afford everything, and so they do not try to find every stem and every tumbler; instead they purchase only one or two different size tumblers or stems.

All of the miniature pieces in Cameo are new! No small size Cameo was ever made during the Depression era. See the ***Reproduction Section*** in the back of the book for information on this and the reproduced Cameo shakers. A new importer is making a weakly patterned shaker in pink, cobalt blue and a darker shade of green than the original color.

Yellow Cameo cups, saucer/sherbet plates, grill and dinner plates were heavily promoted by Hocking. These four yellow pieces are still plentiful today. In fact, they are now difficult to sell . While the trend for Cameo's prices in general has been upward, the prices on common yellow pieces have been the opposite. All other yellow is hard to find with the butter and milk pitchers being rare. I have had a yellow butter bottom for over ten years looking for a top without success. In green, it is the bottom that is harder to find. You can seen both the butter and the milk pitcher in my book called ***Very Rare Glassware of the Depression Years.***

I receive letters or calls about yellow saucers in Cameo each year. The real Cameo saucer has an indented cup ring, but it has never been seen in yellow. Hocking made few indented saucers. They made a dual purpose saucer/sherbet plate for most patterns. If you will look on page 27, the difference can be seen in green. The saucer on the right has a distinct indented ring (1¾" center)while the saucer/sherbet plate (2¾" center) on the left does not.

A difference in the short 3½" and 4" wines can be seen on the closed handled plate between the saucers discussed above. It has been since the third Depression book that I have been able to show this difference. Rarely found glassware eludes me also.

Another question that needs to be addressed is the difference between grill plates. A grill plate is a sectioned or divided plate which keeps the food separated. They were used mostly in the restaurants and "grills" of that day. In the picture of yellow Cameo, both styles are shown. One has tab handles and one does not. Both are common in yellow. In green, the grill with the tab or closed handles is harder to find. For years collectors did not pay much attention to these varieties, but there are so many new collectors who came from collecting fields in which variations made a big difference that it has now carried over into the Depression glass field.

For novice collectors I need to reiterate some basic information shown in the pictures on page 27. In the top picture there are two vases shown in the back on the right. The 8" vase is the bulbous one in the back. The smaller 5¾" is shown in front of it. This smaller vase is often confused with the tall candy bottom. There is no Cameo "rope" design at the top of the vase. There is on the candy. The two handled bowl on the left is a cream soup bowl; and the tray that the creamer is sitting in on the right is called a Domino sugar tray. This one is indented for the creamer although some are not indented.

In the bottom picture please note the plates in the back. The dinner plate is on the right with a large center area. The plate on the left with the smaller center is called a sandwich plate. I also should point out the color variations in the cups as well as the handle styles. The cups on the right have plain handles (abbreviated "ph" in ads) and the cup on the right has a fancy handle (abbreviated "fh" in ads). The darker green bottle is marked "Whitehouse Vinegar" on the bottom. These originally came with a cork.

	Green	Yellow	Pink	Crystal, Plat		Green	Yellow	Pink	Crystal, Plat
Bowl, 4¼" Sauce				4.50	Cake Plate, 10", 3 Legs	15.00			
Bowl, 4¾" Cream Soup	47.50				Cake Plate, 10½" Flat	80.00		110.00	
Bowl, 5½" Cereal	25.00	24.00	50.00	6.00	Candlesticks, 4" Pr.	75.00			
Bowl, 7¼" Salad	37.50				Candy Jar, 4" Low				
Bowl, 8¼" Large Berry	25.00		125.00		and Cover	45.00	60.00	425.00	
Bowl, 9" Rimmed Soup	28.00		85.00		Candy Jar, 6½" Tall				
Bowl, 10" Oval Vegetable	15.00	30.00			and Cover	100.00			
Bowl, 11", 3-Legged					Cocktail Shaker (Metal				
Console	45.00	60.00	27.50		Lid) Appears in				
Butter Dish and Cover	150.00	1250.00			Crystal Only				395.00
Butter Dish Bottom	85.00	425.00			Comport, 5" Wide				
Butter Dish Top	65.00	825.00			Mayonnaise	22.00		165.00	

Please refer to Foreword for pricing information

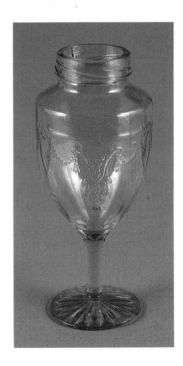

CAMEO, "BALLERINA" or "DANCING GIRL" (Con't.)

	Green	Yellow	Pink	Crystal, Plat
Cookie Jar and Cover	40.00			
Creamer, 3¼"	17.50	13.00		
Creamer, 4¼"	19.00		65.00	
Cup, 2 Styles	12.00	6.50	60.00	5.00
Decanter, 10" With Stopper	110.00			175.00
Decanter, 10" With Stopper, Frosted (Stopper Represents ⅓ Value of Decanter)	25.00			
Domino Tray, 7" With 3" Indentation	80.00			
Domino Tray, 7" With No Indentation			175.00	100.00
Goblet, 3½" Wine	450.00			
Goblet, 4" Wine	50.00		195.00	
Goblet, 6" Water	40.00		150.00	
Ice Bowl or Open Butter, 3" Tall x 5½" Wide	125.00		425.00	225.00
Jam Jar, 2" and Cover	130.00			150.00
Pitcher, 5¾", 20 oz. Syrup or Milk	155.00	450.00		
Pitcher, 6", 36 oz. Juice	45.00			
Pitcher, 8½", 56 oz. Water	40.00		1,100.00	375.00
Plate, 6" Sherbet	2.00	2.00	75.00	1.75
Plate, 7" Salad				3.00
Plate, 8" Luncheon	7.50	7.50	25.00	3.50
Plate, 8½" Square	30.00	110.00		
Pate, 9½" Dinner	12.50	6.00	55.00	
Plate, 10" Sandwich	10.00		35.00	
Plate, 10½" Rimmed Dinner	80.00		110.00	
Plate, 10½" Grill	7.50	5.00	40.00	
Plate, 10½" Grill With Closed Handles	47.50	5.00		
Plate, 10½" With Closed Handles	7.00	5.00		
Platter, 12", Closed Handles	15.00	30.00		
Relish, 7½" Footed, 3 Part	22.00	95.00		100.00
Salt and Pepper, Footed Pr.	55.00		600.00	
Sandwich Server, Center Handle	2,650.00			
Saucer With Cup Ring	110.00			
Saucer, 6" (Sherbet Plate)	2.00	2.00	75.00	
Sherbet, 3⅛" molded	10.00	30.00	50.00	
Sherbet, 3⅛" blown	12.00		60.00	
Sherbet, 4⅞"	25.00	32.00	75.00	
Sugar, 3¼"	13.00	10.00		
Sugar, 4¼"	17.50		60.00	
Tumbler, 3¾", 5 oz. Juice	22.50		70.00	
Tumbler, 4", 9 oz. Water	19.00		65.00	8.00
Tumbler, 4¾", 10 oz. Flat	21.00		80.00	
Tumbler, 5", 11 oz. Flat	21.00	37.50	75.00	
Tumbler, 5¼", 15 oz.	50.00		100.00	
Tumbler, 3 oz. Footed Juice	45.00		100.00	
Tumbler, 5", 9 oz. Footed	20.00	12.00	90.00	
Tumbler, 5¾", 11 oz. Footed	45.00		100.00	
Tumbler, 6⅜", 15 oz. Footed	350.00			
Vase, 5¾"	130.00			
Vase, 8"	19.00			
Water Bottle (Dark Green) Whitehouse Vinegar	15.00			

* Beware Reproductions

Please refer to Foreword for pricing information

CHERRY BLOSSOM JEANNETTE GLASS COMPANY, 1930-1939

Colors: Pink, green, Delphite (opaque blue), crystal, Jadite (opaque green) and red. *(See Reproduction Section)*

Cherry Blossom has finally made a dramatic recovery from the throes and woes of reproductions. Almost all prices have increased since the last book with the notable exception of the Delphite color. (That color is an opaque light blue if you are not familiar with it.) I have seen some really reasonable prices for these newer pieces in the last year at the flea markets with distributors of new glassware. Finally, there are enough reproductions available to over supply the market and that has caused fewer repros to be made. When they don't sell...!

All that has helped Cherry Blossom which has been the biggest target of the newly made foreign glassware resembling our American Depression ware. Prices have risen to ante-repro days except for the shakers which still have a long way to go. One of the problems with the shakers concerns not only the large number of reproductions made, but that many collectors were willing to purchase these fakes in order to have a pair of shakers for their set and not have to pay the high price of the rarely found older ones. I still get many calls and letters on the pink shakers. Only **two** pair of original pink shakers were ever found; so the likelihood of your finding another **old** pair is fairly remote, at best, particularly at a bargain price.

A 11" platter finally surfaced in green! Measure this platter outside edge to outside edge. The 13" platter measures 11" on the inside rims. Other pieces of Cherry are becoming harder and harder to find. The aforementioned platter, soup and cereal bowls and the 10" green grill plate have all been difficult for collectors to find, especially in mint condition. Be sure to check the inner rims of Cherry Blossom pieces as there is a tendency for them to have chips and nicks.

You will find crystal Cherry Blossom at times. Usually it is the two handled bowl which sells in the $12.00 range. It is scarce, but there is not enough crystal found to be collectible. A few red pieces have been found, but the reproduction red wiped out the demand for those.

The letters AOP stand for "all over pattern" on the footed tumblers and pitcher shown on the right in the pictures. The footed large tumblers and the AOP pitcher come in two styles. One style has a scalloped or indented foot while the other is round with no indentions. PAT stands for "pattern at the top" shown on the flat bottomed tumblers on the left in the pictures.

There are some known experimental pieces of Cherry such as a pink cookie jar, pink five-part relish, orange with green trim slag bowl and amber children's pieces. Pricing on these is difficult to determine, but keep your eye out for them, and don't pass them up if you can buy them!

	Pink	Green	Delphite
Bowl, 4¾" Berry	10.00	12.50	10.00
Bowl, 5¾" Cereal	24.00	27.50	
Bowl, 7¾" Flat Soup	37.00	40.00	
* Bowl, 8½" Round Berry	35.00	35.00	35.00
Bowl, 9" Oval Vegetable	20.00	22.00	40.00
** Bowl, 9" 2-Handled	15.00	18.00	12.50
** Bowl, 10½", 3 Leg Fruit	40.00	42.50	
Butter Dish and Cover	55.00	70.00	
Butter Dish Bottom	15.00	20.00	
Butter Dish Top	40.00	50.00	
Cake Plate (3 Legs) 10¼"	15.00	16.00	
Coaster	10.00	9.00	
Creamer	12.00	13.00	15.00
Cup	14.00	16.00	12.50
Mug, 7 oz.	165.00	145.00	
*** Pitcher, 6¾" AOP, 36 oz.			
Scalloped or Round Bottom	35.00	40.00	
Pitcher, 8" PAT, 42 oz. Flat	35.00	40.00	
Pitcher, 8" PAT, 36 oz.			
Footed	45.00	45.00	65.00
Plate, 6" Sherbet	5.00	5.00	8.50
Plate, 7" Salad	14.00	16.00	
**** Plate, 9" Dinner	14.00	18.00	13.00
Plate, 9" Grill	17.50	20.00	
Plate, 10" Grill		60.00	
Platter, 9" Oval	700.00	750.00	

	Pink	Green	Delphite
Platter, 11" Oval	20.00	23.00	35.00
Platter, 13" and 13" Divided	35.00	40.00	
Salt and Pepper			
(Scalloped Bottom)	1,100.00	750.00	
Saucer	2.50	3.00	3.00
Sherbet	11.00	13.50	11.00
Sugar	10.00	12.00	15.00
Sugar Cover	10.00	13.00	
Tray, 10½" Sandwich	14.00	15.00	15.00
Tumbler, 3¾", 4 oz.			
Footed AOP	12.00	15.00	16.00
Tumbler, 4½", 9 oz. Round			
Foot AOP	24.00	27.00	15.00
Tumbler, 4½", 8 oz.			
Scalloped Foot AOP	24.00	27.00	
Tumbler, 3½", 4 oz.			
Flat Pat	14.00	22.00	
Tumbler, 4¼", 9 oz.			
Flat PAT	14.00	18.00	
Tumbler, 5", 12 oz.			
Flat PAT	42.00	55.00	

*Yellow - $350.00
**Jadite - $275.00
***Jadite - $300.00
****Translucent Green - $175.00   Jadite - $40.00

CHERRY BLOSSOM - CHILD'S JUNIOR DINNER SET

	Pink	Delphite
Creamer	30.00	35.00
Sugar	30.00	35.00
Plate, 6"	7.00	10.00 (design on bottom)
Cup	23.00	27.50
Saucer	3.50	5.00
14 Piece Set	200.00	225.00

Original box sells for $15.00 extra with pink sets.

Please refer to Foreword for pricing information

28

CHERRYBERRY U.S. GLASS COMPANY, Early 1930's

Colors: Pink, green, crystal; some iridized.

Cherryberry has evolved from a pattern hardly noticed by collectors, except those who were buying Strawberry, to a pattern sought on its own merits. This is another of the U.S. Glass patterns that has no cup or saucer and a plain butter base. If all these U.S. Glass patterns are "sister" patterns, then Strawberry and Cherryberry are twins. You can only tell them apart by the fruit.

Crystal and iridescent are much rarer than pink or green, but there are fewer collectors for these colors. Some "antique" dealers will try to charge higher prices for the iridized because they think it is not Depression, but "Carnival" glass. Butter dishes and pitchers are the most desirable iridized pieces. Not only do Cherryberry collectors search for these, but collectors of butters and pitchers seek them, also.

	Crystal, Iridescent	Pink, Green		Crystal, Iridescent	Pink, Green
Bowl, 4" Berry	5.00	7.00	Olive Dish, 5" One-Handled	6.50	10.00
Bowl, 6¼", 2" Deep	25.00	45.00	Pickle Dish, 8¼" Oval	7.00	10.00
Bowl, 6½" Deep Salad	10.00	15.00	Pitcher, 7¾"	150.00	130.00
Bowl, 7½" Deep Berry	12.00	16.00	Plate, 6" Sherbet	4.00	6.00
Butter Dish and Cover	140.00	135.00	Plate, 7½" Salad	7.00	11.00
Butter Dish Bottom	75.00	75.00	Sherbet	5.50	6.50
Butter Dish Top	65.00	60.00	Sugar, Small Open	10.00	12.50
Comport, 5¾"	9.00	13.00	Sugar Large	12.50	15.00
Creamer, Small	9.00	12.50	Sugar Cover	25.00	40.00
Creamer, 4⅝" Large	12.50	20.00	Tumbler, 3⅝", 9 oz.	15.00	22.50

CHINEX CLASSIC MacBETH-EVANS DIVISION OF CORNING GLASS WORKS, Late 1930's - Early 1940's

Colors: Ivory, ivory w/decal decoration.

Chinex collectors got upset with me for exposing the beauty of this pattern in the last book. I have been blamed for higher prices having been caused by new collectors buying it before the long time collectors can find it. Castle decal is still the most desirable, but the pastel, decorated floral pieces are beginning to creep up in price.

The plainer, undecorated beige pieces are still waiting for collectors to notice them. So far, not many have taken on this challenge. Collecting the blue or pink trimmed florals is a challenge. More of this is being found in the western Pennsylvania area. Since it was made in that area, that makes sense. Perhaps, it was only distributed locally.

Remember the butter bottoms look like Cremax instead of Chinex. The butter tops have the "scroll like" design that distinguishes this pattern, but this design is missing from the bottoms. The floral or castle designs will be inside the base of the butter, but not on the top.

	Browntone or Plain Ivory	Decal Decorated	Castle Decal		Browntone or Plain Ivory	Decal Decorated	Castle Decal
Bowl, 5¾" Cereal	4.00	6.00	12.00	Cup	3.50	5.00	10.00
Bowl, 7" Vegetable	12.50	17.50	27.50	Plate, 6¼" Sherbet	1.50	2.00	4.00
Bowl, 7¾" Soup	10.00	15.00	25.00	Plate, 9¾" Dinner	3.00	6.00	13.00
Bowl, 9" Vegetable	9.50	15.00	25.00	Plate, 11½" Sandwich			
Bowl, 11"	15.00	25.00	35.00	or Cake	6.50	10.00	17.50
Butter Dish	47.50	60.00	75.00	Saucer	1.50	2.50	3.00
Butter Dish Bottom	10.00	20.00	25.00	Sherbet, Low Footed	5.00	9.00	15.00
Butter Dish Top	32.50	40.00	50.00	Sugar, Open	4.00	7.50	12.50
Creamer	4.50	7.50	15.00				

Please refer to Foreword for pricing information

"CHRISTMAS CANDY", NO. 624 INDIANA GLASS COMPANY, 1950's

Colors: Teal and crystal. *(See Reproduction Section)*

Christmas Candy, as this pattern has been dubbed, created a few letters for me after the cup was omitted from the listings in the last book. It was pictured, but not listed. That is one of the fun things about writing. There is no way you can catch all the errors, but faithful readers will keep you on your toes.

Teal or "Seafoam" as it was named by the company is the color everyone wants to collect. Unfortunately, there is very little of this color found today. Usually, Christmas Candy is found in sets rather than a piece here and there. Any glassware made in the 1950's is often found in sets. That may occur due to lack of usage for over forty years as happens with the 1930's glassware. It may also mean that many people had more than one set of dishes or that they changed patterns more often and stored what they were not using before they were all broken.

There is still little activity to report in crystal, although my shop, Grannie Bear, sold a set of crystal just yesterday. The mayonnaise, shown in crystal, is the only newly discovered piece since the last book. I suspect that there are additional items waiting to be found.

This is one of Indiana's numbered lines, and almost all the pieces I have purchased over the years have come from trips into Indiana. It may have been only regionally distributed. Dunkirk, the home of Indiana Glass, is not far from Indianapolis where I attend several Depression glass shows each year.

	Crystal	Teal		Crystal	Teal
Bowl, 7⅜" Soup	5.00	20.00	Plate, 8¼" Luncheon	5.50	12.50
Creamer	7.50	15.00	Plate, 9⅝" Dinner	7.50	18.00
Cup	3.50	12.50	Plate, 11¼", Sandwich	10.00	30.00
Mayonnaise w/ladle	15.00		Saucer	1.50	3.00
Plate, 6" Bread and Butter	2.50	7.50	Sugar	7.50	15.00

CIRCLE HOCKING GLASS COMPANY, 1930's

Colors: Green, pink and crystal.

Circle is more noticed by kitchenware collectors (especially reamer collectors) than it is by Depression glass enthusiasts because the pitcher (80 oz.) is collected with a reamer top. Hocking made a reamer top that fits this pitcher. The major problem with that fact is color variations in the pitchers make it difficult to find a reamer that matches the green shade of the pitchers. Notice how yellow looking the pitcher is compared to the other green pieces. (Hopefully, that yellowish tint will show when the book is printed).

There are several new listings for this pattern such as the 60 oz. pitcher, 10 oz. tumbler, and two new bowl sizes. Both of these bowls, 9⅜" and 5¼" have ground bottoms. Both styles of cups are shown in pink and green. I have found cups in pink but for some reason have been unable to come up with a pink saucer or a creamer to go with the sugar. Pink, although rarely collected, is not abundant.

You can find the green colored stems with crystal tops easier than you can find plain green stems. I am beginning to doubt the existence of the 9½" dinner plate; so if you have one in your collection, let me know!

	Green,Pink		Green,Pink
Bowl, 4½"	4.00	Pitcher, 80 oz.	22.50
Bowl, 5¼"	5.00	Plate, 6" Sherbet	1.00
Bowl, 5½" Flared	5.00	Plate, 8¼" Luncheon	3.50
Bowl, 8"	10.00	Plate, 9½" dinner	8.00
Bowl, 9⅜"	12.50	Saucer	1.00
Creamer	7.50	Sherbet, 3⅛"	3.50
Cup (2 Styles)	3.50	Sherbet, 4¾"	5.00
Decanter, Handled	27.50	Sugar	6.00
Goblet, 4½" Wine	9.00	Tumbler, 3½", 4 oz. Juice	7.00
Goblet, 8 oz. Water	8.50	Tumbler, 4", 8 oz. Water	8.50
Pitcher, 60 oz.	25.00	Tumbler, 5", 10 oz. Tea	15.00

Please refer to Foreword for pricing information

CLOVERLEAF HAZEL ATLAS GLASS COMPANY, 1930-1936

Colors: Pink, green, yellow, crystal and black.

Black Cloverleaf has seen a revival of collecting in recent months and the already short supply in the market is becoming extinct. Only the ash trays seem to be ignored. I have noticed that this is true in many patterns. Evidently, the non-smokers are being heard for a change or the smokers are finally "wising up"; and it is affecting the sale of smokers' items even in the glassware business.

Other colors in Cloverleaf are also selling with yellow leading the way. In yellow, shakers and bowls do not seem to be available at any price. In green the 8" bowl and the tumblers are selling briskly, but the limited number of items manufactured in pink and crystal leave only luncheon sets collectible. Of course there is the one flared 10 oz. tumbler in pink, but it does not seem to inspire more collectors of pink. That tumbler is quite sparsely distributed I might add. Crystal makes a nice table display with colored accoutrements.

Actually, Cloverleaf was fairly limited in distribution nationally. About ten years ago I bought a large collection of Cloverleaf in Ohio. It had been gathered from dealers all over the country, but the largest accumulations had come from Ohio and Pennsylvania. One of my favorite buys was a yellow candy bottom marked "large sherbet -$2.00". Because he had kept that sales tag on it, I enjoyed the same chuckle the original collector did when he bought it a flea market years earlier.

I have been asked to point out that the Cloverleaf pattern comes on both the inside and outside. It does not make a difference in value or collectability. In order for the black to show the pattern, moulds had to be designed with the pattern on the outside. On transparent pieces the pattern could be on the bottom or the inside and it would still show. In black, the pattern on the bottom of a plate makes it look like a plain black plate; so it was moved to the top. Over the years, transparent pieces also were made using the moulds designed for the black, so, you now find these pieces made with designs on both sides.

The black sherbet plate and the saucer are the same size. The saucer has no "Cloverleaf" pattern in the center.

	Pink	Green	Yellow	Black		Pink	Green	Yellow	Black
Ash Tray, 4", Match Holder in Center				60.00	Plate, 8" Luncheon	5.00	5.00	10.00	11.00
					Plate, 10¼" Grill		15.00	17.50	
Ash Tray, 5¾", Match Holder in Center				72.50	Salt and Pepper, Pr.		22.50	85.00	65.00
					Saucer	2.00	2.50	3.00	3.00
Bowl, 4" Dessert	8.00	14.00	20.00		Sherbet, 3" Footed	4.50	4.00	8.50	16.00
Bowl, 5" Cereal		20.00	22.00		Sugar, 3⅝" Footed		7.50	12.50	12.50
Bowl, 7" Deep Salad		30.00	40.00		Tumbler, 4", 9 oz. Flat		32.00		
Bowl, 8"		45.00			Tumbler, 3¾", 10 oz. Flat Flared	15.00	27.50		
Candy Dish and Cover		42.50	85.00						
Creamer, 3⅝" Footed		7.50	12.50	12.50	Tumbler, 5¾", 10 oz. Footed			17.00	22.00
Cup	5.00	6.00	8.00	12.00					
Plate, 6" Sherbet		3.50	5.00	27.50					

COLONIAL, "KNIFE AND FORK" HOCKING GLASS COMPANY, 1934-1936

Colors: Pink, green, crystal and opaque white.

Colonial pink and crystal sales have picked up considerably. In fact, I purchased a six piece set of each color; and amazingly, the green took the longest to sell! The pink seems to be the color everyone wants now. One color starts selling and the other colors in that pattern you can hardly give away. Suddenly, the trend of buying changes and another color begins to sell. It is impossible to out guess the buying public. If you could only buy items which would sell in the next year, inventory would not be such a burden.

Supply of stemware in green has finally filled the demand, for now, with prices on crystal stems rapidly approaching prices of their green counterparts. There is a true scarcity of crystal stems as any avid crystal collector will tell you. Have you ever seen a crystal cream soup? I have only seen one!

The spooner is placed next to the sugar bowl in each picture so you can see the height difference. I have been able to find a spooner priced as a sugar bottom numerous times in my travels. It can make your day! Occasionally, mugs are found in pink; but only three have turned up in green. These were found in Washington Court House, Ohio, for $1.00 each. A few bargains still turn up, so keep looking.

The cheese dish lid is ½" shorter than the butter top. So far it has only been found in green, but the pink butter is impossible to find without looking for a cheese dish also. The 3" pink sherbet is more than twice as difficult to find as the normally found 3⅜" sherbert, but it only sells for twice as much. So far no 3" green or crystal sherbets have surfaced.

Soups, both cream and regular, cereals, shakers and dinners are still difficult to find in all colors of Colonial. An abundance (compared to the last few years) of green lemonade tumblers have cropped up. It will take a little time for the market to absorb these; so now might be the time to latch on to some for your collection!

	Pink	Green	Crystal		Pink	Green	Crystal
Bowl, 3¾" Berry	25.00			Plate, 6" Sherbet	3.50	4.00	2.50
Bowl, 4½" Berry	7.00	10.00	4.50	Plate, 8½" Luncheon	6.00	7.00	3.25
Bowl, 5½" Cereal	40.00	55.00	15.00	Plate, 10" Dinner	30.00	47.50	17.50
Bowl, 4½" Cream Soup	40.00	40.00	42.00	Plate, 10" Grill	17.50	20.00	10.00
Bowl, 7" Low Soup	37.50	42.00	15.00	Platter, 12" Oval	22.00	17.00	12.00
Bowl, 9" Large Berry	15.00	22.00	12.00	Salt and Pepper, Pr.	110.00	110.00	45.00
Bowl, 10" Oval Vegetable	22.00	25.00	15.00	Saucer (White 3.00)			
Butter Dish and Cover	500.00	45.00	30.00	(Same as Sherbet Plate)	3.50	4.00	2.50
Butter Dish Bottom	350.00	27.50	20.00	Sherbet, 3"	15.00		
Butter Dish Top	150.00	17.50	10.00	Sherbet, 3⅜"	7.50	11.00	5.00
Cheese Dish		125.00		Spoon Holder or Celery	95.00	95.00	60.00
Creamer, 5", 8 oz.				Sugar, 5"	18.00	10.00	7.00
(Milk Pitcher)	13.50	17.50	10.00	Sugar Cover	27.00	15.00	10.00
Cup (White 7.00)	9.00	9.00	6.00	Tumbler, 3", 5 oz. Juice	12.00	22.00	10.00
Goblet, 3¾", 1 oz. Cordial		24.00	15.00	** Tumbler, 4", 9 oz. Water	12.00	16.00	10.00
Goblet, 4", 3 oz. Cocktail		20.00	12.00	Tumbler, 10 oz.	30.00	35.00	15.00
Goblet, 4½", 2½ oz. Wine		20.00	12.00	Tumbler, 12 oz. Iced Tea	37.00	42.00	20.00
Goblet, 5¼", 4 oz. Claret		20.00	14.00	Tumbler, 15 oz. Lemonade	50.00	60.00	30.00
Goblet, 5¾", 8½ oz. Water	30.00	22.50	13.00	Tumbler, 3¼", 3 oz. Footed	11.00	15.00	9.00
Mug, 4½", 12 oz.	400.00	700.00		Tumbler, 4", 5 oz. Footed	17.00	23.00	12.00
+ Pitcher, 7", 54 oz.	37.50	40.00	22.50	*** Tumbler, 5¼", 10 oz. Footed	35.00	35.00	20.00
+* Pitcher, 7¾", 68 oz.	45.00	55.00	25.00	Whiskey, 2½", 1½ oz.	8.00	10.00	6.00

*Beaded top in pink $1000.00   **Royal Ruby $95.00   ***Royal Ruby $150.00   +With or without ice lip

COLONIAL BLOCK HAZEL ATLAS GLASS COMPANY, Early 1930's

Colors: Green, crystal and pink; white in 1950's.

Including Colonial Block in the book has stopped the letters about round Block Optic butter dishes! Most pieces of Colonial Block are marked HA , but not all are so marked. The **H** and **A** are on top of each other confusing some novice collectors into believing that this is the symbol for Anchor Hocking. The anchor is a symbol used by Anchor Hocking and that was not used until after the 1930's.

The candy dish, butter tub and pitcher are the most sought after items in both pink and green. (Actually, I have never seen a pink pitcher or ever heard of one; so it may not exist). The white creamer, sugar and lid are the only white pieces available to date. I had reports of a white butter, but it was never verified.

The Goblet pictured in the center is Colonial Block and not Block Optic as it is so often mislabeled. If you like the heavier appearance of Colonial Block goblets as compared to the thinner Block Optic, then by all means use these realizing that they are less costly and more durable.

U.S. Glass made a similar pitcher to the one shown here. There is little difference in them except most Hazel Atlas pitchers are marked. Collectors today are not as rigid in collecting as they once were. Many collectors will buy either pitcher to go with their set. That is why I call items that are similar to a pattern but not actually a part of it - "go-with" pieces. Many times these "go-with" pieces are more reasonably priced.

	Pink, Green	White		Pink, Green	White
Bowl, 4"	5.00		Candy Jar w/Cover	30.00	
Bowl, 7"	14.00		Creamer	8.50	5.50
Butter Dish	30.00		Goblet	8.50	
Butter Dish Bottom	7.50		Pitcher	30.00	
Butter Dish Top	22.50		Sugar	9.00	4.50
Butter Tub	35.00		Sugar Lid	7.50	3.00

COLONIAL FLUTED, "ROPE" FEDERAL GLASS COMPANY, 1928-1933

Colors: Green and crystal

Though no longer very plentiful, Colonial Fluted is another set of Depression glass that is usually a starter set for beginning collectors. Afterwards it can be blended with another set or used for occasions such as bridge parties or small gatherings. It is a pattern that was used extensively originally. It is still priced moderately enough that it can be used today without fear of a piece or two being broken by guests. My experiences have shown me that most guests recognize this old glass as "antique" and treat it very gently.

Although listed in an early catalogue as being made in pink, I have never received reports of any of this being found in that color. The crystal is collected rarely, but there is a demand for the decaled pieces with hearts, spades, diamonds and clubs which make up a bridge set.

There is no dinner plate in Colonial Fluted, but there is a dinner size plate having the roping effect around the outside of the plate (without the fluting) made by Federal which goes very well with this if you are willing to overlook the missing flutes.

The "F" in a shield found in middle of many Colonial Fluted pieces is the trademark used by the Federal Glass Company. Not all pieces are marked.

	Green		Green
Bowl, 4" Berry	4.00	Plate, 6" Sherbet	1.50
Bowl, 6" Cereal	6.00	Plate, 8" Luncheon	3.25
Bowl, 6½", Deep (2½") Salad	13.00	Saucer	1.00
Bowl, 7½" Large Berry	12.00	Sherbet	5.00
Creamer	4.50	Sugar	3.00
Cup	3.50	Sugar Cover	10.00

Please refer to Foreword for pricing information

COLUMBIA FEDERAL GLASS COMPANY, 1938-1942

Colors: Crystal, some pink.

Columbia keeps adding surprises for collectors! First of all was the discovery of a water tumbler that was shown in the last book; and now there is a juice tumbler to go with the water! You can see both pictured here. I also hope you can see the elusive snack tray shown behind the juice on the right. The juice which holds four ounces looks a little more hidden now than it did in the photography studio. It has been at least four editions since I have had it pictured. Many collectors have not known what to look for since it is an unusual piece and shaped differently than most Columbia. These were found in a boxed set about fifteen years ago in northern Ohio. The box was labeled "Snack Sets" by Federal Glass Company.

There has been a lot of activity in buying pink Columbia. That is surprising since there are only four different pieces to be found and they are in very short supply. The price increases for this pattern have been in the harder to find items and the pink.

One piece of Columbia that was abundantly produced was the butter dish. You can find these with all sorts of multi-colored flashed decorations and floral decals. Federal must have tried everything to sell these and it must have worked since there are so many found today!

Some plates have also been discovered with pastel bands. It may have been a special order or a promotional idea. I suspect that there are luncheon sets decorated this way. Were there a creamer and sugar for this pattern, it would have even more devotees.

	Crystal	Pink		Crystal	Pink
Bowl, 5" Cereal	10.00		Cup	4.50	14.50
Bowl, 8" Low Soup	12.00		Plate, 6" Bread & Butter	1.50	8.00
Bowl, 8½" Salad	12.00		Plate, 9½" Luncheon	5.00	20.00
Bowl, 10½" Ruffled Edge	14.00		Plate, 11" Chop	6.00	
Butter Dish and Cover	15.00		Saucer	1.50	5.50
Ruby Flashed (17.50)			Snack Plate	30.00	
Other Flashed (16.00)			Tumbler, 2⅞", 4 oz., Juice	15.00	
Butter Dish Bottom	5.00		Tumbler, 9 oz., water	14.00	
Butter Dish Top	10.00				

CREMAX MacBETH-EVANS DIVISION OF CORNING GLASS WORKS, Late 1930's-Early 1940's

Colors: Cremax, cremax with fired-on color trim.

Cremax has never been given the credit it should be due. It is a difficult pattern to find. It has several different floral patterned decals that can be collected. Maybe it is the rarity which keeps collectors from buying it the way they do Chinex which is like a sister pattern. Often the bottom to the butter in Chinex is thought to be Cremax. The scalloped edges of the butter bottom are just like the edges on Cremax plates; however, the only tops to the butter ever found have the Chinex scroll-like pattern. If you find only the bottom of a butter, it is a Chinex bottom and not Cremax!

The other confusing problem concerns the name. The beige-like color made by MacBeth-Evans is also called cremax so you have to be aware of that and watch out for a Capital "C" when you see Cremax in advertisements.

The blue creamer and sugar shown in the last book were "Pyrex" pieces made in Canada by Corning. There is a whole set of this pattern available in blue with many of the characteristics of Cremax. I will try to include more on that pattern in my next book.

Demitasse sets are being found in sets of eight. Some have been found on a wire rack. The usual make-up of these sets has been two sets of each of four colors: pink, yellow, blue and green.

	Cremax	Decal Decorated		Cremax	Decal Decorated
Bowl, 5¾" Cereal	2.50	6.00	Plate, 9¾" Dinner	3.00	6.00
Bowl, 9" Vegetable	5.50	10.00	Plate, 11½" Sandwich	3.50	7.50
Creamer	3.00	6.00	Saucer	1.00	1.50
Cup	3.00	3.50	Saucer, Demitasse	2.50	5.00
Cup, Demitasse	10.00	15.00	Sugar, Open	3.00	6.00
Plate, 6¼" Bread and Butter	1.00	2.50			

Please refer to Foreword for pricing information

CORONATION, "BANDED RIB", "SAXON" HOCKING GLASS COMPANY, 1936-1940

Colors: Pink, green, crystal and Royal Ruby.

It has been six years since I first showed green Coronation in the book; and as I was writing this pattern today, I received a call from Pennsylvania where a small green berry bowl without handles was found! It stands to reason that there would be a small bowl to go with the large, but no one knows for sure until it shows up some place. It is a shame that Hocking did not make more of this pattern in green.

The tumbler in Coronation has always received all the publicity since it has been confused with the rarely found Lace Edge tumbler. Note the fine ribs above the middle of the Coronation tumbler. These ribs are missing on a Lace Edge glass. Many collectors buy the Coronation tumblers and use them with Lace Edge since they cost a third as much. Both are the same shape and color since both were made by Hocking. Just don't confuse the two since there is quite a price discrepancy!

By the way, that larger green tumbler in the lower photograph is 5⁷⁄₁₆" tall and holds 14¼ oz. For new readers the lower photo was taken at Anchor-Hocking of glassware from their morgue. The morgue is so called since it has examples of past (dead production) patterns made by the Company. Unfortunately, this was not well kept. Many examples have "walked out" over the years. It is now under lock, but the disappearance of items began long ago. Who knew Depression glass was going to be so important!

I have to laugh every time I see a big price on the commonly found red berry bowl with handles. They have always been plentiful and years ago a large accumulation was found sitting in an old warehouse. They are hard to sell; yet, I see them in my travels priced by unknowing dealers for two to three times their worth. They are usually marked "rare" or "old" or "pigeon blood".

Note that the handles on the red are open; handles on the pink are closed and handles on the green are missing. If you find another style of handle on a different color than these, let me know.

There are many red cups found but no red saucer/sherbet plates have ever been seen. I would not go so far as to say that red saucers were never made. If I have learned any thing in the last twenty years, it is never to say some piece of glass was never made. I do know the red cups were marketed on crystal saucers.

	Pink	Royal Ruby	Green
Bowl, 4¼" Berry	3.00	5.00	
Bowl, 4¼", No Handles			15.00
Bowl, 6½" Nappy	3.50	9.00	
Bowl, 8" Large Berry, Handled	7.00	11.50	
Bowl, 8" No Handles			75.00
Cup	3.50	4.50	
Pitcher, 7¾", 68 oz.	175.00		
Plate, 6" Sherbet	1.25		
Plate, 8½" Luncheon	3.00	6.00	25.00
*Saucer (Same as 6" Plate)	1.25		
Sherbet	3.50		40.00
Tumbler, 5", 10 oz. Footed	15.00		75.00

*crystal $0.50

CUBE, "CUBIST" JEANNETTE GLASS COMPANY, 1929-1933

Colors: Pink, green, crystal, amber, white, ultramarine, canary yellow and blue.

Cube is a pattern that catches the eye of non-collectors. I guess it is the cubed design that catches the light and makes it stand out in the crowd. There is the same appeal for Fostoria's American pattern which is also recognized by non-collectors of that pattern. Cube is often misidentified as American by beginning collectors, but it is easily corrected when the two patterns are compared in quality. The crystal 3" creamer and sugar on the 7" round tray are the most often confused pieces. Cube is very dull and wavy in appearance when compared to the bright, clearer quality of Fostoria's American pattern.

The ultramarine salad bowl listed below was shown in some of my early editions. Several people have written to ask if there is such a piece. It went to a collector in Pensacola who later moved to the Northeast and I lost contact with her. That bowl was the only one I have seen.

Green Cube is harder to find than the pink, but there are more collectors of the pink. The major difficulty in collecting pink is not in finding it, but in finding it with the right shade of pink. The pink varies from a light pink to an orangish-pink. This only shows how difficult it was for glass factories to consistently produce the same quality of glassware in the Depression era. As the glass tanks got hotter, the color got lighter. The orange shade of pink is difficult to sell. I have a beautiful pitcher in my shop that has been there longer than normal because it has an orange cast to the pink. Prices for the pitcher and tumblers continue to rise. Both colors are hard to find, but green seems to be better at hiding than pink.

The powder jar is three legged and shown directly behind the pink butter dish in the picture. Occasionally, the jars are found with celluloid or another similar lid. Powder jars were not made with those lids at the factory. These were possibly replacements when tops were broken. Another possibility is that powder bottoms were bought from Jeannette and non-glass lids were made up elsewhere to fit the bottoms. In any case, prices below are for intact, original glass lids. The powder jars with other types of lids sell for half or less.

Lack of a dinner size plate is the only drawback of collecting Cube. At least this pattern has a pitcher for the tumblers (and all the other basic pieces including cups and saucers)!

	Pink	Green			Pink	Green
Bowl, 4½" Dessert	4.00	5.00		Plate, 6" Sherbet	1.50	2.50
Bowl, 4½" Deep	4.50			Plate, 8" Luncheon	3.00	5.00
* Bowl, 6½" Salad	7.00	11.00		Powder Jar and Cover 3 Legs	15.00	17.50
Butter Dish and Cover	42.50	47.50		Salt and Pepper, Pr.	25.00	27.50
Butter Dish Bottom	10.00	12.50		Saucer	1.25	1.50
Butter Dish Top	30.00	32.50		Sherbet, Footed	4.50	6.00
Candy Jar and Cover, 6½"	22.00	25.00		** Sugar, 2"	2.00	
Coaster, 3¼"	3.50	4.50		Sugar, 3"	5.00	6.00
** Creamer, 2"	2.00			Sugar/Candy Cover	7.50	9.00
Creamer, 3"	5.00	7.00		Tray for 3" Creamer		
Cup	4.50	7.00		and Sugar, 7½" (Crystal Only)	4.00	
Pitcher, 8¾", 45 oz.	150.00	175.00		Tumbler, 4", 9 oz.	40.00	45.00

* Ultramarine - $40.00
**Amber or white - $3.00; crystal $1.00

Please refer to Foreword for pricing information

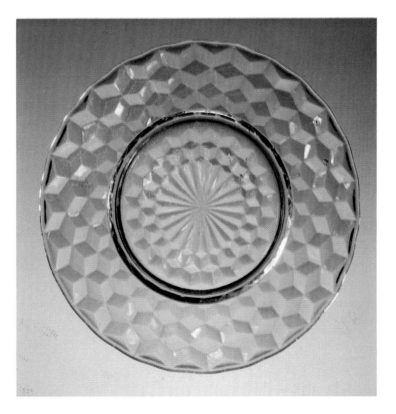

"CUPID" PADEN CITY GLASS COMPANY, 1930's

Colors: Pink, green, light blue, peacock blue, black, canary yellow.

You will notice several new listings and there have been reports of other new pieces that have not been confirmed to me by pictures as yet. Paden City is a company that new discoveries are the norm rather than unusual! Most pieces are shown in catalogues with no etchings; and until a piece shows up with a Paden City etching, there is no way to know that it does exist.

The only piece of black Cupid known is the covered casserole shown in the top picture. The silver decorated edges give this an elegance all its own.

Prices on this Paden City pattern continue to soar. People have been known to buy a piece of Cupid just to own an pretty piece of glass. After a while this one little purchase creates a Cupid collector. There is a mystique about the pattern which attracts new converts. Everyone buying a pattern that was already in short supply, raises the price very quickly. You do not have to own a large number of Cupid pieces to enjoy using what you have!

I would not be too surprised if a cup and saucer were found. After all, there are several of Paden City's lines which have cups and saucers. Samovars are rarely found, but are fetching "big bucks" when they do! So far these have only been reported in green and blue. There should be other colors available.

Those center-handled trays were called sandwich trays and the center-handled bowls of Paden City were called candy trays. I had always wondered what you could serve in these bowls without getting fingers into the contents. Candy, at least, makes sense!

I wish someone else would report a piece of blue. Surely, the blue plate used for a pattern shot is not an experimental piece or color. I certainly hope that there are other pieces in this lovely color! Let me know what you find in Cupid!

	All colors		All colors
Bowl, 8½" Oval-Footed	75.00	Creamer, 5" Footed	52.50
Bowl, 9¼" Footed Fruit	65.00	Ice Bucket, 6"	95.00
Bowl, 9¼" Center-handled	60.00	Ice Tub, 4¾"	100.00
Bowl, 10¼", Fruit	65.00	Lamp, Silver Overlay	300.00
Bowl, 10½", Rolled Edge	65.00	Mayonnaise, 6" Diameter,	
Bowl, 11" Console	60.00	Fits on 8" Plate	85.00
Cake Plate, 11¾"	70.00	Plate, 10½"	55.00
Cake Stand, 2" High, Footed	60.00	Samovar	650.00
Candlestick, 5" Wide, Pr.	85.00	Sugar, 4¼" Footed	50.00
Candy w/Lid, Footed, 4¾" High	100.00	Sugar, 5" Footed	52.50
Candy w/Lid, 3 Part	95.00	Tray, 10¾" Center-handled	55.00
Casserole, covered	250.00	Tray, 10⅞" Oval-Footed	75.00
Comport, 6¼"	50.00	Vase, 8¼" Elliptical	195.00
Creamer, 4½" Footed	50.00	Vase, Fan-Shaped	125.00

Please refer to Foreword for pricing information

46

"DAISY," NUMBER 620 INDIANA GLASS COMPANY

Colors: Crystal, 1933; fired-on red, 1935; amber, 1940; dark green and milk glass, 1960's, 1970's.

Daisy green is catching on with collectors! Remember that it was made in the 1960's and 1970's instead of the Depression era. I received a floral bouquet in 1983 in a green 7⅜" berry bowl when I was in the hospital. It was embossed 1981 in the bottom! This avocado colored green Daisy was marketed by Indiana as "Heritage" and not under the name Daisy or No. 620 as it was when it was first produced in the late 1930's. I mention this because Federal Glass Company also made a "Heritage" pattern that is rare in green. Amber still is the color predominantly collected, but several pieces in amber are causing headaches, particularly the 12 oz. footed tea, 9⅜" berry and the cereal bowls.

I receive more mail than I have time to answer and on occasion, I get one that amuses me. Not long ago, I received a letter blessing me out for the HIGH prices in my book. The lady went on to list prices such as the cereal bowls in amber Daisy and cereal bowls in amber Rosemary than she could not sell for $10.00, let alone get $20.00 for them. There were several other pieces in the same hard to find category that she could not sell at half price. My wife was reading this letter as we were driving to lunch one day. I told her to write the lady and tell her I would be more than happy to purchase her glass at half price. (I pay 60% in my shop for major patterns). To make a long story short, there was no SASE (Self Addressed Stamped Envelope) which means I normally would not answer it; but even worse, there was no return address at all; so I couldn't even answer her to buy her glass! There are a few pieces of red fired-on Daisy being found. A reader's letter this year said that her family had a red set that was purchased in 1935. So, that helps date this production.

	Green, Crystal	Red, Amber		Green, Crystal	Red, Amber
Bowl, 4½" Berry	4.00	7.00	Plate, 10⅜" Grill w/Indent		
Bowl, 4½" Cream Soup	3.00	8.00	for Cream Soup	10.00	25.00
Bowl, 6" Cereal	10.00	22.50	Plate, 11½" Cake or Sandwich	5.00	9.00
Bowl, 7⅜" Deep Berry	6.00	10.00	Platter, 10¾"	5.00	10.00
Bowl, 9⅜" Deep Berry	12.00	25.00	Relish Dish, 8⅜", 3 Part	10.00	20.00
Bowl, 10" Oval Vegetable	8.00	13.00	Saucer	1.00	1.50
Creamer, Footed	4.50	6.50	Sherbet, Footed	2.50	7.00
Cup	2.50	4.50	Sugar, Footed	3.00	6.50
Plate, 6" Sherbet	1.00	2.00	Tumbler, 9 oz. Footed	7.00	15.00
Plate, 7⅜" Salad	2.00	5.50	Tumbler, 12 oz. Footed	17.50	30.00
Plate, 8⅜" Luncheon	2.00	5.00			
Plate, 9⅜" Dinner	3.50	7.00			

DIANA FEDERAL GLASS COMPANY, 1937-1941

Colors: Pink, amber and crystal.

Diana is not as available as it once was. Of course that goes for other Depression glass patterns as well. There are more collectors of crystal than ever before. Crystal collectors have found out what collectors of the other colors found out years ago. There are very few tumblers available. I met a crystal collector in Georgia who had only purchased three of a desired eight tumblers in five years of collecting. She had eight of everything else in that time. Besides the tumblers, there are a limited number of candy dishes, shakers, sherbets and even platters being found. This is true for all colors, but especially amber.

New collectors confuse Diana with some of the other swirled patterns such as Swirl and Twisted Optic. The centers of Diana's pieces are swirled where the centers of the other patterns are plain.

There are very few pink demitasse sets being found. Crystal seems to be more plentiful and so are the cranberry or red sprayed-on sets. These flashed red sets are selling in the $10.00 to $12.00 range. So far, there is little demand for the frosted or satinized pieces that have shown up in crystal or pink. Some crystal frosted pieces have been trimmed in colors, predominantly red.

	Crystal	Pink	Amber		Crystal	Pink	Amber
* Ash Tray, 3½"	2.00	3.00		Plate, 6" Bread & Butter	1.00	1.50	1.50
Bowl, 5" Cereal	3.50	4.50	8.50	Plate, 9½"	4.00	6.00	6.50
Bowl, 5½" Cream Soup	2.50	8.00	9.00	Plate, 11¾" Sandwich	4.50	6.00	6.50
Bowl, 9" Salad	5.00	6.50		Platter, 12" Oval	5.00	8.00	9.00
Bowl, 11" Console Fruit	5.00	6.50	8.00	Salt and Pepper, Pr.	19.50	50.00	85.00
Bowl, 12" Scalloped Edge	6.50	8.50	12.00	Saucer	1.00	1.50	1.50
Candy Jar and Cover,				Sherbet	2.50	5.50	6.00
Round	12.00	20.00	25.00	Sugar, Open Oval	2.50	4.00	4.00
Coaster, 3½"	2.00	3.50		Tumbler, 4⅛", 9 oz.	15.00	20.00	20.00
Creamer, Oval	3.00	6.00	7.00	Junior Set: 6 Cups and			
Cup	2.50	4.00	4.00	Saucers with Round Rack		55.00	135.00
Cup, 2 oz. Demitasse							
and 4½" Saucer Set	6.50	20.00					

* Green $3.00

Please refer to Foreword for pricing information

DIAMOND QUILTED, "FLAT DIAMOND"

IMPERIAL GLASS COMPANY, Late 1920's-Early 1930's

Colors: Pink, blue, green, crystal, black; some red and amber.

A few more Diamond Quilted punch bowls have surfaced. In fact, there were both pink and green sets at a recent show in Chicago! I had never before seen both sets at the same show. Both were sold to the same collector. I guess it will be a long time before they are split up again because the collector was ecstatic with his purchases! More and more of the harder to find pieces are going into collections. Until those collections are sold, those rarely found items are not seen again. Believe me, they're just becoming more and more valuable as they remain in those collections, too!

I caution collectors of green to be aware of the two distinct shades available. You can see that in the top photograph with the two styles of candlesticks. The darker green candle is Diamond Quilted as shown in the catalogue ad at the bottom of the page. I have sometimes seen these candlesticks misidentified as Windsor Diamond.

Those console sets at 65 cents and a dozen candy dishes in assorted colors for $6.95 would be quite a bargain today. No, I do not have any for sale at that price. This ad is from a 1930's catalogue and not my store. I mention that since I get several orders a year from people trying to order glass from these old catalogue ads placed throughout the book!

There is a Hazel Atlas quilted diamond pitcher and tumbler set made in pink, green, cobalt blue and a blue similar to the blue shown here that is confused with Imperial's Diamond Quilted. The quilting on Hazel Atlas pieces ends in a straight line around the top of each piece. Notice this Diamond Quilted pattern ends unevenly in points. You may also notice that the diamond designs on Diamond Quilted pieces are flat as opposed to those others that are curved.

Black pieces have the design on the bottom. Thus, the design on the plate can only be seen if it is turned over. A black creamer is shown satinized with painted flowers. It is the only piece I have seen with such treatment.

	Pink, Green	Blue, Black		Pink, Green	Blue, Black
Bowl, 4¾" Cream Soup	6.50	15.00	Pitcher, 64 oz.	40.00	
Bowl, 5" Cereal	4.50	10.00	Plate, 6" Sherbet	2.50	3.50
Bowl, 5½" One Handle	5.50	12.50	Plate, 7" Salad	4.00	6.50
Bowl, 7" Crimped Edge	5.50	12.00	Plate, 8" Luncheon	4.00	10.00
Bowl, 10½", Rolled Edge Console	15.00	40.00	Punch Bowl and Stand	350.00	
Cake Salver, Tall 10" Diameter	45.00		Plate, 14" Sandwich	8.50	
Candlesticks (2 Styles), Pr.	20.00	40.00	Sandwich Server, Center Handle	20.00	40.00
Candy Jar and Cover, Footed	50.00		Saucer	2.00	3.50
Compote and Cover, 11½"	60.00		Sherbet	4.00	12.50
Creamer	6.00	12.50	Sugar	6.00	12.50
Cup	8.00	12.00	Tumbler, 9 oz. Water	6.50	
Goblet, 1 oz. Cordial	8.00		Tumbler, 12 oz. Iced Tea	7.50	
Goblet, 2 oz. Wine	8.00		Tumbler, 6 oz. Footed	6.00	
Goblet, 3 oz. Wine	8.00		Tumbler, 9 oz. Footed	9.50	
Goblet, 6", 9 oz. Champagne	7.50		Tumbler, 12 oz. Footed	12.50	
Ice Bucket	37.50	75.00	Vase, Fan, Dolphin Handles	40.00	60.00
Mayonnaise Set: Ladle,			Whiskey, 1½ oz.	6.50	
Plate, Comport	30.00	50.00			

Covered Bowl—6⅜ in. diam., deep round shape with 3 artistic feet, dome cover, fine quality brilliant finish **pot glass**, allover block diamond design, transparent Rose Marie and emerald green.
I C5603—Asstd. ½ doz. in carton, 20 lbs.
Doz $6.95

I C989—3 piece set, 2 transparent colors (rose and green), good quality, 10½ in. rolled rim bowl, TWO 3½ in. wide base candlesticks. Asstd. 6 sets in case, 30 lbs. . . . . **SET (3 pcs)** **65c**

Please refer to Foreword for pricing information

DOGWOOD, "APPLE BLOSSOM," "WILD ROSE" MacBETH-EVANS GLASS COMPANY, 1929-1932

Colors: Pink, green, some crystal, Monax, Cremax and yellow.

Pink and green Dogwood are both selling very well. I recently purchased an eight place setting in green with sherbets! I had only owned one green sherbet in all the years I have been buying and selling Depression glass. I once bought four pink platters at one flea market on the same day . Several years later, I purchased nine pink platters at one time in Pennsylvania. Platters are consider rare, and I have owned three times as many of these as I have green sherbets. I was amazed how fast these sherbets sold.

Even more amazing was a customer coming into the shop and buying the whole eight place setting at one time. You normally sell a newly purchased pattern a little at a time. The sherbets had been sold at a show the week before, and the new customer was happy I had not taken the rest of the pattern to that show. Whole patterns selling at one time is a new concept that has not been prevalent before. It has been happening more and more. (Three times in my shop in two weeks)!

Plain (undecorated) tumblers and pitchers made by Macbeth-Evans are not Dogwood! An example in the picture is the shot glass next to the juice tumbler. It is only made in the shape of Dogwood! Do not buy this as "undecorated Dogwood." (In the case of the fat pitcher on the right, it is also not American Sweetheart if it has no pattern etched on it!) These are blanks which became Dogwood only **after** a silk screen decoration was added.

Few pieces of yellow are being found, but there is not much demand for it either. Cremax is another rare color of Dogwood which does not excite many collectors. The Monax salver (12" plate) was once thought of as hard to find, but, over the years it has turned out to be more of a novelty than rare.

The ash tray shown in the foreground is not Dogwood. This ash tray was made by Macbeth-Evans and packed with all of their patterns. It can be found packed in original boxes of American Sweetheart and "S" Pattern also. These sell for $2.00 to $3.00 in pink and $3.00 to $4.00 in green.

The pink sugar, creamer and cup represent the thick style while the green show the thin style. Pink is found in both styles, but the green is only found in thin. The thin creamers were made by adding a spout to the cups. Some of these thin creamers have a very undefined spout. Although there are thick pink cups, the saucers for both style cups are the same.

The pink juice tumbler, platter, large bowl and the American Sweetheart style pitcher have become the items to own. Grill plates come in two styles. Some of these have the Dogwood pattern all over the plate and others have only the pattern around the rim of the plate. Besides the sherbets already discussed, grill plates (rim pattern only), pitcher and tumblers are also difficult to accumulate in green Dogwood.

Sherbets come in two styles. Some have a Dogwood blossom etched on the bottom; some have no blossom on the bottom. I have been told that this gives mail order dealers a problem. Please be sure to specify which style you are trying to match if that is important to you. It really makes no difference as they are only different moulds.

Be aware that there are stemmed pieces with a "Dogwood-like" pattern on them. These come in several sizes and many collectors buy them to go with their sets.

	Pink	Green	Monax Cremax		Pink	Green	Monax, Cremax
*Bowl, 5½" Cereal	17.50	20.00	2.00	Plate, 10½" Grill AOP or Border Design Only	15.00	15.00	
Bowl, 8½" Berry	40.00	85.00	32.00	Plate, 12" Salver	20.00		15.00
Bowl, 10¼" Fruit	245.00	125.00	65.00	Platter, 12" Oval (Rare)	285.00		
Cake Plate, 11" Heavy Solid Ft.	195.00			Saucer	4.00	5.00	15.00
Cake Plate, 13" Heavy Solid Ft.	70.00	65.00	150.00	Sherbet, Low Footed	22.00	75.00	
Creamer, 2½" Thin	14.00	37.50		Sugar, 2½" Thin	12.00	37.50	
Creamer, 3¼" Thick, Footed	15.00			Sugar, 3¼" Thick, Footed	12.00		
Cup, Thin or Thick	11.00	20.00	32.00	Tumbler, 3½", 5 oz. Decorated	225.00		
Pitcher, 8", 80 oz. Decorated	130.00	450.00		Tumbler, 4", 10 oz. Decorated	27.00	65.00	
Pitcher, 8", 8 oz. (American Sweetheart Style)	450.00			Tumbler, 4¾", 11 oz. Decorated	32.00	75.00	
Plate, 6" Bread and Butter	4.50	6.00	20.00	Tumbler, 5", 12 oz. Decorated	35.00	85.00	
* Plate, 8" Luncheon	4.75	6.00		Tumbler, Moulded Band	12.00		
Plate, 9¼" Dinner	18.00						

*Yellow - $50.00

Please refer to Foreword for pricing information

DORIC JEANNETTE GLASS COMPANY, 1935-1938

Colors: Pink, green, some Delphite and yellow.

Doric is a popular pattern—but a little tricky to collect!. Because of all the new collectors, the scarce tumblers are becoming even more so. Tumblers, especially the footed ones, cereal and cream soup bowls, and pitchers have all become THE pieces to own in Doric. Green is more scarce and has more collectors than pink; and therefore, the price for green is higher than the pink. I have only found two cereals and two footed teas in green in the last two years of buying. I might mention that the mould seams on all the footed tumblers are usually rough as is the case on many of the cereals. Many collectors have not seen either piece! In other words, don't let a little roughness keep you from owning these if you see them for sale!

That yellow pitcher in the bottom photo is still the only one known. In January 1973, that pitcher sold for $300.00 which was almost a monthly pay check for me as a teacher. I thought I was not able to buy it.Today, the only Doric pitchers that sell for less than $300.00 are the juice pitchers in pink or green! I should have borrowed the money!

Speaking of the pitchers, the large footed ones come with or without an ice lip as shown in the pink. All these pitchers are difficult to find, with the green nearly impossible. Green Doric collecting is a challenge. It probably will not break you at one time since you will need years to complete a large set unless you get extremely lucky!

Unlike several of Jeannette's other patterns, the candy and sugar lids in this pattern are not interchangeable. The candy is taller and more domed. See the pictures on the right with a green candy and pink sugar.

I still get a lot of letters about rare Delphite (opaque blue) pieces. Actually, the sherbet and the cloverleaf candy are common in Delphite. All other pieces of Delphite ARE rare in Doric; however, there are few collectors; and so the price is reasonable for so rare a color. This could change. Numerous people are buying still "rare but reasonable" glassware as their "retirement" plan.

A three part candy in an iridized color was made in the 1970's and sold for 79 cents in our local dish barn. All other colors of the three part candy are old.

The pink shaker lids are original old nickel plated tops; those on the green are newly made aluminum tops. Original lids are preferable when available, but there are alternatives to having no lids at all.

	Pink	Green	Delphite		Pink	Green	Delphite
Bowl, 4½" Berry	5.00	5.50	27.50	Plate, 6" Sherbet	2.50	3.00	
Bowl, 5" Cream Soup		200.00		Plate, 7" Salad	12.50	13.00	
Bowl, 5½" Cereal	30.00	40.00		Plate, 9" Dinner			
Bowl, 8¼" Large Berry	9.50	12.50	85.00	(Serrated 50.00)	8.00	11.00	
Bowl, 9" 2-Handled	9.50	10.00		Plate, 9" Grill	10.00	14.00	
Bowl, 9" Oval Vegetable	15.00	2000		Platter, 12" Oval	13.00	15.00	
Butter Dish and Cover	55.00	70.00		Relish Tray, 4" x 4"	5.00	7.50	
Butter Dish Bottom	17.50	25.00		** Relish Tray, 4" x 8"	6.50	9.50	
Butter Dish Top	37.50	45.00		Salt and Pepper, Pr.	25.00	27.50	
Cake Plate, 10", 3 Legs	12.50	12.50		Saucer	2.00	2.50	
Candy Dish and				Sherbet, Footed	8.00	10.00	5.00
Cover, 8"	25.00	27.50		Sugar	9.00	10.00	
* Candy Dish, 3-Part	4.50	5.50	4.50	Sugar Cover	10.00	17.50	
Coaster, 3"	10.00	12.00		Tray, 10" Handled	8.00	10.00	
Creamer, 4"	7.50	8.50		Tray, 8" x 8" Serving	9.00	12.00	
Cup	6.00	7.00		Tumbler, 4½", 9 oz.	35.00	55.00	
Pitcher, 6", 36 oz. Flat	25.00	30.00	850.00	Tumbler, 4", 10 oz.			
Pitcher, 7½", 48 oz.				Footed	35.00	60.00	
Footed	350.00	700.00		Tumbler, 5", 12 oz.,			
(Also in Yellow				Footed	45.00	70.00	
at $1,250.00)							

* Candy in metal holder - $40.00. Iridescent made recently. Ultramarine $15.00

Please refer to Foreword for pricing information

DORIC AND PANSY JEANNETTE GLASS COMPANY, 1937-1938

Colors: Ultramarine; some crystal and pink.

Doric and Pansy price doldrums continue with more and more discoveries of this pattern being made in Canada and England. No wonder we always thought Doric and Pansy was rare. It was in the continental United States, but not so outside these boundaries! I now know of over a dozen butter dishes found in England in the last few years. Those are just the ones that have contacted me and I am sure there are others. The price on the butter has continued to slide with so many butters on the market. Hopefully, these will eventually be absorbed into the market; but for now, they are more plentiful than the demand for them.

Watch out for the weak patterned shakers. These should fetch less than the price listed below by 20 or 25 percent. Sugars and creamers are also being found along with those butter dishes; however, their price has not been as adversely effected since they were not so highly priced as the butters. For some reason tumblers and large and small berry bowls are not being found in the accumulations abroad. There have also been no reported findings of the children's sets; so there have been price increases in Doric and Pansy to go along with some decreasing prices.

The major problem facing ultramarine collectors of Doric and Pansy is the color variations. Many pieces have a distinct green cast instead of blue. Few collectors buy the green shade of ultramarine, so it is hard for dealers to sell. Unless you are able to buy the green cast as a large lot, you may have trouble if you ever go to resell it. However, there is the plus side to this greener shade if you like it. Oft times you can purchase it at a bargain price! Future generations may prefer the greener color. You never know!

Only berry and children's sets have been found in pink. Crystal creamer and sugar sets are rare, but there are few collectors. Most of these sets are purchased by collectors of sugar and creamers rather than Doric and Pansy collectors.

I suppose you may have noticed the newly found odd shaped tumbler in the center of the picture. Two of these were found in Pittsburgh and sold in California to a Michigan dealer. I purchased the one below which did not survive a helper's accidental box dropping after our photo session. (That was not the way I had planned it, since George had been kind enough to lend it to me for you to see). The plus to this is I succeeded in making his other tumbler twice as rare. This tumbler stands 4¼" tall and holds 10 ounces. The remaining tumbler had a price tag of $495.00 the last time I saw it. Believe me, it is a rare tumbler!

	Green, Teal	Pink, Crystal		Green, Teal	Pink, Crystal
Bowl, 4½" Berry	10.00	6.50	Plate, 6" Sherbet	7.00	6.00
Bowl, 8" Large Berry	65.00	17.50	Plate, 7" Salad	25.00	
Bowl, 9" Handled	25.00	10.00	Plate, 9" Dinner	18.00	5.00
Butter Dish and Cover	400.00		Salt and Pepper, Pr.	300.00	
Butter Dish Bottom	75.00		Saucer	3.00	2.25
Butter Dish Top	325.00		Sugar, Open	100.00	60.00
Cup	15.00	7.50	Tray, 10" Handled	15.00	
Creamer	105.00	60.00	Tumbler, 4½", 9 oz.	45.00	

DORIC AND PANSY
"PRETTY POLLY PARTY DISHES"

	Teal	Pink		Teal	Pink
Cup	30.00	22.00	Creamer	30.00	22.50
Saucer	4.00	3.00	Sugar	30.00	22.50
Plate	7.00	5.00	14-Piece Set	210.00	160.00

Please refer to Foreword for pricing information

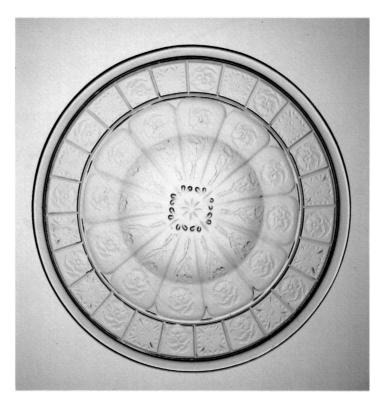

57

ENGLISH HOBNAIL WESTMORELAND GLASS COMPANY, 1920's-1970's

Colors: Crystal, pink, amber, turquoise, cobalt, green, blue and red.

English Hobnail collectors have begun to make their voices heard in the collecting world. The demise of Westmoreland has spurred many new collectors of blue, pink and green. I have only seen a little activity begun in collecting crystal, but I suspect that collectors will soon spring up for crystal also. There have been many rumors of reproduction Westmoreland glass being made. Rumors are facts when it comes to some of the old reamer moulds being used, but to my knowledge as of now (June 1989) no pieces of English Hobnail have been made since the factory closed. This book is written approximately every two years, so I can only update fakes at that time.

Cobalt blue pieces of English Hobnail are found very rarely. A new listing in cobalt is the wine shown in the top photograph! Now, if I could only find a cordial in either blue color for my cordial collection. The turquoise blue has more collectors than the cobalt because so many more pieces can be found in that shade of blue. The turquoise blue vase is particularly nice as an accessory piece. At a recent show, there was a display of blue with a beautiful bouquet of flowers in that vase as a centerpiece. That is a problem that faces collectors attending Depression glass shows. The beautiful displays of glass arranged by the club members makes you want to start collecting even more new patterns! Make a point to attend a show if you've never done so. You'll love it!

Collecting a whole set of English Hobnail is a difficult proposition. This, too, is a pattern that has many color variances. Pink is the easiest color to find, but there are two distinct shades of pink. There are also two distinct shades of amber. One of these is a light yellow amber while the other is dark, and even that varies from piece to piece. There are three different greens from a light yellow green to a deep, dark green. Many collectors mix shades of color, but others can not abide mixing them. That only becomes a problem when you have searched for eons for a particular piece, and when you find it, the coloring is wrong.

There is a story behind the 15" candy shown in green at the back of the lower photo. The first time one of these appeared in pink years ago, it was thought to be Miss America and brought a huge price. It was later determined to be English Hobnail when another was found in green. Another pink one turned up and was sold to an English Hobnail collector, also for a big price. A collector of Miss America tried to buy it from the English Hobnail collector even though she knew it was not Miss America. She offered $1500.00 for it and was turned down. A few years later the English Hobnail collector decided to sell the collection and called the Miss America collector who had since stopped collecting and was therefore no longer interested at any price. Remember the old "bird in hand" adage? A dealer called the next one found in green a "rare master candy" and it sold in Houston for around $700.00. The one in the photograph sold this year in Houston for $250.00. Originally there were a pair of these on a mantle in Cincinnati, Ohio, bought for family ashes I'm told. The new owner will probably not put candy in it as I told him about the intended usage when I sold it.

For beginning collectors, I offer the following observations to distinguish English Hobnail from Miss America. The centers of English Hobnail pieces have center rays of varying distances. Note the pieces set upright in the photographs for the six pointed star effect. In Miss America on page 123, the center rays all end equidistant from the center. The hobs on English Hobnail are more rounded and "feel" smoother to the touch; goblets flair and the hobs go directly into a plain rim area. On Miss America the hobs are sharper to touch and the goblets do not flair at the rim with both goblets and tumblers having three sets of rings above the hobs before entering a plain glass rim.

	Cobalt, Amber, Turquoise, Pink, Green		Cobalt, Amber, Turquoise, Pink, Green
* Ash Tray, Several Shapes	18.50	** Goblet, 6¼ oz.	20.00
Bowls, 4½", 5" Square and Round	9.50	Grapefruit, 6½" Flange Rim	14.00
Bowl, Cream Soup	13.50	Lamp, 6¼" Electric	40.00
Bowls, 6" Several Styles	10.00	** Lamp, 9¼"	90.00
Bowls, 8" Several Styles	20.00	Lamp Shade, 17" Diameter (Crystal)	125.00
** Bowls, 8" Footed and 2-Handled	45.00	Marmalade and Cover	32.50
** Bowls, 11" and 12" Nappies	37.50	Pitcher, 23 oz.	140.00
Bowls, 8", 9" Oval Relish	15.00	Pitcher, 39 oz.	165.00
Bowl, 12" Oval Relish	18.00	Pitcher, 60 oz.	200.00
Candlesticks, 3½" Pr.	30.00	Pitcher, ½ gal. Straight Sides	225.00
Candlesticks, 8½" Pr.	50.00	** Plate, 5½", 6½" Sherbet	3.50
Candy Dish, ½ lb. Cone-Shaped	45.00	Plate, 7¼" Pie	4.00
Candy Dish and Cover, Three Feet	65.00	** Plate, 8" Round or Square	7.50
Candy Dish and Cover, 15" High	250.00	Plate, 10" Dinner	20.00
Celery Dish, 9"	16.50	Salt and Pepper, Pr., Round or Square Bases	67.50
Celery Dish, 12"	20.00	Salt Dip, 2" Footed and with Place Card Holder	20.00
** Cigarette Box	25.00	Saucer	3.50
** Cologne Bottle	25.00	** Sherbet	12.50
Creamer, Footed or Flat	20.00	Sugar, Footed or Flat	20.00
Cup	15.00	Tumbler, 3¾", 5 oz. or 9 oz.	13.00
Decanter, 20 oz. with Stopper	95.00	Tumbler, 4", 10 oz. Iced Tea	15.00
Demitasse Cup and Saucer	30.00	Tumbler, 5", 12 oz. Iced Tea	20.00
Egg Cup	35.00	Tumbler, 7 oz. Footed	13.50
Goblet, 1 oz. Cordial	22.50	Tumbler, 9 oz. Footed	15.00
** Goblet, 2 oz. Wine	20.00	Tumbler, 12½ oz. Footed	20.00
Goblet, 3 oz. Cocktail	15.00	Vase	125.00
Goblet, 5 oz. Claret	18.00	Whiskey, 1½ oz. and 3 oz.	22.00

* Add about 50% more for Turquoise

** Cobalt double price listed

Please refer to Foreword for pricing information

FIRE-KING DINNERWARE "ALICE", "JANE RAY", "SQUARE"

ANCHOR HOCKING GLASS CORPORATION, 1940's-1960's

Colors: Jade-ite, white w/trims of blue or red

    "Alice" dinner plates are as elusive as will-o-the-wisps. Since the cup and saucers were packed in "Mother's" oats and the dinners had to be purchased, it may be that no one was willing to buy dinner plates to go with the cup and saucers. If anyone else has a better explanation, let me know. You will find "Alice" with white plates trimmed in red or blue. It is a shame no more pieces were added to this line.

    The "Square" is harder to find in blue, but more collected in green; so prices for each color are still comparable.

"Jane Ray" is the most collected of the three patterns shown here. A Jade-ite set is possible to attain in this color, with a newly listed demitasse set the hardest piece to find. The soups and platter are the next most difficult to find items. Price is beginning to rise due to the ever increasing demand of these patterns by new collectors. You may find additional pieces of this pattern.

    "Alice" is pictured below, "Jane Ray" on the top right and "Square" on the bottom right.

"Alice" prices*

	Jade-ite	White/trim
Cup	1.50	4.50
Plate, 9½"	10.00	7.50
Saucer	.50	1.50

"Square" prices

	All Colors
Bowl, 4¾", Dessert	3.00
Bowl, 7⅜", Salad	5.75
Cup	2.25
Plate, 8⅜", Luncheon	3.00
Plate, 9¼", Dinner	5.00
Saucer	.50

"Jane Ray" prices

	Jade-ite
Bowl, 4⅞", Dessert	1.50
Bowl, 5⅞", Oatmeal	2.25
Bowl, 7⅝", Soup	3.50
Bowl, 8¼", Vegetable	6.00
Cup	1.25
Cup, Demitasse	7.50
Creamer	2.00
Plate, 7¾", Salad	1.50
Plate, 9⅛", Dinner	2.50
Platter, 12"	8.50
Saucer	.50
Saucer, Demitasse	1.00
Sugar	1.75
Sugar Cover	2.75

FIRE-KING DINNERWARE "PHILBE" HOCKING GLASS COMPANY, 1937-1938

Colors: Blue, green, pink and crystal.

Fire-King dinnerware always elicits the same question at shows. Where is it? I can't seem to find any to buy. It is one of the rarest patterns in Depression Glass, but also one of the most desirable. Some people only collect one piece of each pattern and this is one pattern missing from their collection. The blue is very similar to Mayfair's blue, but many pieces have an added platinum trim as can be seen in the photograph.

Many of the pieces shown on the right are the only ones ever found. Of the five pitchers shown on the right, only another pink juice has been found. All three blue pitchers are the only blue known. The blue cup is still the only one ever found in any color. The two green tumblers are the only green tumblers ever found. You get the picture. It is not found except in a very few pieces that are found over and over again.

The more commonly found items include the blue footed tumblers of which the footed tea is the more easily found. Ask the dealer who bought eight of the iced teas and who has given them a tour of the country more than once trying to sell them at a high price. Pink oval vegetable bowls are the only common pink piece although that same bowl is also common in green. Green grill plates or luncheon plates might end up in your collection with more ease than anything else in "Philbe."

I finally saw another goblet in blue. It will be pictured in the second edition of *The Very Rare Glassware of the Depression Years* when it is released next year. It is a shame a whole set of this can not be collected. I have mentioned in previous books that on my very first trip to Anchor-Hocking in 1972 a whole set was displayed in the office window. I have never forgotten it, because at the time, I didn't even know what the pattern was. It was several years later, as more and more pieces were being found in shapes of pieces in Cameo and Mayfair, that I realized what I had seen. The next trip to the factory produced the revelation that it had been packed and to this day only a few pieces remain at Hocking. The cookie jar shown below is one of those pieces still left there in storage.

I explained how the footed blue tumblers arranged to miss the photo in the last book, so I promise to make sure they are shown in the next edition. The photography sessions for this and other books are major productions. Organizing the multitude of glass for these pictures is quite a process. Ask those collectors who have helped! They have a hard time believing what we do year after year - even after going through a session with us. Hopefully, you will find everyone's effort worthwhile.

	Crystal	Pink, Green	Blue		Crystal	Pink, Green	Blue
Bowl, 5½" Cereal	15.00	30.00	40.00	Plate, 10½" Salver	20.00	35.00	50.00
Bowl, 7¼" Salad	20.00	40.00	60.00	Plate, 10½" Grill	20.00	30.00	45.00
Bowl, 10" Oval				Plate, 11⅝" Salver	20.00	30.00	45.00
Vegetable	20.00	45.00	90.00	Platter, 12" Closed			
Candy Jar, 4" Low,				Handles	22.00	50.00	100.00
with Cover	200.00	400.00	500.00	Saucer, 6" (Same as			
Cookie Jar with Cover	500.00	750.00	950.00	Sherbet Plate)	15.00	30.00	50.00
Creamer, 3¼" Footed	30.00	75.00	95.00	Sugar, 3¼" Footed	30.00	75.00	95.00
Cup	30.00	75.00	125.00	Tumbler, 4", 9 oz.			
Goblet, 7¼", 9 oz.				Flat Water	30.00	100.00	125.00
Thin	47.50	117.50	150.00	Tumbler, 3½" Footed			
Pitcher, 6", 36 oz.				Juice	30.00	90.00	125.00
Juice	250.00	600.00	850.00	Tumbler, 5¼", 10 oz.			
Pitcher, 8½", 56 oz.	350.00	850.00	1,000.00	Footed	20.00	65.00	50.00
Plate, 6" Sherbet	15.00	30.00	50.00	Tumbler, 6½", 15 oz.			
Plate, 8" Luncheon	18.00	25.00	35.00	Footed Iced Tea	25.00	45.00	40.00
Plate, 10" Heavy							
Sandwich	20.00	50.00	75.00				

Please refer to Foreword for pricing information

FIRE-KING OVEN GLASS ANCHOR HOCKING GLASS CORPORATION, 1941-1950's

Colors: Pale blue, crystal; some ivory and Jade-ite.

Fire-King is more easily recognized by non-collectors than any of the other patterns in this book! It was popular and almost everyone remembers Grandma's cooking bread pudding or baking a pie in some piece of Fire-King. Many pieces were handed down from mother to daughter and it is amazing how many Fire-King pieces are still being used! That will give you an idea of the durability of this oven proof glassware.

The skillet and nipple cover are shown compliments of Anchor-Hocking's photographer. As I said previously, now that these are shown, you may turn one up. The skillets are still hiding, but a couple of the nipple covers have surfaced. The blue covers are embossed " BINKY'S NIP CAP U.S.A." (and not Fire-King). No, I have no idea who Binky is or was. Now, go and find a skillet! Yes, it is blue!

For novice collectors I have re-listed the 4⅜" individual pie plate and the 5⅜" deep dish plate (as they were listed by Anchor-Hocking) under "bowls" since I had so many calls and letters wanting to know about the unlisted bowls being found. These are both shown on the left in front of the big roaster.

Be careful using this in the microwave. It is fine for normal ovens, but it tends to develop heat cracks from sudden temperature changes when used in the microwave.

The dry cup measure is not one of the two style mugs being found. However, if you have what you think is a mug with ounce measurements up the side, then you really have the rarely found dry measure. If you do, let me know about your good luck. I'd like to get an idea how many of these exist.

The juice saver pie plate is still being found, but one of the major problems with this pie plate is the heavy usage that most received. I have never seen one chipped so they must have broken along the outward rim which held the pie's juice off of the oven bottom. Many of these are heavily scratched. To obtain the price below, this pie plate has to be mint.

There are two styles of table servers being found; and you can find a casserole lid atop a Bersted Mfg. Co. popcorn popper. One of these can be seen in the fourth edition of my *Kitchen Glassware of the Depression Era.*

	Blue		Blue
Baker, 1 pt., Round or Square	4.00	Custard Cup, 5 oz.	3.00
Baker, 1 qt.	5.00	Custard Cup, 6 oz., 2 Styles	3.50
Baker, 1½ qt.	9.00	Loaf Pan, 9⅛" Deep	20.00
Baker, 2 qt.	10.00	Nipple Cover	75.00
Bowl, 4⅜", Individual Pie plate	10.00	Nurser, 4 oz.	12.00
Bowl, 5⅜", Cereal or Deep Dish Pie Plate	11.00	Nurser, 8 oz.	17.50
Bowl, Measuring, 16 oz.	18.00	Pie Plate, 8⅜"	7.00
Cake Pan (Deep), 8¾" (Roaster)	15.00	Pie Plate, 9"	8.00
Casserole, 1 pt., Knob Handle Cover	10.00	Pie Plate, 9⅝"	9.00
Casserole, 1 qt., Knob Handle Cover	10.00	Pie Plate, 10⅜" Juice Saver	55.00
Casserole, 1½ qt., Knob Handle Cover	12.00	Percolator Top, 2⅛"	3.50
Casserole, 2 qt., Knob Handle Cover	15.00	Refrigerator Jar & Cover, 4½" x 5"	8.50
Casserole, Individual, 10 oz.	12.00	Refrigerator Jar & Cover, 5⅛" x 9⅛"	25.00
Casserole, 1 qt., Pie Plate Cover	15.00	Roaster, 8¾"	35.00
Casserole, 1½ qt., Pie Plate Cover	15.00	Roaster, 10⅜"	50.00
Casserole, 2 qt., Pie Plate Cover	18.00	Table Server, Tab Handles (Hot Plate)	12.00
Coffee Mug, 7 oz., 2 Styles	17.50	Utility Bowl, 6⅞"	9.00
Cup, 8 oz., Dry Measure, No Spout	125.00	Utility Bowl, 8⅜"	12.00
Cup, 8 oz. Measuring, 1 Spout	12.00	Utility Bowl, 10⅛"	15.00
Cup, 8 oz., Measuring, 3 Spout	16.00	Utility Pan, 8⅛" x 12½"	15.00

Please refer to Foreword for pricing information

FIRE-KING OVEN WARE, "TURQUOISE BLUE" ANCHOR HOCKING GLASS CORPORATION, 1950's

Colors: Turquoise blue.

"Turquoise Blue" pattern dishes were our everyday dishes for about five years. There are several observations that years of buying and using this pattern have taught us. The 10" plates are rare and not available in any quantity. It is an ideal size dinner plate (the normal 9" dinner does not hold enough with its upturned edges) as far as I am concerned. Soup and cereal bowls are not commonly found and are probably under priced in today's market. My sons feel the 8" vegetable bowl is a better cereal or soup bowl than the one that the company actually designated as a soup. There are a lot of big eaters in this family, and we like the dishes to hold the food without a dozen refills.

The cups, saucers, creamer and sugar are found easily. The 9" dinner plates and mugs are the next easiest pieces to accumulate. The 6⅛" and 7" plates are not as hard to find as the 10" plates, but they both are scarce. There have been many collectors of this pattern that told me they have never seen either one. Although the 9" plate with cup indent is not as plentiful as the dinner plate, it does not command the price of the dinner since not everyone wants to own these snack sets.

"Turquoise Blue" egg plates and relish plates are usually trimmed in gold and are not good candidates for the microwave since the gold "sparks". Other pieces handle the microwave quite well although I have never tried the teardrop shaped mixing bowls or the coffee cups since we always used mugs. There is also a handled batter bowl with spout in this pattern, but I have only seen a couple of them.

	Blue		Blue
Ash Tray (three sizes)	6.00		
Batter Bowl w/spout	30.00	Creamer	4.00
Bowl, 4½", Berry	4.00	Cup	2.50
Bowl, 5", Cereal	4.50	Egg Plate	10.00
Bowl, 6⅝", Soup/Salad	10.00	Mug, 8 oz.	7.50
Bowl, 8", Vegetable	9.00	Plate, 6⅛"	3.75
Bowl, Tear, Mixing, 1 pt.	4.00	Plate, 7"	5.00
Bowl, Tear, Mixing, 1 qt.	5.00	Plate, 9"	4.50
Bowl, Tear, Mixing, 2 qt.	6.00	Plate, 9", w/Cup Indent	4.00
Bowl, Tear, Mixing, 3 qt.	7.00	Plate, 10"	17.50
Bowl, Round, Mixing, 1 qt.	7.00	Relish, 3 Part	7.50
Bowl, Round, Mixing, 2 qt.	5.00	Saucer	.50
Bowl, Round, Mixing, 3 qt.	6.00	Sugar	3.75
Bowl, Round, Mixing, 4 qt.	7.00		

FIRE-KING OVEN WARE, "SWIRL" ANCHOR HOCKING GLASS CORPORATION, 1955-1960's

Colors: Blue, pink, white w/gold trim, ivory w/trims and Jade-ite.

Swirl" and "Turquoise Blue" are both embossed Oven Ware on the bottom. Each of the colors shown on the right have names found on original labels. The blue is "Azur-ite"; pink is "Pink"; white trimmed in gold is "22K-Gold"; red trimmed is "Sun Rise", and the green is "Jade-ite." The pink and black tumbler shown in the center of the Swirl picture was found in a boxed set of "Pink." I do not know if any tumblers were packed in other colored "Swirl" sets; but if you find a boxed set with tumblers in any other color, let me know.

Since this is heat proof, I suspect that it, too, can be put in the microwave. If you have done so with success, I will pass it on to readers next time. Blue Swirl may bring a higher price in some areas; except for the white, all other colors seem to be selling equally. It will take a longer time for price patterns to develop on this later made glassware.

	Jade-ite	*Other Colors		Jade-ite	*Other Colors
Bowl, Berry, 4⅞"	2.25	3.00	Plate, Dinner, 9⅛"	2.75	4.00
Creamer	2.25	3.50	Platter, 12"	8.00	12.00
Cup	2.00	2.50	Saucer	.50	.75
Plate, 6⅞", Salad	1.50	2.00	Sugar	1.50	2.00
			Sugar Cover	2.00	2.50

* White - 20 to 25% less

Please refer to Foreword for pricing information

FLORAGOLD, "LOUISA" JEANNETTE GLASS COMPANY, 1950's

Colors: Iridescent, some shell pink, ice blue and crystal.

Floragold is often thought to be "Carnival" glass by antique dealers who do not sell much glassware. In fact, this pattern wasn't made until the early 1950's which is forty years too late to be considered true "Carnival" glass. Floragold was designed similar to "Louisa" which was an early "Carnival" glass pattern. Often the rose bowl in "Louisa" is offered for sale as Floragold which turns the confusion around the other way.

I am amazed at how fast the price continues to rise on the Floragold vase. The large tumbler, which is also not very common, was fluted and turned into a small vase. It can be seen next to the butter dish on the left side of the photo. Many of these large, 15 oz. tumblers can be found in crystal selling in the $10.00 range. Crystal tumblers were sprayed with the iridized color and refired to make it stay. Evidently, many of these tumblers were never sprayed. That is unusual since few other crystal pieces are found.

The smaller butter dish (which was shown in earlier editions) remains a mystery. Only one of these has ever been found. It is 5½" square by 3" tall. The normally found square butter shown on the left is 6¼" square and 3½" tall.

There are two different 5¼" comports in Floragold. These were a non-production item. One has a ruffled top and the other has a plain top. These were first shown in my first edition *Very Rare Glassware of the Depression Years* and you can see them here as the pattern shots.

Perfect tops to shakers are hard to find. Because the tops were plastic many were broken by tightening them too much. Some of these tops were made in white and others were brown. Both were made only in plastic; metal tops are replacements.

There is a tid-bit tray in this pattern made up of two ruffled bowls and a white, wooden post. Normally, tid-bits are made from plates.

There are an abundance of cups in Floragold. Cups were sold without saucers in two ways. The large bowl and the pitcher were both sold with twelve cups as "egg nog" sets for the Christmas market. Each set added to the cup production; so today, saucers seem scarce. The 5¼" saucer has no cup ring and is the same as the sherbet plate.

Ice blue, crystal, red-yellow, shell pink and iridized large size comports were made in the early 1960's and into the early 1970's.

	Iridescent		Iridescent
Bowl, 4½" Square	4.50	Cup	4.50
Bowl, 5½" Round Cereal	22.50	Pitcher, 64 oz.	25.00
Bowl, 5½" Ruffled Fruit	7.50	Plate, 5¼" Sherbet	8.50
Bowl, 8½" Square	12.00	Plate, 8½" Dinner	22.00
Bowl, 9½" Deep Salad	27.50	Plate or Tray, 13½"	12.50
Bowl, 9½" Ruffled	7.50	Plate or Tray, 13½", with indent	35.00
Bowl, 12" Ruffled Large Fruit	6.50	Platter, 11¼"	13.50
Butter Dish and Cover, ¼ lb. Oblong	20.00	* Salt and Pepper, Plastic Tops	36.00
Butter Dish and Cover, Round	35.00	Saucer, 5¼" (No Ring)	8.50
Butter Dish Bottom	12.00	Sherbet, Low Footed	10.00
Butter Dish Top	23.00	Sugar	5.00
Candlesticks, Double Branch Pr.	37.50	Sugar Lid	7.50
Candy or Cheese Dish and Cover, 6¾"	40.00	Tid-bit, Wooden Post	20.00
Candy, 5¼" Long, 4 Feet	4.50	Tumbler, 10 oz. Footed	14.00
Candy Dish, 1 Handle	6.50	Tumbler, 11 oz. Footed	14.00
Coaster/Ash Tray, 4"	4.50	Tumbler, 15 oz. Footed	55.00
Creamer	6.50	Vase or Celery	185.00

* Tops $8.00 each

Please refer to Foreword for pricing information

FLORAL, "POINSETTIA" JEANNETTE GLASS COMPANY, 1931-1935

Colors: Pink, green, Delphite, Jadite, crystal, amber, red and yellow.

Floral green pieces continue to be found in England and Canada. It is the more unusual and thought to be rare pieces which are being found. They were rare in our country until collectors in Canada discovered Depression glass and started digging in the nooks and crannies up there. Many Canadians have ancestry in England who continued the search over there. The green Floral flat bottomed pitchers and flat bottomed tumblers are blossoming and the prices are moderating because of the many discoveries. Much of this Floral found in Canada and England is a slightly lighter color green, and the flat pieces all have ground bottoms. This Floral is also panelled to the extent that it stands out from normally found Floral. Rose bowls, and vases in all sizes are found in England; so if you vacation in Europe, remember to try England for Depression glass. If you take my book, you can show the customs inspectors that it was American made and save the import duty on your purchases so one reader informed me.

The big news in Floral is that **reproduction shakers** are now being found in pink, cobalt blue and a dark green color. Cobalt blue and the dark green Floral shakers are of little concern since they were never made in these colors originally. The green is darker than the original green shown here but not as deep as Forest green. The pink shakers are not only a very good pink, but they are also a very good copy. There are lots of minor variations in design and leaf detail to someone who knows glassware well, but I have always tried to pick out a point that anyone can use to determine validity whether he be a novice or professional. There is one easy way to tell the Floral reproductions. Take off the top and look at the threads where the lid screws onto the shaker. On the old there are a PAIR of parallel threads on each side or at least a pair on one side which end right before the mould seams down each side. The new Floral has **ONE CONTINUOUS LINE** thread which starts on one side and continues around the shaker until it ends above the beginning line on the other side. There is approximately one inch of overlapped thread making two lines for that inch; but the whole thread is **ONE CONTINUOUS LINE** and not two separate ones as on the old. No other Floral reproductions have been made as of June 1989.

Floral lemonade pitchers are still being found in the Northwest, but the pink substantially outnumber the green. There are more collectors for green than pink; so these two factors cause the price differences.

There are several pieces of the dresser set being found (shown on page 73), but the set shown here is the only completed set known. Quantities of the 9¼" tray for the set have been found, but the powder jars are not available.

Floral is one of Jeannette's patterns in which the sugar and candy lids are interchangeable.

There are two distinct varieties of pink 11" platters. One has a normal flat edge as shown in the back left of the photo; and the other has a scalloped edge like the platter in Cherry Blossom.

Unusual items in Floral (so far) include the following:
- a) an entire set of DELPHITE Floral
- b) a YELLOW two-part relish dish
- c) an AMBER plate, cup and saucer
- d) green and crystal JUICE PITCHERS w/ground bottoms (shown)
- e) footed vases in green and crystal, flared at the rim (shown); some hold flower frogs with THE PATTERN ON THE FROGS (shown)
- f) a crystal lemonade pitcher
- g) lamps (shown in green and pink)
- h) A green GRILL plate
- i) an octagonal vase with patterned, round foot (shown)
- j) a RUFFLED EDGED berry and master berry bowl
- k) pink and green Floral ICE tubs (shown)
- l) oval vegetable with cover
- m) a rose bowl (shown)
- n) a 9" comport in pink and green (shown)
- o) 9 oz. flat tumblers in green (shown)
- p) 3 oz. footed tumblers in green (shown)
- q) 8" round bowl in cremax and opaque red
- r) CARAMEL colored dinner plate
- s) cream soups (shown in pink)

	Pink	Green	Delphite	Jadite
Bowl, 4" Berry (Ruffled 50.00)	11.00	12.00	25.00	
Bowl, 5½" Cream Soup	650.00	650.00		
* Bowl, 7½" Salad (Ruffled 95.00)	10.00	12.00	45.00	
Bowl, 8" Covered Vegetable	25.00	35.00	37.50 (no cover)	
Bowl, 9" Oval Vegetable	10.00	12.00		
Butter Dish and Cover	70.00	75.00		
Butter Dish Bottom	17.50	20.00		
Butter Dish Top	52.50	55.00		
Canister Set: Coffee, Tea, Cereal Sugar, 5¼" Tall, Each				30.00
Candlesticks, 4" Pr.	52.50	67.50		
Candy Jar and Cover	27.50	33.00		
Creamer, Flat (Cremax $50.00)	9.00	10.00	65.00	
Coaster, 3¼"	10.00	7.00		
Comport, 9"	600.00	700.00		
*** Cup	7.50	8.50		
Dresser Set (As Shown)		1000.00		
Frog for Vase (Also Crystal $500.00)		650.00		
Ice Tub, 3½" High Oval	600.00	650.00		
Lamp	225.00	245.00		
Pitcher, 5½", 23 or 24 oz.		400.00		
Pitcher, 8", 32 oz. Footed Cone	20.00	25.00		
Pitcher, 10¼", 48 oz. Lemonade	165.00	195.00		
Plate, 6" Sherbet	3.50	4.00		
Plate, 8" Salad	7.00	8.00		
** Plate, 9" Dinner	11.00	13.00	110.00	
Plate, 9" Grill		150.00		
Platter (Like Cherry Blossom)	55.00			
Platter, 10¾" Oval	11.00	12.50	125.00	
Refrigerator Dish and Cover, 5" Square		55.00		15.00
*** Relish Dish, 2-Part Oval	10.00	11.00		
**** Salt and Pepper, 4" Footed Pair	37.50	42.50		
Salt and Pepper, 6" Flat	40.00			
*** Saucer	6.50	7.50		
Sherbet	11.00	13.00	75.00	
Sugar (Cremax $50.00)	7.50	8.50	55.00 (open)	
Sugar/Candy Cover	9.50	13.00		
Tray, 6" Square, Closed Handles	9.50	12.00		
Tray, 9¼", Oval for Dresser Set		150.00		
Tumbler, 4½", 9 oz. Flat		145.00		
Tumbler, 3½", 3 oz. Footed		95.00		
Tumbler, 4", 5 oz. Footed Juice	13.00	16.00		
Tumbler, 4¾", 7 oz. Footed Water	13.00	16.00	150.00	
Tumbler, 5¼", 9 oz. Footed Lemonade	32.50	35.00		
Vase, 3 Legged Rose Bowl		400.00		
Vase, 3 Legged Flared (Also in Crystal)		400.00		
Vase, 6⅞" Tall (8 Sided)		375.00		

*Cremax $110.00

**These have now been found in amber and red.

***This has been found in yellow.

****Beware reproductions!

Please refer to Foreword for pricing information

FLORAL AND DIAMOND BAND U.S. GLASS COMPANY, Late 1920's

Colors: Pink, green; some iridescent, black and crystal.

Floral and Diamond is one of U.S. Glass Company's patterns that is collectible even without a cup and saucer. Pink luncheon plates and sugar lids or iced tea tumblers in all colors are THE pieces to find. Many butter bottoms in Floral and Diamond have been robbed to use on other U.S. Glass patterns such as Strawberry and Cherryberry. This occurred because all U.S. Glass butter bottoms are plain. They are all interchangeable with the pattern on the top only. Floral and Diamond butter dishes were very cheaply priced in comparison to Strawberry, so collectors bought these to use their bottoms for other tops. This has now created a shortage of bottoms in pink.

One collecting problem is the various shades of green. Some of the green is blue tinted. It is up to you as how seriously you consider color matching. Another thing that new collectors need to be aware of is mould roughness along the seams of the tumblers and plates. This is "normal" for Floral and Diamond and not considered a detriment.

One of the many interesting things that has happened to Floral and Diamond since I have been associated with Depression glass happened when Carnival glass collectors picked the iridized pitcher shown here as the "find" of the year in "Mayflower" pattern . As you can see by the 1928 ads below, sometimes this pattern was described as "Floral and Diamond" and sometimes as "Diamond and Floral". Carnival glass is normally thought of as being made prior to 1920.

Only the small creamer and sugar have been found in black. This same sized sugar and creamer are often found with a cut flower over the normally found moulded flower.

The iridized and crystal pitcher and butter dishes are rare! In fact, crystal is not commonly found except creamers and sugars.

	Pink	Green			Pink	Green
Bowl, 4½" Berry	5.00	6.00	* Pitcher, 8", 42 oz..		70.00	80.00
Bowl, 5¾" Handled Nappy	7.00	7.00	Plate, 8" Luncheon		22.50	20.00
Bowl, 8" Large Berry	9.50	10.00	Sherbet		5.00	6.00
* Butter Dish and Cover	110.00	95.00	Sugar, Small		7.00	8.00
Butter Dish Bottom	75.00	75.00	Sugar, 5¼"		10.00	10.00
Butter Dish Top	35.00	20.00	Sugar Lid		40.00	50.00
Compote, 5½" Tall	9.50	10.00	Tumbler, 4" Water		13.00	15.00
Creamer, Small	7.00	8.00	Tumbler, 5" Iced Tea		18.00	22.00
Creamer, 4¾"	12.00	15.00				

* Iridescent - $145.00
  Crystal - $100.00

Seven-Piece Berry Set

You'll really be most satisfied with the purchase of this set. It's very attractive, and affords a fitting and stylish addition to your present pieces. In green pressed glass, with diamond and floral design. Large bowl, 8 inches in diameter, and six sauce dishes to match. 4½ inches in diameter.
35N6838—Weight, packed, 7 pounds. Per set...... **68c**

Seven-Piece ☕ Water Set

Made from green pressed glass, with a floral and diamond design. You'll find that the sparkling scintillating pitcher and glasses are a set you'll be mighty proud to own when serving cold drinks. 3-pint pitcher. Six 8-ounce tumblers.
35N6837—Weight, packed, 12 pounds. Per set. **$1.18**

Five-Piece∧ Table Set

Heavy pressed glass in light green, with pressed diamond and floral design. Creamer, covered sugar bowl and covered butter dish. Weight, packed, 9 pounds.
35N6836......... **65c**

FLORENTINE NO. 1, "OLD FLORENTINE", "POPPY NO. 1"
HAZEL ATLAS GLASS COMPANY, 1932-1935

Colors: Pink, green, crystal, yellow and cobalt.

One of the most confusing things for new collectors is learning the differences between Florentine No. 1 and No. 2. It is simple to distinguish once you see the differences. Notice the outline of the pattern shot on the right. The scalloped edges occur on all flat pieces of Florentine No. 1. All footed pieces such as tumblers, shakers or pitchers have the serrated edge. In Florentine No. 2 all flat pieces have a plain edge and the footed pieces are also plain edged. Florentine No. 1 was once advertised as hexagonal and Florentine No. 2 was once advertised as round. This should also help you to remember the differences.

Florentine No. 1 shakers have been **reproduced** in pink and cobalt blue. There may be other colors to follow. I only have one reproduction sample, and it is difficult to know if all shakers will be as badly moulded as this one. I can say by looking at this one shaker that there is little or no design on the bottom. No cobalt blue Florentine No. 1 shakers have ever been found, so those are no problem. The pink is more difficult. I am comparing this one to several old pairs from my shop. The old shakers have a major open flower on each side. There is a top circle on this blossom with three smaller circles down each side. The seven circles form the outside of the blossom. The **new** blossom looks more like a strawberry with no circles forming the outside of the blossom. This repro blossom looks like a poor drawing! Do not use the thread Floral test for the Florentine No. 1 shakers, however. It won't work for Florentine although these are made by the same importing company out of Georgia.

Pink is the hardest color to find. Butter dishes in all colors are most desirable. Sets can be collected in green, crystal or yellow with a lot of work. Because the edges are serrated, damage occurs on those edges; so that is the first place to look when you pick up a piece to examine.

The 48 oz. flat bottom pitcher was sold with both sets. It was listed as 54 oz. in catalogues but measures six ounces less. This pitcher is shown in all four colors on page 79.

The 5¼" footed pink tumbler which is shaped like the lemonade in Floral has made a full circle. This tumbler was shown in some of my previous books. I gave it to a Kansas dealer to deliver to a collector of hers in Louisiana. Somehow, my $25.00 was conveniently forgotten and I never collected. Last year in Denver, I walked in a booth where a like tumbler was sitting. In talking to the dealer, I found out it was bought from that Kansas dealer. Thus, I own it again. It cost substantially more than the $3.00 I originally bought it for in 1973.

There have been a multitude of fired-on colors emerging on luncheon sets, but there has also been little collector demand for these. You can find all sorts of colors and colored bands on crystal if that strikes your fancy.

Flat tumblers are being found with ribs in sets with Florentine No. 1 pitchers. Evidently these ribbed tumblers should be considered as Florentine No. 1 rather than Florentine No. 2.

	Crystal, Green	Yellow	Pink	Blue		Crystal, Green	Yellow	Pink	Blue
Ash Tray, 5½"	20.00	25.00	25.00		Plate, 8½" Salad	5.50	9.50	9.00	
Bowl, 5" Berry	8.00	12.00	8.50	13.00	Plate, 10" Dinner	10.00	17.50	18.00	
Bowl, 5", Cream					Plate, 10" Grill	8.00	11.00	11.00	
Soup or Ruffled Nut			9.50	45.00	Platter, 11½" Oval	10.00	16.00	15.00	
Bowl, 6" Cereal	17.00	18.00	15.00		*Salt and Pepper, Footed	30.00	45.00	45.00	
Bowl, 8½" Large Berry	17.50	22.00	22.50		Saucer	2.00	3.50	3.50	
Bowl, 9½" Oval Vegetable					Sherbet, 3 oz. Footed	6.00	8.50	7.50	
and Cover	40.00	45.00	45.00		Sugar	7.50	10.00	10.00	
Butter Dish and Cover	100.00	150.00	125.00		Sugar Cover	12.00	15.00	15.00	
Butter Dish Bottom	40.00	80.00	65.00		Sugar, Ruffled	25.00		25.00	40.00
Butter Dish Top	60.00	70.00	60.00		Tumbler, 3¼", 4 oz.				
Coaster/Ash Tray, 3¾"	14.00	16.00	20.00		Footed	10.00			
Comport, 3½", Ruffled	18.00		8.00	45.00	Tumbler, 3¾", 5 oz.				
Creamer	7.50		10.00	12.00	Footed Juice	10.00	16.00	15.00	
Creamer, Ruffled	30.00		30.00	50.00	Tumbler, 4", 9 oz., Ribbed	10.00		15.00	
Cup	6.00	8.00	6.50	65.00	Tumbler, 4¾", 10 oz.				
Pitcher, 6½", 36 oz.					Footed Water	17.00	15.00	15.00	
Footed	32.50	40.00	40.00	750.00	Tumbler, 5¼", 12 oz.				
Pitcher, 7½", 48 oz.					Footed Iced Tea	20.00	25.00	25.00	
Flat, Ice Lip or None	40.00	145.00	97.50		Tumbler, 5¼", 9 oz.				
Plate, 6" Sherbet	3.00	4.50	3.50		Lemonade (Like Floral)			85.00	

* Beware reproductions

Please refer to Foreword for pricing information

FLORENTINE NO. 2, "POPPY NO. 2" HAZEL ATLAS GLASS COMPANY

Colors: Pink, green, crystal, some cobalt, amber and ice blue.

Be sure to read the differences between the Florentines under Florentine No. 1 if you are having trouble distinguishing between these patterns.

One good thing about the two Florentines is that the butter dish and oval vegetable tops are interchangeable. That ought to mean you have twice the chance of finding a lid for your butter or oval vegetable bowl. It doesn't! It means twice as many collectors are looking for tops broken over the years.

Many collectors are mixing the Florentines together. Some pieces of each pattern have been found in boxed sets over the years, so the factory must have mixed them also.

Florentine fired-on blue shakers were shown in an earlier book. Now, luncheon sets of red and blue have been reported. The fired-on colors are sprayed over crystal. Once it has been fired-on, (baked, so to speak) the colors will not strip off even with paint removers as some collectors have learned. The fired-on colors are not common, but they also are not avidly collected.

The grill plate with the indent for the cream soup has only been found in green and crystal. Not many of these have been seen; and since they were only recently noticed, it stands to reason they are not very plentiful. Green Florentine is more in demand than crystal, but the crystal is more rare.

Amber is the least found Florentine color, but there is not enough available to collect a set. It was either experimental or a small, special order. Most flat tumbler sizes have been found in amber, but no pitcher has turned up to go with them.

Candy lids in Florentine are hard to find; so "entrepreneurs" have been selling the bottoms as mayonnaise dishes. All you need is a glass ladle and you can make your own. Just know that there were never any mayonnaise dishes originally made in Florentine.

I will make a prediction that some day we will discover that the flat bottom tumblers were actually sold with Florentine No. 1 and that the flat bottomed straight sided pitchers were also sold that way. The handles on the flat bottom pitchers match the handles on the footed Florentine No. 1 pitcher. Cobalt tumblers seems to go with all the other pieces of cobalt in No. 1 including the rarely found pitcher. I also suspect that the ruffled comport and ruffled nut cup or cream soup are also not a part of Florentine No. 2. Only a catalogue or a boxed set will help unravel this mystery!

	Crystal, Green	Pink	Yellow	Blue		Crystal, Green	Pink	Yellow	Blue
Bowl, 4½" Berry	9.00	10.00	15.00		Plate, 10" Dinner	10.00	12.00	12.00	
Bowl, 4¾" Cream Soup	10.00	10.00	16.00		Plate, 10¼" Grill	6.50		8.00	
Bowl, 5½"	25.00		32.00		Plate, 10¼", Grill				
Bowl, 6" Cereal	20.00		30.00		w/Cream Soup Ring	25.00			
Bowl, 7½" Shallow			75.00		Platter, 11" Oval	10.00	12.00	12.00	
Bowl, 8" Large Berry	15.00	20.00	20.00		Platter, 11½" for				
Bowl, 9" Oval Vegetable					Gravy Boat			30.00	
and Cover	40.00		50.00		Relish Dish, 10", 3 Part				
Bowl, 9" Flat	20.00				or Plain	15.00	20.00	20.00	
Butter Dish and Cover	85.00		135.00		**Salt and Pepper, Pr.	35.00		40.00	
Butter Dish Bottom	25.00		45.00		Saucer (Amber 15.00)	2.50		3.50	
Butter Dish Top	60.00		90.00		Sherbet, Footed				
Candlesticks, 2¾" Pr.	35.00		50.00		(Amber 40.00)	6.00		7.50	
Candy Dish and Cover	85.00	110.00	135.00		Sugar	6.00		8.50	
Coaster, 3¼"	10.00	13.50	18.00		Sugar Cover	10.00	15.00		
Coaster/Ash Tray, 3¾"	15.00		18.00		Tray, Condiment for				
Coaster/Ash Tray, 5½"	15.00		30.00		Shakers, Creamer and				
Comport, 3½", Ruffled	18.00	8.00		45.00	Sugar (Round)			55.00	
Creamer	6.50		8.50		Tumbler, 3⅜", 5 oz. Juice	9.00	6.00	18.00	
Cup (Amber 50.00)	5.50		7.00		Tumbler, 3⁹⁄₁₆", 6 oz. Blown	8.50			
Custard Cup or Jello	50.00		70.00		***Tumbler, 4",				
Gravy Boat			40.00		9 oz. Water	10.00	7.00	16.00	55.00
Pitcher, 6¼", 24 oz.					Tumbler, 5", 12 oz., blown	12.50			
Cone-Footed			100.00		****Tumbler, 5", 12 oz.				
* Pitcher, 7½", 28 oz.					Iced Tea	25.00		38.00	
Cone-Footed	22.00		25.00		Tumbler, 3¼", 5 oz.				
Pitcher, 7½", 48 oz.	40.00	97.50	140.00		Footed	10.00	12.00'		
Pitcher, 8¼", 76 oz.	75.00	197.50	300.00		Tumbler, 4", 5 oz. Footed	10.00		12.00	
Plate, 6" Sherbet	2.50		4.00		Tumbler, 4½", 9 oz.				
Plate, 6¼" with Indent	15.00		25.00		Footed	17.50		27.50	
Plate, 8½" Salad	6.00	6.00	7.00		Vase or Parfait, 6"	25.00		50.00	

* Amber - $65.00

** Blue - $400.00

*** Fired-On Red, Orange or Blue, Pr. - $40.00

**** Amber - $65.00

Please refer to Foreword for pricing information

FLOWER GARDEN WITH BUTTERFLIES, "BUTTERFLIES AND ROSES",
U.S. GLASS COMPANY, Late 1920's

Colors: Pink, green, blue-green, canary yellow, crystal, amber and black.

Flower Garden attracts collectors as flowers do butterflies, but new collectors beware! It takes a deep pocket to buy it. This pattern is so infrequently found that collectors of ten or more years still get excited over finding pieces. Having been collectors of the blue for over fifteen years, we still need a multitude of pieces for our set including the rest of the atomizer. I understand this can be newly purchased, but having the old would be even better.

This set has three different powder jars; that may be why the oval and rectangular trays are so plentiful. The trays and the 8" plates are the only commonly found pieces (if there are pieces that could be considered common). Evidently more powder jars than trays were broken over the years. There are two different footed powders. The smaller, shown in blue, stands 6¼" tall; the taller, shown in green, stands 7½" high. Lids to the footed powders are interchangeable. The flat powder jar, also shown in green, has a 3½" diameter. (A blue flat powder is one of the pieces eluding our collection). I still have not found out the exact make-up of the dresser set. Judging by other U.S. Glass powder sets, I suspect that there were two cologne bottles and a powder jar. Yet, with the paucity of colognes found today, there may have only been one of those to a set.

Heart shaped candy dishes are the pieces most coveted by collectors. After finding the pink one shown for the first time at the bottom of page 83, Cathy consented to letting the canary yellow (vaseline) be a Valentines Day's gift for a lovely Texas lady. Now, if we can find a green one, then the pink could find a new owner, too. Mostly, we buy the blue and green!

Prices have dipped for the ash trays, as they have in almost all patterns. These are still difficult to find in Flower Garden.

In the last book, I talked about the "Shari" perfume or cologne set. It's a semi-circular footed dresser tray which holds wedge (pie) shaped bottles. It is often confused with Flower Garden. There are **two** dancing girls **and** butterflies on it. This is not Flower Garden! Neither are the 7" and 10" trivets made by U. S. Glass with flowers all over them. They were mixing bowl covers and they do not have butterflies.

Collectors of black Flower garden have reported some satinized pieces being found, but I have yet to see one! There have been no new reports of additional tumblers in any color, but keep searching! A crystal tumbler was shown in the last book.

	Amber Crystal	Pink Green Blue-Green	Blue Canary Yellow		Amber Crystal	Pink Green Blue-Green	Blue Canary Yellow
Ash Tray, Match-Pack Holders	175.00	85.00	195.00	Mayonnaise, footed 4¾" h. x 6¼" w., w/7" Plate & Spoon	65.00	75.00	110.00
Candlesticks, 4" Pr.	40.00	50.00	85.00	Plate, 7"	15.00	20.00	25.00
Candlesticks, 8" Pr.	75.00	90.00	125.00	Plate, 8", Two Styles	13.50	16.50	22.50
Candy w/Cover, 6", Flat	125.00	150.00		Plate, 10"		32.50	42.50
Candy w/Cover, 7½" Cone-Shaped	75.00	100.00	150.00	Plate, 10", Indent for 3" Comport	30.00	35.00	40.00
Candy w/Cover, Heart-Shaped		500.00	850.00	Powder Jar, 3½", Flat		45.00	
* Cologne Bottle w/Stopper, 7½"		140.00	200.00	Powder Jar, Footed, 6¼"h.	65.00	82.50	150.00
Comport, 2⅞" h.		20.00	25.00	Powder Jar, Footed, 7½"h.	75.00	95.00	175.00
Comport, 3" h. fits 10" Plate	17.50	20.00	25.00	Sandwich Server, Center Handle	45.00	55.00	85.00
Comport, 4¼" h. x 4¾" w.			45.00	Saucer		15.00	
Comport, 4¾" h. x 10¼" w.	45.00	60.00	75.00	Sugar		60.00	
Comport, 5⅞" h. x 11" w.	50.00		85.00	Tray, 5½" x 10", Oval	47.50	50.00	
Comport, 7¼" h. x 8¼" w.	55.00	75.00		Tray, 11¾" x 7¾", Rectangular	47.50	57.50	77.50
Creamer		65.00		Tumbler, 7½" oz.	125.00		
Cup		50.00		Vase, 6¼"	67.50	87.50	120.00
				Vase, 10½"		100.00	175.00

* Stopper, if not broken off, ½ price of bottle

Please refer to Foreword for pricing information

FLOWER GARDEN WITH BUTTERFLIES, "BUTTERFLIES AND ROSES",
(Con't)

PRICE LIST FOR BLACK ITEMS ONLY

Bon Bon w/Cover, 6⅝" Diameter	250.00
Bowl, 7¼", w/Cover, "Flying Saucer"	350.00
Bowl, 8½", Console, w/Base	150.00
Bowl, 9" Rolled Edge, w/Base	200.00
Bowl, 11" Footed Orange	225.00
Bowl, 12" Rolled Edge Console w/Base	200.00
Candlestick 6" w/6½" Candle, Pr.	325.00
Candlestick, 8", Pr.	225.00
Cheese and Cracker, Footed, 5⅜"h. x 10"w.	325.00
Comport and Cover, 2¾" h. (Fits 10"Indented Plate)	200.00
Cigarette Box & Cover, 4⅜" long	125.00
Comport, Tureen, 4¼"h. x 10"w.	225.00
Comport, Footed, 5⅝"h. x 10"w.	225.00
Comport, Footed, 7"h.	175.00
Plate, 10", Indented	100.00
Sandwich Server, Center-Handled	100.00
Vase, 6¼", Dahlia, Cupped	135.00
Vase, 8", Dahlia, Cupped	200.00
Vase, 9", Wall Hanging	300.00
Vase, 10", 2 Handled	225.00
Vase, 10½", Dahlia, Cupped	250.00

Please refer to Foreword for pricing information

FOREST GREEN ANCHOR HOCKING GLASS COMPANY CORPORATION, 1950-1957

Color: Forest green.

Forest Green began to be collected primarily as a pattern to be used on holidays, particularly Christmas. There are an abundance of punch bowl sets. These, along with Royal Ruby sets, were heavily promoted at Christmas as egg nog sets. Both the Forest Green and Royal Ruby punch cups were sold on crystal, fan shaped, snack plates. One reader remembers buying four snack sets for $1.00 at a local hardware store. The punch or snack cup is round whereas the coffee cup is square.

An oval vegetable in Forest Green is now listed! This bowl is scalloped along the edges and has a swirled effect on the sides. Not many of these have been discovered! For a pattern made so late, platters and dinner plates are also infrequently found. Maybe the luncheon plates were large enough to satisfy the needs of buyers at that time.

The large quantity of 4" ball ivy, vases testifies to the successful sales of Citronella candles which were packed in these vases. The picture shows a boxed set of two "mosquito repellent" candles which originally sold for $1.19. More of these vases in Forest Green and in Royal Ruby are found in Florida than any other place. Do you wonder why?

No, there are no footed creamers and sugars (at least in Hocking's Forest Green). Although the dark green color of most glassware companies is called "forest green", the pattern name, **Forest Green**, refers only to that color made by Anchor Hocking in the 1950's.

	Green		Green
Ash Tray	3.00	Plate, 10" Dinner	15.00
Batter Bowl w/Spout	10.00	Platter, Rectangular	23.50
Bowl, 4¾" Dessert	4.00	Punch Bowl	12.50
Bowl, 5¼" Deep	5.00	Punch Bowl Stand	10.00
Bowl, 6" Soup	9.00	Punch Cup (Round)	1.75
Bowl, 7⅜" Salad	7.50	Saucer	.75
Bowl, 8½", Oval Vegetable	19.50	Sherbet, Flat	4.00
Creamer, Flat	4.50	Sugar, Flat	4.50
Cup (Square)	2.50	Tumbler, 3½", 5 oz.	2.00
Mixing Bowl Set, 3 Piece	25.00	Tumbler, 4½", 10 oz.	4.00
Pitcher, 22 oz.	12.50	Tumbler, 5", 14 oz.	6.00
Pitcher, 3 qt. Round	20.00	Vase, 4" Ivy	3.00
Plate, 6¾" Salad	2.00	Vase, 6⅜"	4.00
Plate, 8⅜" Luncheon	4.00	Vase, 9"	6.00

FORTUNE HOCKING GLASS COMPANY, 1937-1938

Colors: Pink and crystal.

The best selling piece in this pattern is the candy dish. However, more candy dish collectors purchase these than do Fortune collectors. Because there are more candy dish collectors, other collectors have to compete with them for candies.

With an investment of some time, pink can be collected as a set; crystal is rarely found and rarely collected! I had someone to write who thought they had a crystal sugar and creamer; but without a picture, I do not know if they did or not. I do know there were no creamers or sugars listed in Hocking catalogues.

The two tumblers listed below have been found. A few pitchers are surfacing that are similar to this pattern. So far, no actual Fortune pitcher has turned up; but there is always hope.

Cups, saucers and the luncheon plates are not plentiful. A major problem in collecting Fortune is that many dealers do not stock it or carry it to shows. A cup and saucer in Fortune takes up the same amount of space as does a cup and saucer in any other pattern. A dealer can carry a popular pattern cup and saucer that many collectors are searching for at $25.00 or he could carry a Fortune set for $5.00 that few people are looking to buy. Which would you do? If you want to collect Fortune, leave your name with several dealers who are willing to help you find it. More and more dealers are creating "want list" files of collectors. That way the dealer has a ready made sale when he buys the glass!

	Pink, Crystal		Pink, Crystal
Bowl, 4" Berry	3.00	Cup	3.00
Bowl, 4½" Dessert	3.50	Plate, 6" Sherbet	2.00
Bowl, 4½" Handled	3.50	Plate, 8" Luncheon	7.50
Bowl, 5¼" Rolled Edge	4.50	Saucer	2.00
Bowl, 7¾" Salad or Large Berry	9.00	Tumbler, 3½", 5 oz. Juice	5.00
Candy Dish and Cover, Flat	15.00	Tumbler, 4", 9 oz. Water	7.00

Please refer to Foreword for pricing information

FRUITS HAZEL ATLAS AND OTHER GLASS COMPANIES, 1931-1933

Colors: Pink, green, some crystal and iridized

Fruits collectors have all been trying to find the 5", 12 oz. tumbler. Smaller juice tumblers are not common either, but I have not had as many folks ask for those as the iced teas. Most collectors seek the green since there has been no pitcher found in pink. The crystal pitcher sells for about half the price of green. These pitchers only have cherries in the pattern. Notice that the handle is shaped like that on the flat Florentine pitchers (Hazel Atlas Company) and not like Cherry Blossom (Jeannette Glass Company) flat pitchers. This will keep you from confusing the Cherry pitchers from the Fruits. Other crystal pieces are rarely collected, but tumblers are available if you would like a cheaper beverage set.

Water tumblers (4") in all colors are the most common pieces in Fruits. You can find a multitude of iridized "Pears" tumblers. These were probably Federal Glass Company, but have never been found in a catalog from that company. Tumblers with cherries or other fruits are commonly found in pink, but green is another matter.

The Fruits berry bowl sets are among the hardest to collect in Depression glass. Since this is not one of the larger patterns and does not have the number of collectors that some other patterns do, the true scarcity of these berry bowls is little recognized by collectors.

	Green	Pink
Bowl, 5" Berry	14.00	12.00
Bowl, 8" Berry	40.00	30.00
Cup	4.50	4.00
Pitcher, 7" Flat Bottom	45.00	
Plate, 8" Luncheon	4.00	4.00
Saucer	2.50	2.50
Sherbet	6.00	5.50
Tumbler, 3½" Juice	12.50	10.00
*Tumbler, 4" (1 Fruit)	8.00	7.50
Tumbler, 4" (Combination of Fruits)	17.50	8.00
Tumbler, 5", 12 oz.	50.00	30.00

* Iridized $7.50

HARP JEANNETTE GLASS COMPANY, 1954-1957

Colors: Crystal, crystal with gold trim, some shell pink and ice blue.

Harp collectors are very exacting. One collector in Michigan reports the following styles of cake stands available. You may find others.

1. Crystal with smooth rim
2. Crystal with ruffled rim
3,4. Either of above with gold trim
5. Ice blue, white or shell pink (opaque) with beads on rim and foot
6. Pink transparent

Many collectors love this set to use for their bridge parties. With the ever present cake stand, cups, saucers and the 7" plates, you can make a great small table setting. The Harp cake stand is the only one in any Depression glass pattern in this book outside of those made by Paden City. Cake **stands** are reminiscent of earlier glass.

	Crystal
Ash Tray/Coaster	3.50
Coaster	2.00
Cup	7.00
* Cake Stand, 9"	17.50
Plate, 7"	5.00
Saucer	2.00
Tray, 2-Handled Rectangular	22.00
Vase, 6"	11.00

* Ice blue, white, pink or shell pink - $22.50

Please refer to Foreword for pricing information

GEORGIAN, "LOVEBIRDS" FEDERAL GLASS COMPANY, 1931-1936

Colors: Green and crystal.

Georgian prices continue to rise. What was once a plentiful pattern has been collected into hundreds of sets, now making it hard to find. This pattern has little "lovebirds" sitting side by side on most pieces except for some dinner plates, tumblers, and hot plates. Tumblers only have the basket design on each side. (Baskets usually alternate with the birds on other pieces). The hot plate carries only the center motif; it can be seen in the lower right side of the picture.

Dinner plates are found in two styles. The less easily found style (shown on the left rear of the photo) is the least desired. This style has no "lovebirds", but does have the center design. The more desirable plate (with lovebirds) is pictured in the back center. This is one case where a less plentiful piece of glass is cheaper because of less demand. Demand and not rarity alone affects prices. Even a rare piece can be unsalable if no one wants it.

Tumblers in both sizes are hard to find. The iced teas have now doubled the price of the water tumblers. I have owned ten waters for every one of the teas over the years to give you an idea of how difficult teas are to find. No pitcher has ever been found, but it took years for someone to uncover Parrot pitchers and thirty seven of those were found. So, there's still hope!

Of the last four 6" deep berries I have seen, three were badly scratched. This pattern was heavily used; so look out for all those worn and scratched pieces. Remember that prices listed in this book are for "mint" condition pieces. Damaged or scratched and worn pieces should fetch less depending upon the extent of damage and wear. If you are collecting the glass to use, it may not make as much difference as collecting it to eventually resale. Mint condition glass will sell more readily and for a much better price if you ever decide to part with your collection.

Very few of the lazy susan or cold cuts servers have been found. Recently, one turned up with an original label which read "Kalter Aufschain Cold Cuts Server Schirmer Cincy". That may be why so many have been found in Kentucky and southern Ohio. These lazy susans are made of walnut and are 18½" across with seven 5" openings for holding the hot plates. Maybe someone misnamed these 5" hot plates since they are being found on a cold cuts server!

In my travels there are only a few Georgian pieces commonly found. Berry bowls, cups, saucers and luncheon plates can be seen with regularity. For other pieces you may have to search a while.

There is no true mug in Georgian. A creamer found without a spout was called a mug. There are many patterns that have creamers or pitchers without a spout and one Federal pattern, Sharon, has at least one two spouted creamer known!

	Green
Bowl, 4½" Berry	6.00
Bowl, 5¾" Cereal	15.00
Bowl, 6½" Deep	55.00
Bowl, 7½" Large Berry	45.00
Bowl, 9" Oval Vegetable	50.00
Butter Dish and Cover	70.00
Butter Dish Bottom	40.00
Butter Dish Top	30.00
Cold Cuts Server, 18½" Wood with Seven 5" Openings for 5" Coasters	550.00
Creamer, 3", Footed	9.00
Creamer, 4", Footed	12.00
Cup	7.50
* Hot Plate, 5" Center Design	35.00
Plate, 6" Sherbet	3.00
Plate, 8" Luncheon	5.50
Plate, 9¼" Dinner	20.00
Plate, 9¼" Center Design Only	16.00
Platter, 11½" Closed-Handled	50.00
Saucer	2.00
Sherbet	9.00
Sugar, 3", Footed	7.50
Sugar, 4", Footed	8.50
Sugar Cover for 3"	25.00
Sugar Cover for 4"	75.00
Tumbler, 4", 9 oz. Flat	37.50
Tumbler, 5¼", 12 oz. Flat	75.00

* Crystal-$20.00

Please refer to Foreword for pricing information

89

HERITAGE FEDERAL GLASS COMPANY, Late 1930's - 1960's

Colors: Crystal, some pink, blue, green and cobalt.

Why anyone would want to remake this little pattern is beyond my comprehension. Reproductions of Heritage bowls are being marketed by McCrory's. These are being made in amber, crystal and green. Most are marked "MC" in the center. I say most because not all reports from readers have mentioned this mark. In any case, the smaller berry bowls are selling three for $1.00 and the larger for $1.59 each. The pattern on these pieces is not very good and should not fool even beginning collectors. Just compare the full designed hobs in my picture to the sparsely designed hobs on the reproductions. The green being found is much darker and closer to the avocado colored green of the 1970's than to the pretty shade of green shown here. Amber was never made originally; so, that is no problem.

Actually, there has been quite a demand for Heritage even with the reproduction problems. Creamers and 8½" berry bowls in crystal are more difficult to find than other pieces. The sugar turns up more frequently for some reason. The pink, blue and green berry bowls are all experts at hiding. These are truly rare!

Crystal Heritage sets can be gathered more easily than sets of other patterns due to the lack of different pieces. With only ten separate pieces to find, the limitation you have is whether to search for a six, eight or twelve place setting.

Refer to Daisy for an explanation of Indiana's Heritage pattern in green.

	Crystal	Pink	Blue Green		Crystal	Pink	Blue Green
Bowl, 5" Berry	5.00	30.00	35.00	Plate, 8" Luncheon	4.50		
Bowl, 8½" Large Berry	22.00	75.00	125.00	Plate, 9¼" Dinner	6.50		
Bowl, 10½" Fruit	11.00			Plate, 12" Sandwich	8.50		
Cup	4.00			Saucer	1.75		
Creamer, Footed	18.00			Sugar, Open-Footed	12.00		

HEX OPTIC, "HONEYCOMB" JEANNETTE GLASS COMPANY, 1928-1932

Colors: Pink, green, ultramarine and iridescent in 1950's.

Hex Optic is collected by Kitchenware buyers more than by any other group. The sugar shaker, bucket reamer and butter dish are eagerly sought. Refrigerator dishes, stacking sets and mixing bowls are also desirable; but these are not as much in demand as are the previously listed kitchen pieces.

Green is less available and more desirable than pink. This color preference effects both kitchenware and depression collectors alike. For now, prices for both colors are listed the same. However, if more people spurn the pink and collect only green, prices will begin to reflect that.

Iridized tumblers, oil lamps and pitchers were all made during Jeannette's iridized craze of the 1950's. I have never been able to verify when the company made the ultramarine tumblers. A guess would be in the late 1930's when the company was making Doric and Pansy, but that is only a guess.

	Pink, Green		Pink, Green
Bowl, 4¼" Ruffled Berry	4.00	Platter, 11" Round	8.50
Bowl, 7½" Large Berry	5.00	Refrigerator Dish, 4" x 4"	7.00
Bowl, 7¼" Mixing	10.00	Refrigerator Stack Set, 3 Pc.	40.00
Bowl, 8¼" Mixing	14.00	Salt and Pepper, Pr.	17.50
Bowl, 9" Mixing	15.00	Saucer	1.50
Bowl, 10" Mixing	18.00	Sugar, 2 Styles of Handles	4.00
Bucket Reamer	45.00	Sugar Shaker	120.00
Butter Dish and Cover, Rectangular 1 lb. Size	60.00	Sherbet, 5 oz. Footed	3.50
Creamer, 2 Style Handles	4.00	Tumbler, 3¾", 9 oz.	3.50
Cup, 2 Style Handles	3.00	Tumbler, 5", 12 oz.	5.00
Ice Bucket, Metal Handle	12.50	Tumbler, 4¾", 7 oz. Footed	6.50
Pitcher, 5", 32 oz. Sunflower Motif in Bottom	15.00	Tumbler, 5¾" Footed	4.50
Pitcher, 9", 48 oz. Footed	30.00	Tumbler, 7" Footed	7.50
Plate, 6" Sherbet	1.50	Whiskey, 2", 1 oz.	5.00
Plate, 8" Luncheon	4.50		

HOBNAIL HOCKING GLASS COMPANY, 1934-1936

Colors: Crystal, crystal w/red trim and pink.

Hocking's Hobnail is only one of the many hobnails made by dozens of glass companies. This Hobnail is more readily recognized by the shapes of pieces in this pattern. Shapes of Hobnail items are similar to those found in Miss America and those used in 1942 to make the better known Hocking pattern, Moonstone. There are many beverage sets that can be found in Hobnail, but there is a lack of serving pieces.

The red trimmed crystal has caught the fancy of many collectors, but this is found mostly on assorted stems available as shown by the footed wine. In most patterns this wine (as listed in Hocking's catalogue) is called a "footed juice".

(Terminology in glassware catalogues drives authors batty. Sometimes I have to decide whether to list what the factory said in catalogues or to list items in today's lingo. I have tried to incorporate both where feasible without creating a problem for new collectors. There is a glossary of terms listed in the back of my *Pocket Guide to Depression Glass* for those who have need to refer to it. There is not enough spare space in this book to cover all the glass terms needed; so I try to cover each of them throughout this book. That means you have to read it all to find them. It took a couple of months and some fourteen to sixteen hour days of writing to put this book together. We won't even discuss the rest of the years of gathering, photographing, proofing and worrying to put it all on paper).

For collectors who wish to purchase an economically priced set, this is just the ticket. The major problem in collecting this set is finding dealers who stock it. There are many ways collectors can overcome this handicap. I suggest you make out a want list and give it to dealers to call you when they find your pattern. You can also subscribe to a monthly paper that carries Depression glass advertising. See page 222 for my suggestions of monthly papers.

Pink Hobnail collectors are at a great disadvantage. There are only four different pieces made by Hocking, five, if you count the sherbet plate and saucer as two pieces. As with many Hocking patterns, these serve dual purposes. The saucer and sherbet plate are the same. You can pick another pink Hobnail pattern such as one made by MacBeth-Evans to go along with Hocking's; thereby you add a pitcher and tumbler set to your repertoire, something unavailable in the Hocking ware.

	Pink,	Crystal
Bowl, 5½" Cereal		2.50
Bowl, 7" Salad		3.75
Cup	3.00	3.00
Creamer, Footed		2.50
Decanter and Stopper, 32 oz.		20.00
Goblet, 10 oz. Water		5.00
Goblet, 13 oz. Iced Tea		6.00
Pitcher, 18 oz. Milk		15.00
Pitcher, 67 oz.		21.50
Plate, 6" Sherbet	1.50	1.00
Plate, 8½" Luncheon	2.00	2.00
Saucer (Sherbet Plate in Pink)	1.50	1.00
Sherbet	2.50	2.00
Sugar, Footed		2.50
Tumbler, 5 oz. Juice		3.00
Tumbler, 9 oz., 10 oz. Water		4.50
Tumbler, 15 oz. Iced Tea		6.00
Tumbler, 3 oz. Footed Wine		5.00
Tumbler, 5 oz. Footed Cordial		4.50
Whiskey, 1½ oz.		4.00

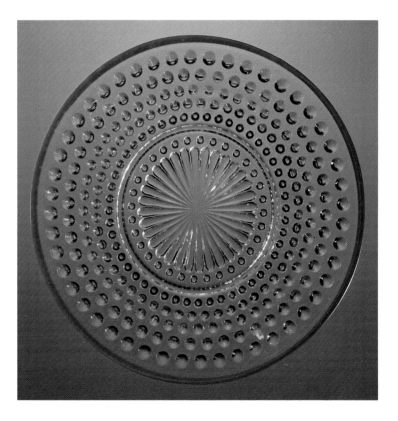

HOLIDAY, "BUTTONS AND BOWS" JEANNETTE GLASS COMPANY, 1947-1949

Colors: Pink, iridescent; some shell pink opaque and crystal.

Holiday seems to have suffered the same fate as Floral and Doric and Pansy. The pieces that we have difficulty in finding in these patterns were exported. Unlike the other patterns which seem to have been sent to England, Holiday was exported to the Philippines. As reported in the Eighth book, iced teas, soups and juices were found in abundance there. The tumblers were sent in boxes of six to be used as premiums for a well known chocolate bar.

Recently, I talked to the sailor who had brought these items back from the Philippines. He is now stationed in Florida and has been unable to get a container of glass back to the United States due to Customs problems in the Philippines. Hopefully, I will be able to report favorably in the next book on this shipment. It has been tied up for three years now. I just want to know what else is there! There must be "finds" being made as I have shipped several books there including one that the air postage cost more than the book itself! I wish someone would let me know what is being found. If you have any friends stationed in the Philippines, teach them about Depression glass. It is easy for them to send packages while stationed in the military. Afterwards, customs can tie up packages for quite a while. You can read a more detailed account in the last book.

Beginning collectors need to know that there are two styles of cup and saucer sets. Some cups and saucers have a plain center and others have a rayed center. You can not mix these together! Rayed cups have to go on rayed saucers and vice versa. You should also be aware in examining Holiday that the points which protrude outward are prone to chips, nicks and "chigger bites", an auction term that varies from place to place. Some auction houses must harbor some big chiggers! Remember, damaged glass can't be "almost" mint. The prices listed here are for mint glassware!

Holiday console bowls, candlesticks and cake plates are the most difficult pieces to find outside of those pieces discussed previously. You wonder how such a lately manufactured glassware could have so many hard to find pieces! Also, Holiday seems to have been a heavily used pattern judging by all the butter bottoms found and the multitude of damaged pieces I have incurred as I have looked at sets over the years. Yes, my Mom still has her set and the six $10.00 iced teas I bought her a long time ago.

I have a report of two styles of 10 oz. tumblers, but no pictures. Collectors, have you noticed any distinctions?

	Pink		Pink
Bowl, 5⅛" Berry	8.00	Pitcher, 6¾", 52 oz.	25.00
Bowl, 7¾" Soup	30.00	Plate, 6" Sherbet	3.00
Bowl, 8½" Large Berry	15.00	Plate, 9" Dinner	10.00
Bowl, 9½" Oval Vegetable	12.50	Plate, 13¾" Chop	70.00
Bowl, 10¾" Console	75.00	Platter, 11⅜" Oval	10.00
Butter Dish and Cover	30.00	Sandwich Tray, 10½"	10.00
Butter Dish Bottom	10.00	Saucer, 2 Styles	3.00
Butter Dish Top	20.00	Sherbet	5.00
Cake Plate, 10½", 3 Legged	65.00	Sugar	6.00
Candlesticks, 3" Pr.	65.00	Sugar Cover	8.50
Creamer, Footed	6.50	Tumbler, 4", 10 oz. Flat	15.00
Cup, Two Sizes	5.00	Tumbler, 4" Footed	27.50
Pitcher, 4¾", 16 oz. Milk	45.00	Tumbler, 6" Footed	75.00

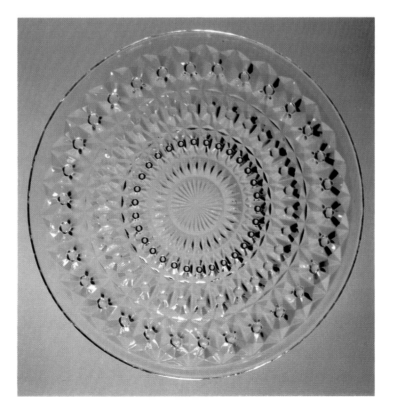

HOMESPUN, "FINE RIB" JEANNETTE GLASS COMPANY, 1939-1949

Colors: Pink and crystal.

Homespun tumblers are a nemesis to collectors of this pattern. Only the commonly found 5 oz. juice is available. Other tumblers range from hard to nearly impossible to find. This is a challenging set to complete. I have had several collectors ask me what I thought was an under valued pink set and this is the one I suggested. Since they have a head start, I hope they will not mind my repeating my feelings about this pattern. Buy every water and tea tumbler you find. You will not go broke as there are not that many to find!

Notice the two styles of 15 oz. footed tumblers in the picture. Unfortunately, the butter dish hides the base of one more than I would like it to do. You can see how that tumbler (6¼") is fatter at the bottom than the other to its right. The one on the right (6⅜") has a pronounced stem and the hidden base of the other tumbler has practically no stem at all. Both of these have been listed at 6¼", but there is ⅛" difference!

The flat iced tea also comes in two styles. One has the pattern all the way to the rim while the other has ½" of plain glass at the top. You can see the latter style pictured.

Finally, I have the child's tea pot and lid together for a picture! I remember the first time I saw this set for $25.00 at a flea market in Ohio. I refused to buy it because there was a creamer with a "sugar lid" and no sugar in the set. Later I found out that this set had a tea pot with lid and no sugar and creamer! That first set stayed on the dealer's table for three shows before I found out about the set's make up. Someone else must have also. The next month the set was gone and I never bought another pink set for less than $65.00. We all have to learn the hard way when we first start out. My books should give you some of my twenty years of experience and help you avoid some of my mistakes.

There is no sugar lid! The lid sometimes found on the Homespun sugar is actually a fine rib pattern powder jar top. It does fit, so many have been added to the sugars over the years. Yet, fitting the sugar does not make it right!

	Pink, Crystal		Pink, Crystal
Bowl, 4½", Closed Handles	4.50	Saucer	2.00
Bowl, 5" Cereal	14.00	Sherbet, Low Flat	7.50
Bowl, 8¼" Large Berry	12.00	Sugar, Footed	6.00
Butter Dish and Cover	42.50	Tumbler, 3⅞", 9 oz. Straight	11.00
Coaster/Ash Tray	5.00	Tumbler, 4", 9 oz. Water, Flared Top	13.00
Creamer, Footed	6.50	Tumbler, 5¼", 13 oz. Iced Tea	20.00
Cup	4.50	Tumbler, 4", 5 oz. Footed	4.50
Plate, 6" Sherbet	2.00	Tumbler, 6¼", 9 oz. Footed	18.00
Plate, 9¼" Dinner	10.00	Tumbler, 6½", 15 oz. Footed	22.50
Platter, 13", Closed Handles	8.50		

HOMESPUN CHILD'S TEA SET

	Pink,	Crystal
Cup	22.50	15.00
Saucer	6.00	4.50
Plate	9.00	6.50
Tea Pot	30.00	
Tea Pot Cover	40.00	
Set: 14-Pieces	225.00	
Set: 12-Pieces		105.00

INDIANA CUSTARD, "FLOWER AND LEAF BAND" INDIANA GLASS COMPANY1930's; 1950's

Colors: Ivory or custard, early 1930's; white, 1950's.

Indiana Custard has few devotees; but that may be because so many pieces are hard to find! Those loyalists who like this pattern are gluttons for punishment. This is the only pattern I know where both cups and sherbets are the hard pieces to find. Many collectors think $75.00 is a lot to pay for a sherbet; but collectors who have searched for several years without success in finding even one, would not agree. Cups are the other Achilles heel to this pattern. I have had a couple more sherbets than cups in the last two years. Both sell quickly, so there is a demand for these. More Indiana Custard collectors are in the central Indiana area than any place. Of course, it is more plentiful there, and easier to get hooked on it!

The white illustrated with the decorated scenic pieces is difficult to market. I still have not met a collector of white Indiana Custard. The decorated pieces which I have bought to photograph have all been more than reasonably priced when I bought them.

I wonder if there is a full set of yellow floral decorated pieces. I now know that there is a full set of glass decorated like the saucer on the right. The biggest fault to this set is that the decorations come off easily. If you can find this set with nicely colored pieces, you will fall in love with it. Finding it a piece or two at a time would be quite a chore! But, then, some people like a challenge!

	French Ivory		French Ivory
Bowl, 4⅞" Berry	7.00	Plate, 7½" Salad	8.50
Bowl, 5¾" Cereal	15.00	Plate, 8⅞" Luncheon	9.00
Bowl, 7½" Flat Soup	25.00	Plate, 9¾" Dinner	15.00
Bowl, 9", 1¾" Deep, Large Berry	22.00	Platter, 11½" Oval	25.00
Bowl, 9½" Oval Vegetable	20.00	Saucer	6.00
Butter Dish and Cover	52.50	Sherbet	75.00
Cup	32.00	Sugar	8.50
Creamer	12.50	Sugar Cover	15.00
Plate, 5¾" Bread and Butter	4.50		

Please refer to Foreword for pricing information

IRIS, "IRIS AND HERRINGBONE" JEANNETTE GLASS COMPANY, 1928-1932; 1950's; 1970's

Colors: Crystal, iridescent; some pink; recently bi-colored red/yellow and blue/green combinations and white.

Iris continues to be one of the **hottest** patterns being collected! Since my shop, Grannie Bear, opened in 1976, there has never been less than twenty five pieces of Iris crystal in stock. Most times there would be more. Recently, there has been a "run" on this pattern and there are only four pieces in stock! Iridized Iris is in better supply, but not by much. Customers used to buy several pieces at a time. Now, they are buying the whole inventory! It is becoming more and more difficult for dealers to find Depression glass as I write this. This has always been the case in a rising market. It is another problem for me in pricing. The deadlines for a book are so far ahead of the release date, that you can not anticipate prices. Prices have to be written for the current market. (In three months ....?)

There are several changes in sizes noted in the listing below. This pattern is wild in that respect. Going back to earlier books taken from catalogue pages and comparing them to today's listings is comical. Whoever measured and listed Iris for Jeannette's catalogues must have been a grade school drop-out and never learned how to round off or read fractional inches.

Both the cocktail and the wine are 4¼" tall. The cocktail (shown on the right behind the tall sherbet with red flowers) holds 4 ozs., and the wine (shown to the left and behind the cocktail) holds only 3 ozs. The large footed tumbler is only 6½" tall and was changed in the last *Pocket Guide* from the listed 7". The 11" ruffled bowl actually measures 11½".

The 11½" bowl really got a workout by Jeannette. This bowl was redesigned into a lamp shade as shown in pastel blue. Note the heavier ribbed center of this piece. This was **designed** as a shade and was not a ruffled bowl with a hole drilled in the center as is sometimes passed off as the lamp shade. The true shade comes in other pastel colors of pink, yellow and beige. Blue and pink are more in demand.

The 11½" bowl was also turned into a fruit or nut set. The one pictured is a nut set including a nut cracker and nut picks in a metal holder with slots for each piece. The fruit set has knives in the center. These were probably a special order and they most likely were not completely made at Jeannette.

Demitasse cups still out number the saucers by a large margin. For new readers, the demitasse cups were once sold in six piece sets with copper saucers in the late 1940's. These were advertised in the back of a women's magazine of the time for an expensive price of $2.00 each or set of six for $11.00. It was referred to as "demi tasse unique" which added "a delightful touch to al fresco dining."

The satinized Iris pieces with painted flowers are not selling well. It's a shame that so many of the 8" luncheon plates were treated that way. It explains one of the reasons that this plate is so hard to find today in regular crystal. I have reports that a man in Pennsylvania has developed a process for removing the iridized spray from Iris. That may be one of the reasons that soup and dinner plates in iridized have taken big price leaps in recent months. If this can be done, the crystal soup prices may suffer! In any case, if you see any crystal, plain bottomed wines which are 4" tall, beware! These would have been made from iridized wines. The crystal wine has a rayed foot and stands 4¼" tall. See the plain footed wine in the iridized picture. Speaking of plain footed items, the crystal candy bottoms and iridized candy bottoms with plain foot were made in the 1970's. There were a multitude of sprayed on color combinations and even a few milk glass candy bottoms made. These were sold along with the 9" vases in the same colors at dish barns for $1.09 to $1.29. You may find white milk glass vases with rayed feet and sprayed on green or pink outsides. These were also made in this time period. This is usually offered in the $5.00 range, but I have never seen one sell!

Price leaps in crystal include the cereal and coasters. I recently bought eight coasters for $30.00 at a local flea market. When I held one up and asked the price, the dealer said $30.00, so I took the eight over and laid down two twenties since I could not tell if he meant the price for each or for all. He said he didn't have change; so I was able to find ten of my own to make it right! Had this been a Depression glass dealer, I would have never bothered to check if he meant each for he would have known better.

The red flowered pieces were a special ordered line. The name and decorating company were given to me in South Carolina a couple of years ago, but I have been unable to put my hands on it as I write. This decorating was not done at Jeannette. Thankfully, with the listings now being in my computer, I can make those notes after each show instead of using napkins, scrap pieces of paper, etc. which sometimes get away from me as I travel from show to show.

	Crystal	Iridescent		Crystal	Iridescent	
Bowl, 4½" Berry, Beaded Edge	28.00	6.50	Goblet, 4" Wine		19.50	
Bowl, 5" Ruffled Sauce	6.00	15.00	Goblet, 4¼", 4 oz., Cocktail	16.00		
Bowl, 5" Cereal	45.00		Goblet, 4¼", 3 oz., Wine	14.00		
Bowl, 7½" Soup	80.00	35.00	Goblet, 5¾", 4 oz.	16.50		
Bowl, 8" Berry, Beaded Edge	52.50	10.00	Goblet, 5¾", 8 oz.	16.00	75.00	
* Bowl, 9½" Ruffled Salad	8.50	8.00	Lamp Shade, 11½"	35.00		
Bowl, 11½" Ruffled Fruit	8.50	6.00	Pitcher, 9½" Footed	25.00	27.50	
Bowl, 11" Fruit, Straight Edge	32.50		Plate, 5½" Sherbet	8.00	7.00	
Butter Dish and Cover	27.50	27.50	Plate, 8" Luncheon	37.50		
Butter Dish Bottom	5.00	7.50	Plate, 9" Dinner	35.00	30.00	
Butter Dish Top	22.50	22.50	Plate, 11¾" Sandwich	12.00	15.00	
Candlesticks, Pr.	20.00	25.00	Saucer	6.00	4.00	
Candy Jar and Cover	75.00		Sherbet, 2½" Footed	16.00	10.00	
Coaster	40.00		Sherbet, 4" Footed	13.00		
Creamer, Footed	7.00	8.00	Sugar	6.00	6.00	
Cup	8.50	7.50	Sugar Cover	6.50	6.00	
** Demitasse Cup	20.00	95.00	Tumbler, 4" Flat	52.50		
** Demitasse Saucer	75.00	100.00	Tumbler, 6" Footed	12.00	12.00	
Fruit or Nut Set	35.00		Tumbler, 6½" Footed	15.00		
			Vase, 9"	17.50	14.00	75.00

*Pink - $50.00

**Ruby, Blue, Amethyst priced as Iridescent

Please refer to Foreword for pricing information

JUBILEE LANCASTER GLASS COMPANY, Early 1930's

Colors: Yellow and pink.

Jubilee collectors are amazing. They do not get stymied by going to show after show and finding very little to buy. They just bide their time and stock up when they find it. The basic luncheon set consisting of cups, saucers, luncheon plates, creamer and sugar are readily found. After finding those pieces, you have a problem getting anything else.

As I have mentioned before, **TRUE** Jubilee has twelve petal flowers and an open-centered flower. There are other Lancaster "look-alike" patterns that have sixteen petals or twelve petals with a smaller petal in between the larger ones. Many collectors are willing to settle for these at a lesser price; however, purist collectors will accept nothing but the real thing. As an advertiser of glass or a dealer who is offering glass for sale as Jubilee, you had better know the difference or be prepared for an onslaught of returns. Personally, I find the patterns that are similar a welcome addition to the short supply of Jubilee and my customers enjoy buying "look-alike" pieces for less than prices paid for "the real thing."

Shown for the first time are the center-handled server and the 8", three-footed bowl which stands 5⅛" high! I still have not personally seen the 9", two-handled fruit bowl shown in the old catalogues. Keep looking!

The mayonnaise has been fetching some wild prices. According to the catalog, the liner plate to the mayonnaise is the 8¾" plate. There is no plate shown in the catalogues with an indent for the mayonnaise. Yet, some collectors have sworn their sets have an indented plate. I have not seen that plate. There is a scarcity of 7" plates in comparison to the regular luncheon plates. Some day this will pass the luncheons in price.

A cordial has also been found! It is on the panelled-type blank that some tumblers have, but it is hard to get the whole pattern on this smaller piece. It stands 4" tall and holds 1 oz.! I have now (this minute) added it to my cordial collection. Cathy bought it for me as a birthday present. The shock was not so much that she bought it as it was to receive it six weeks late! She was proofing my ramblings on the cordial, and remembered that she had not given it to me on my birthday. After twenty five years, she is still full of surprises. A cocktail was also reported, but I have not seen it (or a picture of it) as yet.

Pink Jubilee still eludes me, but there have been several sets reported to me. The sugar pictured is all I have been able to buy. If pink is shown to me at shows, it is never for sale!

	Pink,Yellow
Bowl, 8", 3-Footed, 5⅛" High	165.00
Bowl, 9" Handled Fruit	65.00
Bowl, 11", 3-Footed	165.00
Candlestick, Pr.	125.00
Cheese & Cracker Set	115.00
Creamer	17.50
Cup	12.00
Goblet, 4", 1 oz., Cordial	150.00
Goblet, 5", 6 oz., Juice	55.00
Goblet, 6", 10 oz., Water	32.50
Goblet, 6⅛", 12½ oz., Tea	85.00
Mayonnaise & Plate	165.00
w/Original Ladle	175.00
Plate, 7" Salad	9.00
Plate, 8¾" Luncheon	10.00
Plate, 13½" Sandwich	35.00
Saucer, Two Styles	5.50
Sherbet/Champagne, 4¾"	30.00
Sugar	16.00
Tray, 11", 2-Handled Cake	30.00
Tray, 11", Center-Handled Sandwich	75.00

Please refer to Foreword for pricing information

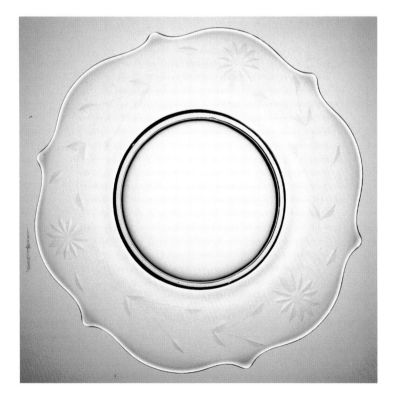

LACE EDGE, "OPEN LACE" HOCKING GLASS COMPANY, 1935-1938

Colors: Pink and some crystal.

Lace Edge still confuses new collectors because there were other companies that made an "open lace" type pattern. Both Lancaster and Standard made very similar designs, but the glass is better quality and "rings" when flipped on the edge with your finger. Hocking's Lace Edge makes a "clunk" sound. The pink color of other companies' glass is usually a prettier shade of pink. If the piece is not shown in my listing or in any color other than pink or crystal, the likelihood of your having a Lace Edge piece is slim at best.

Notice the 9" comport shown as a pattern shot. There is a comport similar to this that measures 9" also. It was made by another glass company and is better quality glass. The Lace Edge "pretender" has a plain foot with no rays as does the real comport. Amazingly, these comports keep turning up in the Cincinnati area. The last two reports came from there! Sadly, both comports were damaged to some extent. Candlesticks, console bowls and vases are other hard to find **mint** pieces in this pattern.

The major problem to collecting Lace Edge (besides finding it) concerns the damaged lace on the outside of the pieces. It chipped and cracked very easily. Plates and bowls have to be stacked cautiously because of that.

The base of the footed tumbler is hidden in the picture behind the flat tumbler. The ribs on this tumbler only extend about half way up the side as they do on the cup. This tumbler is often confused with the Coronation tumbler with a similar shape and design. You can see the Coronation tumbler under that pattern. Notice the fine ribbed effect from the middle up on the Coronation tumbler. This is missing on the Lace Edge tumbler.

The butter bottom also serves as a 7¾" salad bowl according to old catalogues, but many collectors like to think the true salad bowl is ribbed. Ribbing makes a big difference in pricing on this bowl! The 9½" bowl is also found ribbed or plain, but the price remains the same for both types.

Satinized or frosted pieces have already been discussed elsewhere in this book (page 20). Frosted Lace Edge pieces such as the vase shown here sell for only a fraction of their unfrosted counter parts. Lack of demand is the main reason. Although some collectors think frosted Lace Edge is beautiful, most do not! My Mom handles frosted glass rarely. It affects her as a squeaky chalkboard does other people.

	*Pink		*Pink
** Bowl, 6⅜" Cereal	12.50	Plate, 8¼" Salad	14.00
Bowl, 7¾" Ribbed Salad	37.50	Plate, 8¾" Luncheon	12.50
Bowl, 8¼" (Crystal)	10.00	Plate, 10½" Dinner	20.00
Bowl, 9½" Plain or Ribbed	13.50	Plate, 10½" grill	13.00
***Bowl, 10½", 3 Legs, (Frosted, $30.00)	145.00	Plate, 10½", 3-Part Relish	20.00
Butter Dish or Bon Bon with Cover	45.00	Plate, 13", Solid Lace	20.00
Butter Dish Bottom, 7¾"	15.00	Plate, 13", 4-Part Solid Lace	18.50
Butter Dish Top	30.00	Platter, 12¾"	19.00
***Candlesticks, Pr. (Frosted $40.00)	145.00	Platter, 12¾", 5-Part	18.00
Candy Jar and Cover, Ribbed	32.50	Relish Dish, 7½", 3-Part Deep	45.00
Comport, 7"	16.00	Saucer	7.50
Comport, 7" and Cover, Footed	30.00	***Sherbet, Footed	60.00
Comport, 9"	550.00	Sugar	15.00
Cookie Jar and Cover	45.00	Tumbler, 3½", 5 oz. Flat	15.00
Creamer	16.00	Tumbler, 4½", 9 oz. Flat	11.00
Cup	17.50	Tumbler, 5", 10½ oz. Footed	50.00
Fish Bowl, 1 gal. 8 oz. (Crystal Only)	22.00	Vase, 7", (Frosted $45.00)	265.00
Flower Bowl, Crystal Frog	17.50		

* Satin or frosted items 50% lower in price or less

** Officially listed as cereal or cream soup

*** Price is for absolute mint condition

Please refer to Foreword for pricing information

LACED EDGE, "KATY BLUE" IMPERIAL GLASS COMPANY, Early 1930's

Colors: Blue w/opalescent edge and green w/opalescent edge.

Laced Edge, as this pattern was named by Imperial, is often called "Katy" by older collectors. The white edging technique was called "Sea Foam" by Imperial and was put on many other Imperial colors and also on other patterns besides Laced Edge.

You will find pieces in this design without the white edging technique. Blue and green pieces without the white sell for about half of the prices listed if you can find a buyer. Crystal pieces do not seem to be selling at any price. I have never seen crystal pieces with white edging in this pattern; so if you have a piece, let me know.

Prices for the blue are beginning to creep up again. The green follows along since it is much rarer than the blue. Notice the lack of green in my picture. I have not been able to find it in my travels. Presently, there are few collectors looking for green which holds the price line on this color.

Platters, oval bowls and other serving pieces are in shorter supply than originally thought. Collectors are grabbing all the serving bowls they see. You may not find these available for much longer!

There have been several Depression shows where Laced Edge has been displayed as a table setting. It really catches the public's eye. Many a non-collector has asked, "What is the name of that pattern and where can I get some?" If I only knew where to find a big lot, I'd be there first!

	Opalescent		Opalescent
Bowl, 4½" Fruit	15.00	Plate, 6½" Bread & Butter	9.50
Bowl, 5"	20.00	Plate, 8" Salad	15.00
Bowl, 5½"	20.00	Plate, 10" Dinner	35.00
Bowl, 7" Soup	25.00	Plate, 12" Luncheon (Per Catalogue Description)	37.50
Bowl, 9" Vegetable	50.00	Platter, 13"	65.00
Bowl, 11" Divided Oval	50.00	Saucer	7.50
Bowl, 11" Oval	55.00	Sugar	22.00
Cup	20.00	Tidbit, 2-Tiered, 8" & 10" Plates	55.00
Creamer	25.00	Tumbler, 9 oz.	27.50
Mayonnaise, 3-Piece	75.00	Vase 5½"	40.00

LAKE COMO HOCKING GLASS COMPANY, 1934-1937

Color: White with blue scene.

Lake Como sells very quickly when displayed at shows. This, too, is a pattern that is rarely seen. Collectors do not buy a piece at a time, but usually buy all that is available. It sounds great for the dealer; but it is also discouraging to have several weeks (or months) of buying disappear in one fell swoop. It may take the dealer months to replace what he has just sold.

Notice the flat soup standing up on the left. The floral decoration is embossed instead of painted in blue. I have only seen two of these in my travels. I just found a platter that will be shown the next book. One of the disappointments in finding Lake Como is that the design wears so easily. The prices below are for mint condition glass with little wear on the design. Evidently, this pattern was used heavily. Part of all the collections I have purchased have been worn. The collectors told me that they had "settled" on buying less than mint glass in order to be able to have some of the pieces. Cups are hard to find that are not worn.

You should be able to buy worn Lake Como at 50 % to 80% of the prices listed depending upon the amount of wear.

	White		White
Bowl, 6" Cereal	15.00	Plate, 9¼" Dinner	15.00
Bowl, 9¾" Vegetable	25.00	Platter, 11"	30.00
Bowl, Flat Soup	65.00	Salt & Pepper, Pr.	30.00
Creamer, Footed	15.00	Saucer	5.00
Cup, Regular	20.00	Saucer, St. Denis	5.00
Cup, St. Denis	15.00	Sugar, Footed	13.50
Plate, 7¼" Salad	10.00		

Please refer to Foreword for pricing information

LAUREL McKEE GLASS COMPANY, 1930's

Colors: French Ivory, Jade Green, White Opal and Poudre Blue.

"Poudre Blue" Laurel is still the hard to find color, but more collectors are turning to the "Jade Green" for a change. The "French Ivory" color attracts few new collectors; so prices have remained rather steady. Serving bowls in all colors are in short supply.

A new listing is a 5" high sherbet or champagne! A long time collector of Laurel now has four of these. I also have received a picture of a Jade decanter and wine which I have tried to contact the owner about with little success. Stay tuned for next time.

Several people are beginning to buy the trimmed ivory. The red trimmed is the most plentiful, but a set can also be gathered with green trim. Children's sets continue to be the hot ticket in Laurel. The Scotty Dog Collectors Club has really dried up the market for those children's pieces. Red, green or orange trimmed children's sets are found in a limited supply with orange the most difficult color to find.

The shakers are hard to find with strong patterns. Many of the designs are weak or obscure. Better to find a patterned pair than a pair that has only the right shape.

	White Opal, Jade Green	French Ivory	Poudre Blue
Bowl, 5" Berry	4.00	5.00	10.00
Bowl, 6" Cereal	5.00	6.00	15.00
Bowl, 6", Three Legs	10.00	10.00	
Bowl, 8" Soup		25.00	
Bowl, 9" Large Berry	15.00	17.00	30.00
Bowl, 9¾" Oval Vegetable	15.00	15.00	30.00
Bowl, 10½", Three Legs	25.00	27.50	45.00
Bowl, 11"	22.00	27.50	45.00
Candlestick, 4" Pr.	25.00	25.00	
Cheese Dish and Cover	40.00	50.00	
Creamer, Short	7.50	9.00	
Creamer, Tall	9.00	10.00	22.00
Cup	6.00	6.00	15.00
Plate, 6" Sherbet	2.50	3.50	5.00
Plate, 7½" Salad	8.00	8.00	10.00
Plate, 9⅛" Dinner	9.00	9.00	15.00
Plate, 9⅛" Grill	8.00	9.00	
Platter, 10¾" Oval	15.00	20.00	27.50
Salt and Pepper	45.00	35.00	
Saucer	2.00	2.50	5.00
Sherbet	6.50	9.50	
Sherbet/Champagne, 5"		25.00	
Sugar, Short	6.50	7.50	
Sugar, Tall	8.50	9.50	22.00
Tumbler, 4½", 9 oz. Flat	35.00	25.00	
Tumbler, 5", 12 oz. Flat		35.00	

CHILDREN'S LAUREL TEA SET

	Plain	Decorated Rims	Scotty Dog Decal	Green
Creamer	20.00	32.50	50.00	32.50
Cup	15.00	20.00	35.00	20.00
Plate	7.50	12.50	25.00	12.50
Saucer	5.50	7.50	45.00	7.50
Sugar	20.00	32.50	50.00	32.50
14-Piece Set	150.00	225.00	400.00	225.00

Please refer to Foreword for pricing information

LINCOLN INN FENTON GLASS COMPANY, Late 1920's

Colors: Red, cobalt, light blue, amethyst, black, green, green opalescent, pink, crystal, amber and jade (opaque).

Lincoln Inn tumblers, stems and high sherbet/champagnes abound. I believe you can find a high sherbet in any color made in this pattern. Whether this is true for other pieces, I am not sure. The only older pitchers known are made in the colors shown in the picture. Fenton remade an iridized dark carnival colored pitcher several years ago. Light blue pitchers keep turning up in Florida. Another was found near Jacksonville recently. Florida readers, take note!

Several years ago I visited a lady whose grandfather worked at Fenton early in this century. She had the largest set of crystal Lincoln Inn I have ever seen! She uses them for every day dishes.

Shakers are difficult to find in all colors. The red and black are the most desired colors, but don't pass by any color in your travels. I found a red pair tucked away with Royal Ruby in a corner of a shop not long ago for only $45.00! Sometimes you have to look in some not so obvious places as you check out the shops. Many dealers who specialize in other areas do not take time to learn some of the lesser known patterns; and you can find a bargain once in a while.

Lincoln Inn plates can also be found with a fruit design in the center according to a 1930's catalogue; however, I have never seen or heard of one. Have you? If you have one of these, let me know!

Many of the red pieces are more amberina in color. Amberina is a red which has a yellowish cast to it. Red glass is made by reheating glass that comes out of the furnace yellow. Uneven reheating causes some of this to remain yellow.

Actually, red and cobalt blue are the easiest colors to find in Lincoln Inn. This helps, since those are the colors most desired by collectors.

	Cobalt Blue, Red	All Other Colors		Cobalt Blue, Red	All Other Colors
Ash Tray	15.00	10.00	Nut Dish, Footed	15.00	10.00
Bon bon, Handled Square	12.50	10.00	Pitcher, 7¼", 46 oz.	750.00	650.00
Bon Bon, Handled Oval	12.50	10.00	Plate, 6"	6.00	3.00
Bowl, 5" Fruit	9.50	7.00	Plate, 8"	10.00	6.00
Bowl, 6" Cereal	10.00	6.50	Plate, 9¼"	12.50	10.00
Bowl, 6" Crimped	11.00	7.00	Plate, 12"	17.50	10.00
Bowl, Handled Olive	12.00	7.00	* Salt/Pepper, Pr.	150.00	110.00
Bowl, Finger	15.00	10.00	Saucer	3.00	2.00
Bowl, 9", Shallow		18.00	Sherbet, 4½", Cone Shape	15.00	10.00
Bowl, 9¼" Footed	25.00	15.00	Sherbet, 4¾"	15.00	10.00
Bowl, 10½" Footed	35.00	25.00	Sugar	16.50	11.50
Candy Dish, Footed Oval	17.50	10.00	Tumbler, 4 oz. Flat Juice	20.00	7.50
Comport	20.00	12.00	Tumbler, 9 oz. Flat Water		17.50
Creamer	17.50	12.00	Tumbler, 5 oz. Footed	20.00	8.50
Cup	12.50	7.50	Tumbler, 9 oz. Footed	22.00	12.00
Goblet, Water	20.00	12.00	Tumbler, 12 oz. Footed	30.00	15.00
Goblet, Wine	25.00	15.00	Vase, 12" Footed	125.00	65.00

* Black $165.00

Please refer to Foreword for pricing information

LORAIN, "BASKET", No. 615 INDIANA GLASS COMPANY, 1929-1932

Colors: Green, yellow and some crystal.

Collectors of Lorain green and yellow please notice that all pieces in each color are shown except for one size plate in yellow. The snack plate, which has only been found in crystal, is the only Lorain piece not included here. I have bought several collections in the last few years and have found further information from people who searched for Lorain for years. Cereal bowls are the hardest to find item and the inner rims are usually rough. The 8" deep berry in yellow is the next hardest piece to find, but only having to buy one of these instead of four, six or more cereals is a small blessing. Green dinner plates are almost as hard to find as green cereals. Mould roughness is the biggest concern of these very particular collectors. Most Lorain suffers from that malady!

Mint condition saucers are harder to locate than cups! Trust me.

I need to remind new collectors that the white and green avocado colored sherbets (which have a Lace Edge border) are a later issue and should be treated as such. These have always been assumed to be an Indiana product; but several turned up with Anchor Hocking stickers. I have not been able to corroborate this, but the sticker attached was used in the late 1950's and early 1960's. Some one may have just attached labels to these as sometimes happens. If any one out there has some information on these, please help.

You may notice a general rise in prices in both colors. There have been more new collectors starting green than yellow. Price may have something to do with that. Green is less expensive. Although there are a few pieces found in crystal, I would not suggest you try to complete a set. It would be nearly impossible.

Snack trays in crystal (with colored borders of red, yellow, green and blue) have an off center indent for the cup. The cups that go with these trays are sometimes decorated in the same colored borders, but many times these are plain crystal.

	Crystal, Green	Yellow		Crystal, Green	Yellow
Bowl, 6" Cereal	27.50	47.50	Plate, 10¼" Dinner	30.00	42.50
Bowl, 7¼" Salad	32.00	50.00	Platter, 11½"	20.00	32.50
Bowl, 8" deep Berry	70.00	110.00	Relish, 8", 4-Part	15.00	25.00
Bowl, 9¾" Oval Vegetable	30.00	40.00	Saucer	3.50	4.50
Creamer, Footed	12.00	17.00	Sherbet, Footed	15.00	25.00
Cup	8.50	11.50	Snack Tray, Crystal/Trim	17.50	
Plate, 5½" Sherbet	5.50	7.50	Sugar, Footed	11.00	16.00
Plate, 7¾" Salad	8.00	12.00	Tumbler, 4¾", 9 oz. Footed	15.00	20.00
Plate, 8⅜" Luncheon	13.00	22.00			

Please refer to Foreword for pricing information

MADRID FEDERAL GLASS COMPANY, 1932-1939; INDIANA GLASS COMPANY, 1980's

Colors: Green, pink, amber, crystal and "Madonna" blue. (See Reproduction Section)

Madrid gravy boats and platters still are being found in Iowa. One is shown in front of the cookie jar in the center of the amber picture. The wooden lazy susans are still being found in Eastern Kentucky and southern Ohio. A recent label found on one of these says "Kalter Aufschain Cold Cuts Server Schirmer Cincy." You have to go back to the Fifth Edition to see one of these pictured.

Ash trays and mint condition sugar lids in any color are finds! Footed tumblers are harder to find than the flat ones. Collectors of green Madrid have turned out to be almost as scarce as the pattern.

Madrid has been a genuine headache for collectors since 1976 when Federal reissued this pattern for the Bicentennial under the name "Recollection" glassware. Fine, it was dated 1976; but it **WAS** issued in the older color of amber instead of another color. Everyone was informed and many collectors assumed it would be collectible later. However, Indiana bought the moulds when Federal went bankrupt and there have been problems for collectors ever since. First Indiana removed the 1976 and made crystal. The old crystal butter was selling for several hundred dollars and the new one sold for $2.99. Prices plummeted!

Next, Indiana made pink and although it was lighter in color than the original, prices went down on the old. Now, Indiana has made blue; and although it is a brighter, harsher blue than the original, it has not helped the prices of the older blue. You can see the new pink in the *Reproduction Section* in the back. All the pieces made in pink have now been made in blue.

Blue Madrid collectors will have to be careful with their purchases for now. Only the items listed below were made in blue originally. Some of the old items have been remade, so know from whom you are buying your glass if you do not know the glass well. If a piece is found in blue that is not priced below, rest assured it is new!

	Amber	Pink	Green	Blue		Amber	Pink	Green	Blue
Ash Tray, 6" Square	175.00		125.00		Pitcher, 8", 60 oz.				
Bowl, 4¾" Cream					Square	37.50	32.50	125.00	125.00
Soup	10.00				Pitcher, 8½", 80 oz.	50.00		195.00	
Bowl, 5" Sauce	5.00	5.50	6.00		Pitcher, 8½",				
Bowl, 7" Soup	10.00		12.00	25.00	80 oz. Ice Lip	50.00		200.00	
Bowl, 8" Salad	11.50		15.00		Plate, 6" Sherbet	2.50	3.00	3.00	6.50
Bowl, 9⅜" Large					Plate, 7½" Salad	8.00	8.00	7.50	15.00
Berry	15.00	17.50			Plate, 8⅞" Luncheon	5.50	6.00	7.50	15.00
Bowl, 9½" Deep					Plate, 10½" Dinner	25.00		26.00	55.00
Salad	22.00				Plate, 10½" Grill	8.00		13.50	
Bowl, 10" Oval					Plate, 10¼" Relish	8.50	8.50	12.50	
Vegetable	12.50	12.00	13.50	30.00	Plate, 11¼" Round				
* Bowl, 11" Low					Cake	10.00	8.50		
Console	11.50	8.00			Platter, 11½" Oval	10.00	9.00	12.50	17.50
Butter Dish and					Salt/Pepper, 3½"				
Cover	52.50		70.00		Footed, Pr.	57.50		77.50	120.00
Butter Dish Bottom	22.50		32.50		Salt/Pepper, 3½"				
Butter Dish Top	30.00		37.50		Flat, Pr.	37.50		50.00	
* Candlesticks,					Saucer	2.50	3.00	3.50	5.00
2¼" Pr.	15.00	13.50			Sherbet, Two Styles	6.50		7.50	9.50
Cookie Jar and					Sugar	6.50		7.50	10.00
Cover	32.50	25.00			Sugar Cover	25.00		30.00	145.00
Creamer, Footed	6.00		8.00	13.00	Tumbler, 3⅞",				
Cup	5.00	6.00	6.50	12.00	5 oz.	12.50		30.00	32.00
Gravy Boat and					Tumbler, 4¼", 9 oz.	11.00	11.00	17.50	20.00
Platter	1000.00				Tumbler, 5½",				
Hot Dish Coaster	30.00		30.00		12 oz. 2 Styles	17.00		26.00	32.50
Hot Dish Coaster					Tumbler, 4", 5 oz.				
w/Indent	30.00		30.00		Footed	20.00		35.00	
Jam Dish, 7"	17.50		13.50	25.00	Tumbler, 5½",				
Jello Mold, 2⅛"					10 oz. Footed	20.00		35.00	
High	9.00				Wooden Lazy				
** Pitcher, 5½"					Susan, 7 Hot				
36 oz. Juice	30.00				Dish Coasters	500.00			

* Iridescent priced slightly higher

** Crystal - $150.00

Please refer to Foreword for pricing information

MANHATTAN, "HORIZONTAL RIBBED" ANCHOR HOCKING GLASS COMPANY, 1938-1943

Colors: Crystal, pink; some green, ruby and iridized.

Manhattan's collectability has not been affected by the making of **PARK AVENUE** by Anchor Hocking. **PARK AVENUE** was a new pattern line introduced in 1987 to "re-create the Glamour Era of 1938 when Anchor Hocking first introduced a classic" according to the *Inspiration '87* catalogue issued by the company. Anchor Hocking went to the trouble to preserve the integrity of their older glassware, however! None of the pieces in this line are exactly like the old Manhattan! They are only similar and Manhattan was never made in blue as this line has been. Many collectors of Manhattan have bought this new pattern to use as everyday dishes. Thus, everyone remains happy, company and collector alike.

There are disbelievers among the collectors of pink about the existence of some items. There are cups (see top photo on the right), saucers and dinner plates. The former owner of the cup had saucers before he found two cups. He sold the saucer/ sherbet plates believing he would never find cups to go with them! I have seen dinner plates, but even I have not seen the saucers. The saucer/sherbet plates of Manhattan are like many of Hockings saucers; they have no cup ring.

The cereal bowl measures 5½" and has no handles. The handled berry measures 5⅜". These closed handled bowls are not the cereal! We photographed the real cereal, but it was in a picture that was omitted from the book. One can be seen in the foreground of the top picture in the last book. I mention the differences because there is a vast price difference. In fact, the reason the 5⅜" handled berry has increased in price so much has come from dealers selling these as cereals!

In the top photograph are several Manhattan "look-alikes." The five crystal pieces were placed here to help differentiate them from the true Manhattan. The little wine on the left (3½" tall and 2½" wide) has a similar friend which stands 3¾" tall and is 3" wide. These sell for a similar price. The two water bottles are both Hocking and sold about the same time as Manhattan, but there are no indications in the catalogue that they were considered to be a part of that line. The bottle with the flat top sells for $8.00 to $10.00 while the one with the "Cameo" type stopper sells for $12.50 to $15.00 . The double branched candle and the candy are both products of L.E. Smith. The candy is listed below since so many people consider it Manhattan and the candle sells in the $10.00 to $12.50 range.

In the bottom photo there are three ash trays of interest. Evidently, there was a bridge set of ash trays made since you can see the "club" design. The "Jan & Bills" advertising piece is nice, but the ash tray to its left is embossed "Anchor Hocking Glass Corp. 1903-1943; 38 yrs. of Progress." These sell for up to twice the price of a normal ash tray depending upon demand in a local area.

The sherbet in Manhattan has a beaded bottom as can be seen to the left of the cup in the top picture. The center insert to the relish tray does not have these beads.

	Crystal	Pink		Crystal	Pink
* Ashtray, 4" Round	9.00		Relish Tray, 14", 4-Part	15.00	15.00
Ashtray, 4½" Square	17.50		Relish Tray, 14" With Inserts	40.00	40.00
Bowl, 4½" Sauce, Handles	6.00		*** Relish Tray Insert	3.50	4.00
Bowl, 5⅜" Berry w/Handles	12.00	12.00	Pitcher, 24 oz.	20.00	32.50
Bowl, 5½" Cereal, No Handles	20.00		Pitcher, 80 oz. Tilted	25.00	37.50
Bowl, 7½" Large Berry	8.50	8.50	Plate, 6" Sherbet or Saucer	4.00	30.00
Bowl, 8", Closed Handles	13.00	17.50	Plate, 8½ Salad	9.00	
Bowl, 9" Salad	12.00	15.00	Plate, 10¼" Dinner	11.00	75.00
Bowl, 9½" Fruit Open Handle	20.00	25.00	Plate, 14" Sandwich	14.00	
Candlesticks, 4½" (Square) Pr.	12.00		Salt & Pepper, 2" Pr. (Square)	20.00	30.00
Candy Dish, 3 Legs		7.50	Saucer/Sherbet Plate	4.00	30.00
** Candy Dish and Cover	30.00		Sherbet	6.50	6.00
Coaster, 3½"	7.50		Sugar, Oval	7.50	7.50
Comport, 5¾"	17.50	17.50	**** Tumbler, 10 oz. Footed	12.00	12.00
Creamer, Oval	8.00	8.00	Vase, 8"	13.00	
Cup	13.00	125.00	** Wine, 3½"	5.00	

   * Ad for Hocking $15.00
   ** "Look-Alike"
   *** Ruby-$3.50
   **** Green or iridized-$10.00

Please refer to Foreword for pricing information

MAYFAIR FEDERAL GLASS COMPANY, 1934

Colors: Crystal, amber and green.

Federal's Mayfair has been a pattern with collecting ups and downs. It was a very limited production because of pattern name difficulties. Amber and crystal are the colors that can be collected in the true form of this pattern. Green is found only in the TRANSITIONAL pieces of this pattern. Let me explain.

Hocking patented the name "Mayfair" first which caused Federal to redesign these glass moulds into what became the "Rosemary" pattern. The green pieces pictured here (as well as the amber sugar, cup and cream soup) represent a "transitional period" of glassware made between the old "Mayfair" pattern and what was to become "Rosemary." Notice these transitional pieces have arching in the bottom of each piece rather than the waffle design, and there is no waffling between the top arches. If you turn to the Rosemary (168-169) for reference, you will see that the glass under the arches is perfectly plain. Most collectors consider the TRANSITIONAL pieces a part of Mayfair rather than Rosemary which was the final design after working on Mayfair at least twice. I suspect that after examining the reworking of the moulds, someone decided that the changes made were not different enough and so they were done again.

I have never seen a piece of crystal except in Mayfair or green in anything except the TRANSITIONAL. Amber is found in both.

Personally, I prefer the style lines of the Mayfair to that of Rosemary, but that is only my viewpoint. You will find this a hard set to assemble; but once you have it together, you will not be sorry. Mix the transitional with the regular pattern in amber. They go well together and only an experienced collector will notice the difference.

There are no sherbets. The sugar, as in Rosemary, looks like a large sherbet since it does not have handles. Both the Mayfair and the changed pattern differences can be seen in the amber creamer and sugar.

You might try carrying a four leaf clover or a rabbit's foot when searching for this pattern. You'll need all the extra help you can get in finding some! However, when you do get lucky enough to find the pattern, you often find several pieces together, rather than a piece here and there.

	Amber	Crystal	Green		Amber	Crystal	Green
Bowl, 5" Sauce	6.00	4.00	8.00	Plate, 9½" Dinner	10.00	7.00	10.00
Bowl, 5" Cream Soup	15.00	9.00	15.00	Plate, 9½" Grill	10.00	7.00	10.00
Bowl, 6" Cereal	14.00	7.50	16.00	Platter, 12" Oval	20.00	15.00	22.00
Bowl, 10" Oval Vegetable	20.00	12.50	20.00	Saucer	2.00	1.25	2.00
Creamer, Footed	10.00	9.50	13.50	Sugar, Footed	10.00	9.00	13.00
Cup	6.50	3.50	6.50	Tumbler, 4½", 9 oz.	17.50	10.00	20.00
Plate, 6¾" Salad	4.50	3.00	6.00				

MAYFAIR, "OPEN ROSE" HOCKING GLASS COMPANY, 1931-1937

Colors: Ice blue, pink; some green, yellow and crystal. *(See Reproduction Section)*

Mayfair is one of the three most collected patterns of Depression glass. I spend more time answering questions and calls about pieces in Mayfair than for any other pattern. Reproductions and rare pieces are the major concerns. I have updated the *Reproduction Section* in the back to take care of the odd colors of cookie jars and shakers now being found; and I have tried to show all the rarer stems that have not been shown for several books.

The stem that causes the most concern is shown in the middle of the lower photograph. I found three of these in an ex-factory workers house in Lancaster, Ohio, years ago. Although this may be listed in one of Hocking's 1935 catalogues as a 4", 2½ oz. wine, I had the chance to measure this again and conclude that this goblet does hold 2½ ozs., but it stands 4⅛" high! Notice the cocktail which is to the left of this stem. The cocktail measures 4" and holds 3 oz., but these measurements on ounces vary a little. Notice the shape of this rarer stem. The bowl is more shallow and more pointed. The stem is thinner and the pink color is brighter.

Why make such a point of these differences? Price is the reason! While the cocktail is selling for $60.00, the rarer goblet has been sold for $750.00. I will get lots of calls and letters about this; so let me reiterate. Only three of these have ever been found! All came out of a factory worker's home! Also from that home came the only known green Mayfair juice pitcher, the first five round Mayfair cups, the first little liqueur and the first claret ever found. These are shown to the front, right of center in the lower photo. This was the find of the year in 1977.

I used to have time to get out and find rare glass. After eight weeks of self imposed prison at this computer, I would prefer to be out this weekend among all the Memorial Day flea markets. I wish you luck in finding rare and unusual glassware! It is usually found by those who really work at finding it.

I have eliminated the green and yellow Mayfair pictures for this book in order to show you the blue and pink that can be found more easily. For those of you who have trouble identifying stemware and tumblers, all known pink and blue styles are represented in these pictures. Pink has five flat tumblers if you count the shot glass; blue has only four. Pink has three styles of footed tumblers; blue has only two. Pink has seven stemmed goblets with two additional sherbets; blue has only one goblet and one sherbet.

Now you can see why an eight place setting in pink can cost you more than the same size setting in blue. There are so many more pieces in pink that do not exist in blue. It really makes a difference when you consider there is no known sugar lid or three legged bowl in blue to find. Blue is a bargain!

Speaking of blue, there was an omission in the last type setting of the book. The blue divided celery was omitted from the price listing. It is common in blue, but rare in pink. It is pictured on the left at the top of page 121. When you have to check thousands of prices, an omission or a misplaced decimal point can get by you. Not many do, but that is one of the hazards of working with pricing such a comprehensive book.

The vase with the blue flowers is known as a sweet pea vase. I get several letters asking what is a sweet pea so we added some flowers to make it noticeable.

A few pink sugar lids and another yellow one have been found. Finally, another yellow sugar turned up; but to my amazement, it was a different style of sugar and my sugar lid would not fit! This sugar is shaped like the odd sized footed Princess that was found years ago. It is 3½" tall and measures 3⅝" by 3½" across the top. The normally found sugar bowl is 2⅝" tall and 4" x 4" across the top

Crystal Mayfair occurs in only a few pieces. Most commonly found are the pitcher, shakers and the divided platter. A reader writes that this was given as a premium with the purchase of coffee or spices in late 1930's.

	*Pink	Blue	Green	Yellow		*Pink	Blue	Green	Yellow
Bowl, 5" Cream					Bowl, 12" Deep				
Soup	35.00				Scalloped Fruit	40.00	55.00	27.50	125.00
Bowl, 5½" Cereal	17.50	37.50	60.00	60.00	Butter Dish and				
Bowl, 7" Vegetable	17.50	37.50	100.00	100.00	Cover or 7"				
Bowl, 9", 3⅛ High,					Covered Vegetable	45.00	235.00	1,100.00	1,100.00
3 Leg Console	3,500.00		3,500.00		Butter Bottom				
Bowl, 9½" Oval					With Indent				265.00
Vegetable	19.00	40.00	90.00	95.00	Butter Dish Top	30.00	185.00	1,000.00	1,000.00
Bowl, 10" Vegetable	17.00	42.00		95.00	Cake Plate, 10"				
Bowl, 10" Same					Footed	20.00	42.00	85.00	
Covered	72.50	80.00		400.00	Candy Dish				
Bowl, 11¾"					and Cover	40.00	150.00	425.00	300.00
Low Flat	37.50	45.00	25.00	110.00	Celery Dish, 9"				
					Divided			120.00	120.00

*Frosted or satin finish items slightly lower

Please refer to Foreword for pricing information

MAYFAIR, "OPEN ROSE" (Cont.)

	*Pink	Blue	Green	Yellow
Celery Dish, 10"	25.00	32.00	90.00	90.00
Celery Dish, 10" Divided	125.00	40.00		
Cookie Jar and Lid	32.50	175.00	500.00	750.00
Creamer, Footed	16.00	50.00	175.00	160.00
Cup	14.00	37.00	135.00	135.00
Cup, Round	200.00			
Decanter and Stopper, 32 oz.	115.00			
Goblet, 3¾", 1 oz. Cordial	400.00		400.00	
Goblet, 4⅛", 2½ oz.	750.00		400.00	
Goblet, 4", 3 oz. Cocktail	60.00		330.00	
Goblet, 4½", 3 oz. Wine	60.00		350.00	
Goblet, 5¼", 4½ oz. Claret	600.00		500.00	
Goblet, 5¾, 9 oz. Water	47.50		350.00	
Goblet, 7¼:, 9 oz. Thin	125.00	120.00		
** Pitcher, 6", 37 oz.	35.00	95.00	450.00	400.00
Pitcher, 8", 60 oz.	37.50	115.00	400.00	350.00
Pitcher, 8½", 80 oz.	65.00	135.00	450.00	450.00
Plate, 5¾" (often Substituted as Saucer)	9.50	15.00	70.00	70.00
Plate, 6½" Round Sherbet	10.00			
Plate, 6½" Round, Off-Center Indent	20.00	20.00	100.00	
Plate, 8½" Luncheon	17.50	27.50	60.00	60.00
Plate, 9½" Dinner	37.50	47.50	100.00	100.00
Plate, 9½" Grill	27.50	27.50	60.00	60.00
Plate, 11½" Handled Grill				80.00
Plate, 12" Cake w/Handles	27.50	42.50	27.50	
*** Platter, 12" Oval, Open Handles	17.50	37.50	120.00	120.00
Platter, 12½" Oval, 8" Wide, Closed Handles			190.00	190.00
Relish, 8⅜", 4-part	20.00	37.50	110.00	110.00
Relish, 8⅜" Non-partitioned	125.00		200.00	200.00
**** Salt and Pepper, Flat Pr.	45.00	195.00	1,000.00	750.00
Salt and Pepper, Footed	5,000.00			
Sandwich Server, Center Handle	30.00	45.00	25.00	95.00
Saucer (Cup Ring)	22.50			125.00
Saucer (See 5¾"Plate)				
Sherbet, 2¼" Flat	120.00	70.00		
Sherbet, 3" Footed	12.50			
Sherbet, 4¾" Footed	57.50	52.50	135.00	135.00
Sugar, Footed	17.50	50.00	165.00	165.00
Sugar Lid	1,300.00		1,000.00	1,000.00
Tumbler, 3½", 5 oz. Juice	31.00	80.00		
Tumbler, 4¼", 9 oz. Water	22.50	67.50		
Tumbler, 4¾", 11 oz. Water	110.00	85.00	160.00	160.00
Tumbler, 5¼", 13½ oz. Iced Tea	35.00	125.00		
Tumbler, 3¼", 3 oz. Footed Juice	57.50			
Tumbler, 5¼", 10 oz. Footed	28.50	90.00		160.00
Tumbler, 6½", 15 oz. Ftd. Iced Tea	27.50	110.00	195.00	
Vase (Sweet Pea)	110.00	72.50	195.00	
Whiskey, 2¼", 1½ oz.	50.00			

* Frosted or satin finish items slightly lower

** Crystal-$15.00

*** Divided Crystal-$12.50

**** Crystal-$17.50 pr. - Beware Reproductions.

Please refer to Foreword for pricing information

120

MISS AMERICA (DIAMOND PATTERN) HOCKING GLASS COMPANY, 1935-1937

Colors: Crystal, pink; some green, ice blue jad-ite and red. *(See Reproduction Section)*

Miss America remains one of the shining stars of Depression glass. The costs for pink butter dishes have soared past pre-reproduction prices. Crystal butter sales are still lagging, but most other crystal prices are beginning to show signs of life. Pink is still THE color to collect.

The blue shown in the top picture is quite rare. Notice that the blue sherbet is shaped somewhat differently than that which is normally found. There is a pink sherbet that flairs out slightly at the top rim. Some collectors have confused this with English Hobnail, but it is Miss America from a different mould. Be sure to read the section under English Hobnail about the major differences in these two patterns.

Any time a pattern was made for several years, it will be possible to find pieces that vary in design. There was more than one mould made for each piece; so each item can vary as often as each mould was changed.

One of the toughest reproduction problems has been the shakers. Read about these in the *Reproduction Section* in the back. Suffice to say, there are few green shakers available that are old. In fact, I haven't seen a pair that was old since the early 1970's. Pink shakers are a **HEADACHE!** Rarely, have I had as many questions about Miss America shakers as in the last two years because there have been reproductions of the reproductions and even those have now been copied by another importer. Interesting enough, there are two different moulds used for old shakers. The shakers that stay fat toward the base are the best ones to buy, since they have not been reproduced. The shakers which get thin (as shown in the photographs) are the style that has been reproduced. Both styles were made originally, but only the thin style has been copied. **Buy shakers from a reputable dealer.**

The hardest to find stem is the footed juice goblet. The supply of pink water goblets is more than adequate for the demand. There has only been one report of a pink divided relish being found since the last book. It was found in Ohio!

The gold painted candy dish has been sold! The owner retired from the glass business and I bought all his glass. The only condition I made was no gold candy. (I wonder how much he paid someone to take it off his hands)! It was UGLY!

There are a few odd-colored or flashed pieces of Miss America that are found occasionally. Flashed-on red, green or amethyst make interesting conversation pieces, but are not plentiful enough to collect a set. A jad-ite 8" bowl has now been found to go with the plate shown in the last book!

	Crystal	Pink	Green	Red		Crystal	Pink	Green	Red
Bowl, 4½" Berry			7.00		Goblet, 4¾", 5 oz.				
* Bowl, 6¼" Berry	6.00	14.00	10.00		Juice	20.00	65.00		185.00
Bowl, 8" Curved in at					Goblet, 5½", 10 oz.				
Top	30.00	50.00		350.00	Water	17.50	33.00		160.00
Bowl, 8¾" Straight					Pitcher, 8", 65 oz.	40.00	90.00		
Deep Fruit	22.50	42.50			Pitcher, 8½", 65 oz.				
Bowl, 10" Oval					w/Ice Lip	57.50	100.00		
Vegetable	10.00	17.50			***Plate, 5¾" Sherbet	3.00	5.00	5.00	
Bowl, 11", Shallow				600.00	Plate, 6¾"			6.00	
** Butter Dish and					Plate, 8½" Salad	5.00	15.00	8.00	65.00
Cover	190.00	435.00			****Plate, 10¼" dinner	10.00	18.00		
Butter Dish Bottom	6.00	14.00			Plate, 10¼" Grill	7.50	16.00		
Butter Dish Top	184.00	421.00			Platter, 12¼" Oval	10.00	18.00		
Cake Plate, 12"					Relish, 8¾", 4 Part	7.50	16.00		
Footed	17.50	29.00			Relish, 11¾" Round				
Candy Jar and					Divided	15.00	450.00		
Cover, 11½"	45.00	97.50			Salt and Pepper, Pr.	22.50	42.50	275.00	
Celery Dish, 10½"					Saucer	2.50	4.00		
Oblong	8.00	16.00			***Sherbet	6.50	11.00		
Coaster, 5¾"	12.50	20.00			Sugar	6.00	12.50		140.00
Comport, 5"	11.00	17.50			****Tumbler, 4", 5 oz.				
Creamer, Footed	6.50	13.00		145.00	Juice	12.50	37.50		
Cup	7.50	16.00	8.00		Tumbler, 4½",				
Goblet, 3¾", 3 oz.					10 oz. Water	12.00	20.00	15.00	
Wine	16.00	50.00		175.00	Tumbler, 5¾", 14 oz.				
					Iced Tea	20.00	47.50		

* Also has appeared in Cobalt Blue-$125.00

** Absolute mint price

*** Also in Ice Blue-$35.00

**** Also in Ice Blue-$80.00

Please refer to Foreword for pricing information

MODERNTONE & "LITTLE HOSTESS PARTY DISHES," HAZEL ATLAS GLASS COMPANY, 1934-1942; Late 1940's-Early 1950's

Colors: Amethyst, cobalt blue; some crystal, pink and platonite fired-on colors.

Cobalt Moderntone continues to be a "hot" color. Platonite is also beginning to be "hot" in some colors! Mostly, it is the dark Platonite colors that are in demand. Platters are being found in all pastel colors! Collectors are turning to many of the later made patterns.

I was asked by several collectors about the crystal shot glasses in the metal holder. This came in a boxed set with a Colonial Block creamer. The box was marked "Little Deb" Lemonade Server Set. I paid $20.00 for the set. It's a shame the shots and pitcher were not cobalt!

Iced tea and juice tumblers are still the pieces to find in both cobalt and amethyst. Where have all the ruffled cream soups and sandwich plates gone? The cheese dish lid has been moved to the side to show the wooden cheese plate which fits inside the metal lid.

Thanks to Sherry McClain for the picture shown below. You can see a flat soup in the right foreground of the picture.

Watch those children's dish prices soar! The tea pot is the valuable piece to the sets, but it is the lid that is so hard to find. Little girls must have played house with those quite often. The maroon tea pot is much harder to find than the turquoise. Even Cathy had a turquoise one left over from her childhood! Cathy received her set as a premium from Big Top Peanut Butter.

	Cobalt	Amethyst	Platonite Colors		Cobalt	Amethyst	Platonite Colors
* Ash Tray, 7¾", Match Holder in Center	110.00			Plate, 5⅞" Sherbet	4.00	3.50	
Bowl, 4¾" Cream Soup	14.00	13.00	5.00	Plate, 6¾" Salad	7.00	6.00	
Bowl, 5" Berry	16.00	12.00	3.50	Plate, 7¾" Luncheon	7.00	6.50	4.50
Bowl, 5" Cream Soup, Ruffled	25.00	15.00		Plate, 8⅞" Dinner	11.00	8.00	
Bowl, 6½" Cereal	45.00	35.00	7.00	Plate, 10½" Sandwich	35.00	25.00	
Bowl, 7½" Soup	65.00	55.00		Platter, 11" Oval	25.00	20.00	7.50
Bowl, 8"			8.00	Platter, 12" Oval	40.00	30.00	
Bowl, 8¾" Large Berry	30.00	25.00	6.50	Salt and Pepper, Pr.	30.00	30.00	12.50
Butter Dish with Metal Cover	65.00			Saucer	2.00	2.00	1.00
Cheese Dish, 7" with Metal Lid	250.00			Sherbet	9.00	8.00	3.50
Creamer	8.00	6.00	4.00	Sugar	7.50	6.50	4.00
Cup	7.50	6.00	3.00	Sugar Lid in Metal	25.00		
Cup (Handle-less) or Custard	11.00	10.00		Tumbler, 5 oz.	25.00	17.00	
				Tumbler, 9 oz.	19.50	18.00	6.00
				Tumbler, 12 oz.	65.00	50.00	
				Whiskey, 1½ oz.	18.00		

* Pink—$50.00

LITTLE HOSTESS PARTY SET

	Pastel	Dark		Pastel	Dark
Cup, ¾"	4.00	6.00	Sugar, 1¾"	5.00	7.00
Saucer, 3⅞	1.00	3.00	Teapot and Lid, 3½"		50.00
Plate, 5¼"	4.00	7.00	Set, 14 Piece	45.00	
Creamer, 1¾'	5.00	7.00	Set, 16 Piece		125.00

MOONDROPS NEW MARTINSVILLE GLASS COMPANY, 1932-1940

Colors: Amber, pink, green, cobalt, ice blue, red, amethyst, crystal, dark green, light green, jadite, smoke and black.

Collecting red or cobalt blue Moondrops continues to be the only story in this pattern! There are a few collectors of other colors, but these collectors have a wide range of unusual pieces from which to choose. I recently bought an amethyst bud vase. I was happy to see any bud vase in Moondrops! I did find a cobalt perfume; but, alas, it had no stopper. The butter has to have a glass top to fetch the price listed below. The metal top found with a bird finial on butter bottoms is better than none, but that top sells for about $25.00. However, the metal top with the fan finial brings about $50.00!

	Blue,Red	Other Colors
Ash Tray	30.00	15.00
Bowl, 5¼" Berry	10.00	5.00
Bowl, 6¾" Soup	65.00	
Bowl, 7½" Pickle	18.00	11.00
Bowl, 8⅜" Footed, Concave Top	25.00	15.00
Bowl, 8'" 3-Footed Divided Relish	20.00	12.00
Bowl, 9½" 3-Legged Ruffled	35.00	
Bowl, 9¾" Oval Vegetable	25.00	20.00
Bowl, 9¾" Covered Casserole	125.00	85.00
Bowl, 9¾" Handled Oval	45.00	30.00
Bowl, 11" Boat-Shaped Celery	25.00	20.00
Bowl, 12" Round 3-Footed Console	70.00	25.00
Bowl, 13" Console with "Wings"	95.00	35.00
Butter Dish and Cover	375.00	225.00
Butter Dish Bottom	40.00	35.00
Butter Dish Top	335.00	200.00
Candles, 2" Ruffled Pr.	25.00	17.50
Candles, 4'" Sherbet Style Pr.	22.50	15.00
Candlesticks, 5" Ruffled, Pr.	27.50	17.50
Candlesticks, 5" "Wings" Pr.	75.00	35.00
Candlesticks, 5¼" Triple Light Pr.	85.00	45.00
Candlesticks 8½" Metal Stem Pr.	35.00	25.00
Candy Dish, 8" Ruffled	28.00	15.00
Cocktail Shaker with or without Hdl., Metal Top	30.00	20.00
Comport, 4"	17.50	10.00
Comport, 11½"	45.00	25.00
Creamer, 2¾" Miniature	12.00	7.50
Creamer, 3¾" Regular	12.00	7.50
Cup	10.00	7.50
Decanter, 7¾" Small	50.00	32.50
Decanter, 8½" Medium	60.00	32.50
Decanter, 11¼" Large	70.00	37.50
Decanter, 10¼" "Rocket"	175.00	100.00
Goblet, 2⅞", ¾ oz. Cordial	25.00	15.00
Goblet, 4", 4 oz. Wine	17.00	10.00
Goblet, 4¾", "Rocket" Wine	40.00	25.00
Goblet, 4¾, 5 oz.	18.00	11.00
Goblet, 5¾" 8 oz.	25.00	15.00

	Blue,Red	OtherColors
Goblet, 5⅛", 3 oz. Metal Stem Wine	13.00	8.50
Goblet, 5½", 4 oz. Metal Stem Wine	15.00	8.50
Goblet, 6¼", 9 oz. Metal Stem Water	18.00	13.50
Gravy Boat	100.00	75.00
Mug, 5⅛", 12 oz.	27.50	17.50
Perfume Bottle, "Rocket"	155.00	100.00
Pitcher, 6⅞", 22 oz. Small	135.00	75.00
Pitcher, 8⅛", 32 oz. Medium	150.00	100.00
Pitcher, 8", 50 oz. Large, with Lip	165.00	40.00
Pitcher, 8⅛", 53 oz. Large, No Lip	160.00	115.00
Plate, 5⅞"	7.00	5.00
Plate, 6⅛" Sherbet	5.00	3.00
Plate, 6" Round, Off-Center Sherbet Indent	9.00	7.00
Plate, 7⅛" Salad	9.00	7.00
Plate, 8½" Luncheon	11.00	9.50
Plate, 9½" Dinner	15.00	12.00
Plate, 14" Round Sandwich	25.00	13.50
Plate, 14" 2-Handled Sandwich	35.00	20.00
Platter, 12" Oval	22.00	15.00
Powder Jar, 3 Footed	125.00	85.00
Saucer	3.50	3.00
Sherbet, 2⅝"	10.00	7.50
Sherbet, 4½"	20.00	12.50
Sugar, 2¾"	9.00	7.00
Sugar, 4"	11.50	7.00
Tumbler, 2¾", 2 oz. Shot	12.00	7.50
Tumbler, 2¾", 2 oz. Handled Shot	14.00	9.00
Tumbler, 3¼", 3 oz. Footed Juice	12.50	8.00
Tumbler, 3⅝", 5 oz.	10.00	6.00
Tumbler, 4⅜", 7 oz.	11.00	7.50
Tumbler, 4⅜", 8 oz.	12.00	8.50
Tumbler, 4⅞", 9 oz. Handled	22.00	12.00
Tumbler, 4⅞", 9 oz.	13.50	10.00
Tumbler, 5⅛", 12 oz.	20.00	11.50
Tray, 7½", For Mini Sugar/Creamer	25.00	16.00
Vase, 7¾" Flat, Ruffled Top	45.00	35.00
Vase, 8½" "Rocket" Bud	155.00	110.00
Vase, 9¼ "Rocket" Style	150.00	85.00

MOONSTONE ANCHOR HOCKING GLASS CORPORATION, 1941-1946

Colors: Crystal with opalescent hobnails and some green.

Moonstone has experienced a surge of new collectors. Long time collectors can not find the 5½" berry bowls. The ruffled 5½" are found faster, but even they are not as plentiful as they once were. The straight sided bowl was set on a rack on the right and looks more like a plate. Its counterpart ruffled bowl is set up on a rack on the left.

Given the odd pieces shown in the bottom photograph with Moonstone stickers, it seems that Moonstone may have referred more to the process of white edging than to the actual pattern. It was Imperial who called the same process **Sea Foam** on their patterns such as Laced Edge.

The flashed red candy has a new home with a happy collector. Those pieces shown in the top photograph below are from Hocking's morgue. Evidently, these were experimental pieces or colors. The pink bowl is similar to a green one I pictured in earlier books. The green was issued under the name "Ocean Green" and was made in sets containing goblets, cups, saucers, plates, creamer and sugars. I wonder if the pink had a name.

Notice the yellow hobnail piece under the pink bowl. This is very reminiscent of a color of Fenton's Hobnail pattern. Many Moonstone collectors buy Fenton pitchers and tumblers in white Hobnail to go with their sets since there is no pitcher or tumbler in Moonstone.

Several years ago, there was a 9" vase reported that was shaped just like the 5½" vase. I have not heard about it since then; so if you have one, let me know.

There are no Moonstone shakers. These, too, are Fenton. There is no Moonstone cologne bottle. It, also, is Fenton. The Fenton pieces go well with Moonstone; and, if you would like additional pieces that are similar to your pattern, by all means buy these! The hobs on the Fenton are more pointed than on Moonstone, but the colors match very well.

	Opalescent Hobnail
Bowl, 5½" Berry	12.00
Bowl, 5½" Crimped Dessert	6.00
Bowl, 6½" Crimped Handled	7.00
Bowl, 7¾" Flat	9.00
Bowl, 7¾" Divided Relish	7.50
Bowl, 9½" Crimped	12.50
Bowl, Cloverleaf	9.00
Candle Holder, Pr.	15.00
Candy Jar and Cover, 6"	17.50
Cigarette Jar and Cover	15.00
Creamer	6.00
Cup	6.00
Goblet, 10 oz..	15.00
Heart Bonbon, One Handle	9.00
Plate, 6¼" Sherbet	2.50
Plate, 8" Luncheon	8.50
Plate, 10" Sandwich	16.00
Puff Box and Cover, 4¾" Round	16.00
Saucer (Same as Sherbet Plate)	2.50
Sherbet, Footed	6.00
Sugar, Footed	6.00
Vase, 5½" Bud	9.00

Please refer to Foreword for pricing information

MOROCCAN AMETHYST HAZEL WARE, DIVISION OF CONTINENTAL CAN, 1960's

Color: Amethyst.

Moroccan Amethyst is the color and the pattern name found on several styles and shapes of this Hazel Ware glass. There are all kinds of new pieces being found in this color as you can see by the expanded listing. I have found an interesting boxed set also. This set is called "The Magic Hour" 4 pc. cocktail set. It features a clock showing six o' clock and says "yours" on one side and "mine" on the other. In this boxed set are two 2½", 4 oz. tumblers and a spouted cocktail with glass stirrer to make up the four pieces.

There is a "chip and dip" set in a metal holder. It is made up of the 10¾" bowl on the bottom and the 5¾" bowl on top. This set was purchased after our photography was finished; so you will have to wait until next time to see it. I wanted you to be on the lookout for it.

The three stemmed pieces shown have all been found with Moroccan Amethyst labels so there is no question as to their inclusion in our list. There may be another size or two in this design. The tumbler on the right holds 11 oz. as does the normally found water; but notice the indented, crinkled bottom design. There may be other sizes in this style. That is one of the fun things about collecting a pattern for which I have not found a catalogue listing. You may find new pieces not listed. All I ask is that you send me a picture and the measurements!

I am still amazed to see people paying $12.00 for iced tea tumblers that we sold at our first garage sale for less than a quarter each. We sold these, which had been wedding gifts in 1964, because the top heavy tumblers were a nuisance with small kids. Not only did they turn over easily, but they rolled, spewing the contents in all directions!

You will find these same shaped pieces in blue and crystal. The blue has labels to indicate it was called "Capri", but I have not seen a label on the crystal. These colors may also become collectible! So be on the lookout for them.

	Amethyst		Amethyst
Ash Tray, 6⅞, Triangular	6.00	Ice Bucket, 6"	22.50
Bowl, 4¾, Fruit, Octagonal	4.50	Plate, 5¾",	2.50
Bowl, 5¾", Deep, Square	6.00	Plate, 7¼", Salad	4.00
Bowl, 7¾", Oval	12.00	Plate, 9¾", Dinner	5.50
Bowl, 7¾", Rectangular	10.00	Plate, 12" , Sandwich	7.00
Bowl, 10¾"	20.00	Saucer	.75
Candy w/Lid Short	20.00	Tumbler, Juice, 2½", 4 oz.	5.50
Cocktail w/Stirrer, 6¼", 16 oz., w/Lip	12.50	Tumbler, Old Fashion, 3¼", 8 oz.	7.50
Cup	3.25	Tumbler, Water, Crinkled Bottom, 4¼", 11 oz.	7.50
Goblet, 4", 4½ oz., Wine	8.50	Tumbler, Water, 4⅝", 11 oz.	8.00
Goblet, 4¼", 7½ oz., Sherbet	5.50	Tumbler, Iced Tea, 6½",16 oz.	12.00
Goblet, 4⅜", 5½ oz., Juice	7.50	Vase, 8½" Ruffled	27.50

MT. PLEASANT, "DOUBLE SHIELD" L.E. SMITH GLASS COMPANY, 1920's-1934

Colors: Black amethyst, amethyst, cobalt blue, crystal, pink, green.

Mt. Pleasant seems to have caught the fancy of a new collecting fraternity. The demand for cobalt blue is strongly evidenced at shows as dealers stock rapidly disappears. The black is collected by many collectors of "black" glass that are not necessarily Depression glass collectors per se. Oft times, these collectors of black glass have become Depression glass collectors once they become aware of our glass. More Mt. Pleasant is being found in Kansas, Nebraska and western New York than any place. It seems that this pattern was promoted heavily at hardware stores in those areas. Blue is the color most mentioned in letters from those areas. Many pieces of both colors are found with a platinum (silver) band around them. This band wore off very easily, so many pieces are found with only partial evidence of this decoration. I just purchased eight black sherbets with only two having complete encircling decorations.

If you have two different sized leaf plates in your collection, let me know their sizes. I have the 8" plate, but I do not know if the other is 7" or 9". I received a letter from a reader with a photograph of two sized leaf plates. She gave no sizes and no return address; so I have not been able to follow up on that information.

	Pink, Green	Black Amethyst, Cobalt		Pink, Green	Black Amethyst, Cobalt
Bon Bon, Rolled-Up Handled, 7"	12.50	17.50	Mayonnaise, 5½", 3-Footed	12.50	20.00
Bowl, 4" Opening, Rose	15.00	20.00	Mint, 6", Center Handle	10.00	15.00
Bowl, 4", Square Footed Fruit	10.00	15.00	Plate, 7", 2-Handled, Scalloped	6.50	10.00
Bowl, 6", 2-Handled, Square	10.00	13.00	Plate, 8", Scalloped or Square	7.50	12.00
Bowl, 7", 3 Footed, Rolled Out Edge	12.50	17.00	Plate, 8", 2-Handled	7.50	14.00
Bowl, 8", Scalloped, 2-Handled	15.00	22.00	Plate 8¼, Square w/Indent for Cup		13.00
Bowl, 8", Square, 2-Handled	15.00	25.00	Plate, 9" Grill		8.50
Bowl, 9", Scalloped, 1¾" Deep, Footed		25.00	Plate, 10½", Cake, 2-Handled	13.50	20.00
Bowl, 9¼", Square Footed Fruit	15.00	25.00	Plate, 12", 2-Handled	15.00	25.00
Bowl, 10", Scalloped Fruit		30.00	Salt and Pepper, 2 Styles	20.00	32.50
Bowl, 10", 2-Handled, Turned-Up Edge		27.00	Sandwich Server, Center-Handled		30.00
Candlestick, Single, Pr.	15.00	20.00	Saucer	1.50	2.50
Candlestick, Double, Pr.	20.00	35.00	Sherbet	6.50	12.50
Creamer	15.00	12.50	Sugar	15.00	12.50
Cup (Waffle-Like Crystal)	3.50		Tumbler, ftd.		15.00
Cup	5.00	8.50	Vase, 7¼"		22.00
Leaf, 8"		12.00			

NEW CENTURY, and incorrectly, "LYDIA RAY" HAZEL ATLAS GLASS COMPANY, 1930-1935

Colors: Green; some crystal, pink, amethyst and cobalt.

New Century is the official name for this pattern made by Hazel Atlas. "Lydia Ray" was the name used until an official name was found. I mention this for new collectors since the name "New Century" was also used (incorrectly) by another author to identify the **Ovide**. This has caused confusion in the past, so I want you to be aware of this minor problem.

Collectors seek the green more than any other color; in fact, sets can only be gathered in crystal and green. So far, pink, cobalt blue and amethyst can only be found in water sets except for occasionally found cups and saucers.

Tumblers are difficult to find in any size other than the 9 and 10 ounce. Ash trays in green are rare, but few collectors are purchasing smokers' items at present. The casserole bottom is harder to find than the top. I have often wondered why that is true for New Century and Floral and does not hold true for any of the other patterns which have covered bowls.

It has been a while since I have seen cream soups, wines or a decanter in my travels. Were there more collectors of New Century, the true scarcity of some of these pieces would be exposed. Unless there is new collector interest in a pattern, many times dealers do not stock minor patterns. The time to start collecting New Century is NOW!

	Green, Crystal	Pink Cobalt Amethyst		Green, Crystal	Pink Cobalt Amethyst
Ash Tray/Coaster, 5⅜"	25.00		Plate, 8½" Salad	7.00	
Bowl, 4½" Berry	9.50		Plate, 10" Dinner	10.00	
Bowl, 4¾" Cream Soup	10.00		Plate, 10" Grill	8.00	
Bowl, 8" Large Berry	12.50		Platter, 11" Oval	11.00	
Bowl, 9" Covered Casserole	45.00		Salt and Pepper, Pr.	27.50	
Butter Dish and Cover	47.50		Saucer	2.00	5.00
Cup	5.00	15.00	Sherbet, 3"	7.00	
Creamer	6.00		Sugar	5.00	
Decanter and Stopper	42.00		Sugar Cover	10.00	
Goblet, 2½ oz. Wine	15.00		Tumbler, 3½", 5 oz.	9.00	10.00
Goblet, 3¼ oz. Cocktail	14.00		Tumbler, 4¼", 9 oz.	11.00	10.00
Pitcher, 7¾", 60 oz. with or			Tumbler, 5", 10 oz.	11.00	12.00
without Ice Lip	27.50	25.00	Tumbler, 5¼", 12 oz.	17.00	15.00
Pitcher, 8", 80 oz. with or			Tumbler, 4", 5 oz. Footed	11.00	
without Ice Lip	30.00	35.00	Tumbler, 4⅞", 9 oz. Footed	14.00	
Plate, 6" Sherbet	2.25		Whiskey, 2½", 1½ oz.	12.00	
Plate, 7⅛" Breakfast	6.00				

NEWPORT, "HAIRPIN" HAZEL ATLAS GLASS COMPANY, 1936-1940

Colors: Cobalt blue, amethyst; some pink, "Platonite" white and fired-on colors.

Pink Newport sets were given away as premiums for buying seeds from a catalogue in the 1930's. A few of these sets are entering the market but are not being bought very quickly. It is the cobalt blue and amethyst that draw collectors' praises.

Unfortunately, collectors of blue and amethyst can not find enough cereal bowls or tumblers to make their collections complete. I have listened to many collectors' woeful stories of searching for these two items without success. Amethyst is even harder to find than cobalt blue, but there are fewer amethyst collectors.

The "Platonite" white and white with fired on colors was a popular line for Hazel Atlas. Notice the white edge on the fired-on pink plate in the rear. The edge and back of this plate is white. The pink and other colors are decorating only the top edge. The white shaker shown here is often used by Petalware collectors for shakers in that set since there are no shakers in that MacBeth-Evans set. It is amazing how many people have been fooled into thinking these shakers are really Petalware.

The white color comes in two distinct shades. One is very translucent and the other is a flat white similar to what many collectors know as milk glass.

	*Cobalt	Amethyst		*Cobalt	Amethyst
Bowl, 4¼" Berry	11.00	10.00	Plate, 11½" Sandwich	25.00	22.00
Bowl, 4¾" Cream Soup	13.00	12.00	Platter, 11¾" Oval	30.00	25.00
Bowl, 5¼" Cereal	25.00	20.00	Salt and Pepper	37.50	35.00
Bowl, 8¼" Large Berry	30.00	25.00	Saucer	2.50	2.50
Cup	7.50	6.50	Sherbet	10.00	9.00
Creamer	10.00	9.00	Sugar	10.00	9.00
Plate, 6" Sherbet	3.50	3.00	Tumbler, 4½", 9 oz.	25.00	22.00
Plate, 8½" Luncheon	8.00	8.00			

* White and pink 50% of Cobalt price.

Please refer to Foreword for pricing information

"NORA BIRD", PADEN CITY GLASS COMPANY, LINE 300, 1929-1930's

Colors: Pink, green, crystal.

"Nora Bird" is a name given to this Paden City pattern by collectors. It was a numbered etching on the popular #300 line blank. This blank is found in several additional colors, but pink, green and crystal "Nora Bird" are the only colors on which this etching has been found.

There may be more pieces in this pattern that I do not have listed, so let me know if you find something else. The bird on each piece can be found in flight or getting ready to fly. Some collectors have suggested this is a pheasant.

The candy dish and mayonnaise are the pieces missing from most collections, but cup and saucer sets are not abundant either.

	Pink, Green		Pink, Green
Candlestick, Pr.	45.00	Plate, 8"	17.50
Candy Dish w/Cover, 6½", 3 Part	55.00	Saucer	10.00
Creamer, 4½", Round Handle	27.50	Sugar, 4½", Round Handle	25.00
Creamer, 5", Pointed Handle	27.50	Sugar, 5", Pointed Handle	25.00
Cup	35.00	Tumbler, 3"	25.00
Ice Tub, 6"	75.00	Tumbler, 4"	30.00
Mayonnaise and Liner	55.00	Tumbler, 4¾", Footed	35.00

NORMANDIE, "BOUQUET AND LATTICE" FEDERAL GLASS COMPANY 1933-1940

Colors: Iridescent, amber, pink, crystal.

Pink Normandie dinner plates are not being found at any price. All three sizes of tumblers, pitcher, shakers and sugar lid in pink make this one of the more challenging sets to acquire in today's market. The same pieces are hard to find in amber, but there are not as many collectors buying amber as there are buying pink. Not only that, but amber **is** available with searching.

Paying for the pink will stretch some pocket books out of shape if you do find it. One collector told me that pink had been easy on her purse. Of course, she had only found cups, saucers and sherbets in two years of looking!

The amber will not break your bank account when you do find it, but the sugar lid might dent it a little. There are few collectors of the iridescent color, but the salad plates seem to be unavailable at any price. For those who like the iridized color, this is a set that can be put together economically except for the aforementioned salad plates.

The console bowl and candlesticks sometimes found with the iridized Normandie are Madrid. Maybe these were sold at the same time. Several collectors have reported finding this console set with Normandie.

	Amber	Pink	Iridescent		Amber	Pink	Iridescent
Bowl, 5" Berry	4.00	5.00	4.00	Plate, 11" Grill	12.00	14.00	8.00
*Bowl, 6½" Cereal	10.00	15.00	6.50	Platter, 11¾"	12.50	19.00	10.00
Bowl, 8½" Large Berry	11.00	15.00	9.50	Salt and Pepper, Pr.	37.50	57.50	
Bowl, 10" Oval Veg.	12.00	25.00	12.50	Saucer	1.50	2.00	1.50
Creamer, Footed	6.00	8.50	6.50	Sherbet	5.00	7.00	6.00
Cup	5.50	7.00	5.00	Sugar	6.00	7.50	5.00
Pitcher, 8", 80 oz.	55.00	90.00		Sugar Lid	70.00	110.00	
Plate, 6" Sherbet	2.00	2.00	2.00	Tumbler, 4", 5 oz. Juice	15.00	35.00	
Plate, 7¾" Salad	7.00	9.00	50.00	Tumbler, 4¼", 9 oz. Water	12.50	30.00	
Plate, 9¼ Luncheon	5.50	10.00	7.50	Tumbler, 5", 12 oz. Iced Tea	18.00	50.00	
Plate, 11" Dinner	20.00	75.00	13.00				

* Mistaken by many as butter bottom.

No. 610, "PYRAMID" INDIANA GLASS COMPANY, 1926-1932

Colors: Green, pink, yellow, white, crystal, blue or black in 1974-1975 by Tiara.

The official name of this pattern is No. 610. Collectors long ago began calling it "Pyramid" and that has stuck.

Blue and black pieces of "Pyramid" were made by Indiana in the mid 1970's. Normally, you see black tumblers or the 4-part center handled relish in either color. Berry bowls were also made. These colors are recent and NOT Depression glass! That 4-part relish is sometimes mistaken for Tea Room.

Crystal pitcher and tumblers are harder to find than the other colors, although there are fewer collectors searching for them. The crystal pitcher shown here was purchased about fifteen years ago for $8.00 at a flea market in Ohio. Since then, it has had four additional owners. It is well traveled having gone from Ohio to Kentucky, Georgia, Maryland, California and now to Louisiana!

This deco looking pattern has gotten very popular and prices have risen dramatically the last few years. Be careful in buying "Pyramid" because the points on the outsides of the pieces have a tendency to chip.

Ice buckets are readily found, even in yellow. It is the yellow lid that is nearly impossible to find!

Oval bowls and pickle dishes are both 9½". The oval bowl has pointed edges as can be seen in yellow and the over turned white bowl. It was turned over so you can see the pattern on this opaque color. The pickle dish edges are rounded as shown by the pink one on the left.

	Crystal	Pink	Green	Yellow		Crystal	Pink	Green	Yellow
Bowl, 4¾" Berry	8.00	14.50	15.00	25.00	Pitcher	300.00	200.00	185.00	400.00
Bowl, 8½" Master Berry	12.00	20.00	22.50	45.00	Relish Tray, 4-Part				
Bowl, 9½" Oval	25.00	15.00	22.50	45.00	Handled	18.00	30.00	37.50	50.00
Bowl, 9½" Pickle, 5¾"					Sugar	12.00	17.50	17.50	25.00
Wide	15.00	25.00	22.50	45.00	Tray for Creamer and				
Creamer	12.00	18.00	18.00	25.00	Sugar	10.00	17.50	20.00	40.00
Ice Tub	45.00	65.00	75.00	175.00	Tumbler, 8 oz. Footed	30.00	20.00	25.00	42.50
Ice Tub Lid				475.00	Tumbler, 11 oz. Footed	50.00	35.00	45.00	55.00

No. 612, "HORSESHOE" INDIANA GLASS COMPANY, 1930-1933

Colors: Green, yellow, pink, crystal.

The official name for this Indiana pattern is No. 612, but collectors dubbed it "Horseshoe". Butter dishes have remained in the same price category for several years. This happens when the butter dish reaches so high a price that new collectors decide to do without it. Actually, new collectors have shied away from "Horseshoe" for years since it has so many highly priced pieces. Prices are beginning to rise again!

Grill plates remain elusive. Be aware that many plates and platters are plain in the center, while others have the pattern.

Candy dishes only have the pattern on the top. The bottom is plain. No yellow butter dish, grill plate, candy dish or flat tumblers have ever been found! If you find the first of these, let me know.

Only creamer and sugars have been found in crystal. A crystal sugar is pictured. These sell in the $15.00 range, but they are quite rare!

Catalogues list a 10⅜" dinner plate, but there are doubts about its existence. Does anyone have a stack of these in your set?

	Green	Yellow		Green	Yellow
Bowl, 4½" Berry	17.50	16.00	Plate, 6" Sherbet	3.00	4.50
Bowl, 6½" Cereal	17.50	17.00	Plate, 8⅜" Salad	6.00	7.00
Bowl, 7½" Salad	15.00	17.00	Plate, 9⅜" Luncheon	9.00	9.50
Bowl, 8½" Vegetable	17.00	22.50	Plate, 10⅜" Grill	47.50	
Bowl, 9½" Large Berry	25.00	28.00	Plate, 11½" Sandwich	11.00	13.00
Bowl, 10½" Oval Vegetable	16.00	18.00	Platter, 10¾" Oval	16.00	17.00
Butter Dish and Cover	500.00		Relish, 3 Part Footed	15.00	27.50
Butter Dish Bottom	125.00		Saucer	3.00	3.50
Butter Dish Top	375.00		Sherbet	11.00	12.00
Candy in Metal Holder Motif			Sugar, Open	10.00	10.50
on Lid	95.00		Tumbler, 4¼", 9 oz.	80.00	
Also, Pink	135.00		Tumbler, 4¾", 12 oz.	100.00	
Creamer, Footed	11.50	12.50	Tumbler, 9 oz. Footed	15.00	16.00
Cup	8.00	8.50	Tumbler, 12 oz. Footed	90.00	100.00
Pitcher, 8½", 64 oz.	210.00	235.00			

Please refer to Foreword for pricing information

No. 616, "VERNON" INDIANA GLASS COMPANY, 1930-1932

Colors: Green, crystal, yellow.

Another of Indiana's numbered lines, this pattern is not easily found. I hated to get away from my previous photograph that showed every piece in all three colors, but that box of glass has been missing for several years. The last time I even remember it was years ago when we left glass in Paducah to be photographed. The studio had a fire and most of our glass got soaked in the procedure. The glass was in wax coated boxes but the pads that the glass was packed in mildewed before we returned to finish the session. Maybe some of the glass did get more than soaked! It has never been seen again.

Anyway, the pattern shows better in the photograph even if there are a few less pieces to be seen. We used the crystal No. 616 for everyday dishes for a couple of years. Many of the crystal pieces are found trimmed in platinum (silver). The sandwich plates make great dinner plates. By the way, these are 11½" instead of 11" as has previously been listed.

Yellow and green are both hard to accumulate, but there is less green than yellow available. Green tumblers are especially hard to locate.

	Green	Crystal	Yellow
Creamer, Footed	20.00	10.00	17.50
Cup	13.50	6.00	12.00
Plate, 8" Luncheon	6.50	4.00	6.50
Plate, 11½" Sandwich	20.00	10.00	20.00
Saucer	4.50	2.00	4.50
Sugar, Footed	19.50	9.00	17.50
Tumbler, 5" Footed	25.00	12.00	25.00

No. 618, "PINEAPPLE & FLORAL" INDIANA GLASS COMPANY, 1932-1937

Colors: Crystal, amber; some fired-on red, green; late 1960's, avocado; 1980's pink, cobalt blue etc.

Several fired-on red pitchers have been found with fired-on red sets of "Pineapple and Floral". The pitcher is of poor quality as is most of the red in this color. There is a cross hatching design on the base similar to that of this pattern, but (besides the poor quality and color) there is where the similarity ends.

Indiana has re-made the diamond shaped comport and 7" salad bowl in all kinds of colors. Many of these have sprayed-on colors although the light pink is a nice transparent color. The price of the crystal has dropped because they also remade these in crystal. Amber and fired-on red are safe colors to collect to avoid reproductions. The crystal is a nice set.

Remember that the mould seams on all of this pattern are rough. This is true on all size tumblers! I found two sets of eight water tumblers in an Antique Mall last week. These were priced as "old Pattern Glass" - 8 for $28.00. I bought both sets and only wished they had more. The cups were twelve for $36.00, but there were no saucers. Bargains do exist!

	Crystal	Amber, Red		Crystal	Amber, Red
Ash Tray, 4½"	15.00	16.00	Plate, 11½" w/Indentation	20.00	
Bowl, 4¾" Berry	20.00	14.00	Plate, 11½" Sandwich	12.50	13.50
Bowl, 6" Cereal	20.00	17.50	Platter, 11" Closed Handles	12.00	15.00
* Bowl, 7" Salad	1.00	8.50	Platter, Relish, 11½" Divided	15.00	
Bowl, 10" Oval Vegetable	20.00	16.00	Saucer	3.00	3.00
* Comport, Diamond-Shaped	1.00	6.50	Sherbet, Footed	16.00	16.00
Creamer, Diamond-Shaped	6.50	8.50	Sugar, Diamond-Shaped	6.50	8.50
Cream Soup	7.50	7.00	Tumbler, 4¼", 8 oz.	30.00	
Cup	7.50	7.00	Tumbler, 5", 12 oz.	35.00	
Plate, 6" Sherbet	3.00	4.00	Vase, Cone-Shaped	25.00	
Plate, 8⅜" Salad	5.00	6.00	Vase Holder (17.50)		
** Plate, 9⅜" Dinner	10.00	12.50			

* reproduced in several colors
** Green-$25.00

Please refer to Foreword for pricing information

OLD CAFE HOCKING GLASS COMPANY, 1936-1938; 1940

Colors: Pink, crystal and Royal Ruby.

Old Cafe dinner plates continue to march upward in price! This plate is more rarely found than many which bring $40.00 to $50.00; but, it suffers from being in a small pattern that is not collected by large numbers of collectors. However, smaller patterns often have a good chance to return profits if kept for a long time. Prices doubling on these smaller, economically priced patterns does not seem out of line, while doubling the prices on some of the more expensively priced patterns may take longer.

There is a juice pitcher that seems to be Old Cafe even though it is not shown in Hocking's catalogues. The pitcher shown here is a nice "go-with" piece. It was made by Hocking, but is most often found in green. Notice that the panels are all the same size and this is not true on any other pieces of Old Cafe.

There is a numbered line cookie jar made by Hocking that is a nice "go-with" piece also. It is ribbed up the sides similar to Old Cafe but has a cross-hatched lid which is not even close to this pattern.

Royal Ruby cups are found on crystal saucers just as in Coronation. Not many lamps have been found. Vases were drilled, turned upside down and wired to make these lamps. There is no factory record of these being made, so they may be an outside contracted item. In any case, they are a nice addition to this small set.

	Crystal, Pink	Royal Ruby		Crystal, Pink	Royal Ruby
Bowl, 3¾" Berry	2.00	4.00	Pitcher, 80 oz.	75.00	
Bowl, 5", 1 or 2 Handles	3.00		Plate, 6" Sherbet	1.50	
Bowl, 5½" Cereal	4.00	8.50	Plate, 10" Dinner	20.00	
Bowl, 9", Closed Handles	7.50	11.50	Saucer	1.50	
Candy Dish, 8" Low	5.00	10.00	Sherbet, Low Footed	4.50	
Cup	3.00	6.00	Tumbler, 3" Juice	8.00	7.50
Lamp	12.50	20.00	Tumbler, 4" Water	8.00	
Olive Dish, 6" Oblong	4.00		Vase, 7¼"	9.50	14.00
Pitcher, 6", 36 oz.	50.00				

OLD ENGLISH, "THREADING" INDIANA GLASS COMPANY

Colors: Green, amber, pink, crystal and forest green.

Old English remains a mystery pattern. Flat pieces are harder to find than the serving pieces which is not the normal circumstance. Berry bowl sets are difficult to find in all colors. Pink is the most elusive color. Only the center handled server and the sherbet are shown in the picture. These are the only different pieces I have seen for sale in four years in pink. The sherbet pictured was found years ago in Lancaster, Ohio. That was the same time I found a large group of unlisted Hocking glass, but how this lowly Indiana sherbet found it way to Hocking's home territory is anyone's guess. As an author, I have wished more than once that glassware could talk.

Crystal decorated pitcher and tumbler sets have been found in several different designs. The only one that I have seen more than once has a lot of orange and black painted flowers on each of the pieces in the set including the pitcher lid. The pitcher lid, which is missing in the picture, has the same cloverleaf type knob as shown on the green sugar. This lid was pictured in earlier editions. The flat candy lid is similar in size, but the pitcher lid is notched to allow pouring without removing the top.

An unusual candy dish can be made by using the goblet and a Jeannette Fine Rib powder top. I have seen two of these mismatched "candy jars" in my travels.

The cheese and cracker set uses a 3½" comport on an indented plate. You can see this pictured in amber behind the pink sherbet.

	Pink, Green, Amber		Pink, Green, Amber
Bowl, 4" Flat	12.00	Pitcher	50.00
Bowl, 9" Footed Fruit	22.50	Pitcher and Cover	90.00
Bowl, 9½" Flat	25.00	Plate, Indent for Compote	17.50
Candlesticks, 4" Pr.	22.50	Sandwich Server, Center Handle	40.00
Candy Dish & Cover, Flat	40.00	Sherbet, 2 Styles	16.00
Candy Jar with Lid	40.00	Sugar	12.00
Compote, 3½" Tall, 7" Across	14.00	Sugar Cover	25.00
Compote, Cheese For Plate	12.50	Tumbler, 4½" Footed	15.00
Creamer	14.00	Tumbler, 5½" Footed	25.00
Egg Cup (Crystal only)	6.50	Vase, 5⅜", Fan Type, 7" Wide	40.00
Fruit Stand, 11" Footed	35.00	Vase, 8¼" Footed, 4¼" Wide	35.00
Goblet, 5¾", 8 oz.	25.00	Vase, 12" Footed	40.00

Please refer to Foreword for pricing information

"ORCHID" PADEN CITY GLASS COMPANY, EARLY 1930's

Colors: Yellow, cobalt blue, green, amber, pink, red and black.

Orchid continues to be found in small quantities. There are several different orchid varieties being found on Paden City blanks. This pattern is so sparsely found that collectors do not mind mixing these different Orchid designs together. I received a letter from a collector who had found three different red ruffled comports. Unfortunately, there was no other information as to size or a picture to confirm these. You might keep an eye out for these; and if you should find a comport, please send the measurements.

Although the number of collectors of Heisey's Orchid pattern is staggering, there are a relatively small number for Paden City's Orchid. Supply available and the heavy national promotion for Heisey Orchid are key factors.

Prices for all Paden City patterns continue to rise, but the small amount of glass made in comparison to other companies will always keep collectors driving up prices with each purchase. Console bowls and candlesticks are the only pieces that crop up frequently. You have to realize that "frequently" for this pattern is like "hardly ever" for some major collectible patterns. I have seen more Mayfair sugar lids than Orchid consoles as an example.

	All Other Colors	Red Black Cobalt Blue		All Other Colors	Red Black Cobalt Blue
Bowl, 4⅞" Square	10.00	25.00	Ice Bucket, 6"	50.00	75.00
Bowl, 8½", 2-Handled	22.50	50.00	Mayonnaise, 3 Piece	45.00	70.00
Bowl, 8¾" Square	20.00	45.00	Plate, 8½", Square		42.50
Bowl, 10", Footed	30.00	75.00	Sandwich Server, Center Handled	25.00	50.00
Candlesticks, 5¾" Pr.	30.00	65.00	Sugar	20.00	35.00
Creamer	20.00	35.00	Vase, 10"	40.00	90.00
Comport, 6¼"	15.00	30.00			

OVIDE, incorrectly dubbed "NEW CENTURY" HAZEL ATLAS GLASS COMPANY, 1930-1935

Colors: Green, black, white platonite trimmed with fired-on colors in 1950's.

Ovide Art Deco design continues to elude collectors. My pictures of it have been lusted over by collectors, but little has been seen outside of my books. I have only seen one sugar and creamer priced for sale in all my travels. I purchased those for future pictures, but have been unable to buy the set I have borrowed to photograph.

The "flying ducks" (geese) belongs to the same collector who owns the Art Deco set. Evidently, there was a strong distribution of decorated sets in the north central Ohio region. This seems to be where the decorated sets are being found.

So far, there has been little collector interest in the Platonite with pastel colored bands around the edges. More often, this economically priced glassware is being gathered up to use as everyday dishes. I'm told that it works well in both the microwave and the dishwasher. Those two facts alone will attract more buyers. If it doesn't go in the dishwasher, it is not allowed in our kitchen. (Non-stick coated pans do not last long around Cathy!)

	Black	Green	* Decorated White		Black	Green	* Decorated White
Bowl, 4¾" Berry			6.00	Plate, 8" Luncheon		1.50	6.00
Bowl, 5½" Cereal			10.00	Plate, 9" Dinner			7.00
Bowl, 8" Large Berry			17.50	Platter, 11"			12.50
Candy Dish and Cover	35.00	15.00	25.00	Salt and Pepper, Pr.	22.00	9.00	20.00
Cocktail, Footed Fruit	3.00	2.00		Saucer	2.00	1.25	4.00
Creamer	5.00	2.50	12.00	Sherbet	5.00	1.50	10.00
Cup	5.00	2.00	8.00	Sugar, Open	5.00	2.50	12.00
Plate, 6" Sherbet		1.00	5.00	Tumbler			15.00

*Art Deco Triple Price

OYSTER AND PEARL ANCHOR HOCKING GLASS CORPORATION, 1938-1940

Colors: Pink, crystal, Ruby Red, white with fired-on pink or green.

Oyster and Pearl continues to be bought for its accessory pieces. The relish dish and candlesticks are hard to keep in my shop because they are reasonably priced and are usually purchased as gifts for non-collectors. Several times this has created a "new" collector who knew nothing about Depression glass until they received it as a gift. It has become expected by members of my wife's family to receive a pretty bowl or plate on special occasions. Wedding gifts of antique glass seem to be received better than a toaster or can opener.

Crystal is rarely bought, but some collectors have fallen in love with the red decorated crystal pieces. This decorated red and the Royal Ruby are both used for Christmas and Valentine parties. The 10½" fruit bowl is a great salad bowl, but several collectors have told me that it makes an ideal small punch bowl. I guess you could use the Royal Ruby punch cups with the red bowl, but I do not have any idea what you use as punch cups with the other colors.

The pink color fired-on over white was called "Dusty Rose"; the fired-on green was christened "Springtime Green" by Hocking. Collectors do not seem to have a middle ground on these fired-on colors. They either love them or hate them. One lady told me that these colored sets just "did something" for her table when she served in them. There seem to be more of the fired-on colors available than the plain white.

There has been some activity in all Royal Ruby of late. The candlesticks in this pattern are the easiest pair to find in Royal Ruby; and because of that, the price has been increased by Royal Ruby collectors purchasing them. Collectors of Royal Ruby usually buy all patterns of this color made by Hocking.

The spouted 5¼" bowl is often referred to as heart shaped. The same bowl is also found without the spout. Royal Ruby one handled bowls have never been found with this spout!

	Crystal, Pink	Royal Ruby	White and Fired-On Green Or Pink
Bowl, 5¼" Heart-Shaped, 1-Handled	5.00	5.25	
Bowl, 5½", 1-Handled	5.00	9.50	
Bowl, 6½" Deep-Handled	8.00	15.00	
Bowl, 10½" Deep Fruit	16.00	35.00	11.00
Candle Holder, 3½" Pr.	15.00	35.00	12.50
Plate, 13½" Sandwich	10.00	27.50	
Relish Dish, 10¼" Oblong	7.00		

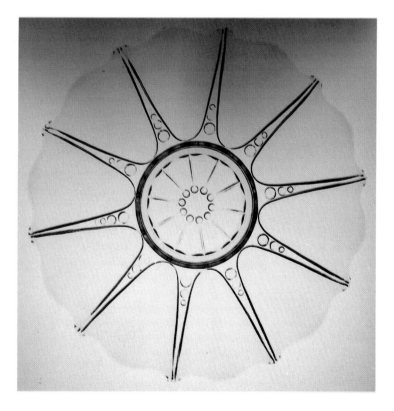

"PARROT", SYLVAN FEDERAL GLASS COMPANY, 1931-1932

Colors: Green, amber; some crystal and blue.

Parrot prices are flying! Amber is not as popular as the green, so this color's prices have not increased as fast as the green even though it is more rare. The amber butter dish, sugar lid and thin footed tumbler are all hard to find. There has only been one MINT condition butter dish top found in amber. The butter bottom has an indented ledge for the top. The jam dish is the same piece without the ledge.

Not as hard to find, but still elusive are the oval vegetable and creamer in amber. The 8½" round plate shown on the right in the amber picture was made by Indiana. These are also found in green. If you see these, you may notice that the birds more closely resemble parakeets than parrots. In any case, they are not a part of Federal's Parrot pattern.

Most people recognize the Madrid shapes on which we find Parrot. You will notice that most Parrot tumblers are found on these Madrid blanks except for the heavy footed tumbler. Evidently, the thin, moulded, footed tumbler did not accept the Parrot design very well and a new style tumbler was made. No thin, footed tumblers in green have ever been found. The supply of amber, heavy, footed tumblers and the thin, flat iced teas have more than met the demand of collectors. The price for these two tumblers has slipped a few dollars. However, other pieces in amber have more than compensated for any decreases in price!

The hot plate has been found in two styles. One is shaped like the Madrid hot plate with the pointed edges. This can be seen in the green photo. The other is round, and more like Federal's other bird pattern, Georgian. (It can be seen below.) It seems the round hot plate may be the harder to find; but right now, **ANY** hot plate is hard to find!

Only the one blue sherbet (shown in previous editions) has been seen.

There are lots of sugar and butter lids found. The major concern is finding MINT condition lids. The pointed edges and ridges on Parrot chipped then and now. You should carefully check these points when purchasing this pattern. Damaged or REPAIRED glassware should not bring MINT prices. I emphasize that here - - for many sugar and butter lids have been repaired. If it has been repaired, it should be sold as repaired with the buyer being told by the seller. I have no qualms with repaired glassware if it is done properly. In fact, I will buy glass to photograph that has been repaired since it is sold cheaper.

My main concern is there are many so-called "glass grinders" who are just that. They grind glass, but they do not repair it. You would not let a doctor cut off your arm if it were broken. By the same token, you should not expect to have a chipped glass cut off below the chip and left so sharp you would have fear of a cut lip if you tried to drink out of it. The glass would have been better off left alone.

Ask to see an example of a glass grinder's work **before** you hand over your treasures. If the edges are rounded and smoothed to the touch and not flattened or sharp, look no further. Can you feel the repair? Are chips and flakes ground away leaving noticeable dips in the surface or can you see scratches and cracks in the work? You should find an edge that is worked to uniformity. Unless it was a badly damaged piece, you should not notice the repair until close examination. If you can find where the piece was repaired without much difficulty, this grinder is not for you.

	Green	Amber
Bowl, 5" Berry	14.00	11.00
Bowl, 7" Soup	30.00	25.00
Bowl, 8" Large Berry	55.00	65.00
Bowl, 10" Oval Vegetable	35.00	50.00
Butter Dish and Cover	240.00	1,000.00
Butter Dish Bottom	27.50	200.00
Butter Dish Top	212.50	800.00
Creamer, Footed	22.00	35.00
Cup	25.00	25.00
Hot Plate, 5", 2 Styles	525.00	
Jam Dish, 7"		25.00
Pitcher, 8½", 80 oz.	1,200.00	
Plate, 5¾" Sherbet	20.00	12.00
Plate, 7½" Salad	18.00	
Plate, 9" Dinner	32.00	27.50
Plate, 10½" Round Grill	22.00	
Plate, 10½" Square Grill		20.00
Plate, 10¼" Square (Crystal only)	25.00	
Platter, 11¼" Oblong	27.50	50.00
Salt and Pepper, Pr.	195.00	
Saucer	8.50	8.50
* Sherbet, Footed Cone	17.00	16.00
Sherbet, 4¼" High	225.00	
Sugar	20.00	20.00

	Green	Amber
Sugar Cover	100.00	325.00
Tumbler, 4¼", 10 oz.	95.00	95.00
Tumbler, 5½", 12 oz.	110.00	100.00
Tumbler, 5¾" Footed Heavy	95.00	95.00
Tumbler, 5½", 10 oz. Footed (Madrid Mould)		110.00

* Blue-$100.00

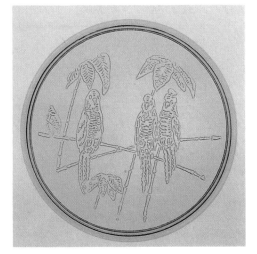

PATRICIAN, "SPOKE" FEDERAL GLASS COMPANY, 1933-1937

Colors: Pink, green, crystal and amber ("Golden Glo").

Amber Patrician is the most prevalent color found and it is also highly prized by collectors. There is nothing in amber that can truly be considered as rare; but mint condition sugar lids, cookie bottoms and footed tumblers are harder to find than other pieces. Be sure to check sugar lids for signs of repair. That same cookie bottom is rare in green. There are several lids found for each bottom. Most people think that all tops are harder to find than bottoms. This does not hold true for butter dishes and cookie jars in Patrician.

There are two styles of pitchers found. The one pictured has the moulded handle and is easier to find in amber than the applied style handle. You will have to refer to an earlier edition to see an applied handled pitcher. In crystal, the applied handle pitcher is the easiest to find! Green Patrician is more easily found than pink or crystal, and is collected more than either of those colors. To complete a set in pink is difficult, but not impossible. It is in crystal. Not all pieces have been found in crystal, so you would have to settle for a smaller set than in other colors.

The hexagonal shape of Patrician pieces has always infatuated new collectors. I still remember buying the first cookie jar and leaving the first pitcher that I saw. I was not sure if the patterns were Madrid or Patrician, but I knew they had to be good buys at $3.00 for the cookie and $5.00 for the pitcher! Alas, $5.00 was a lot of money to gamble on my Kentucky school teacher salary back then.

Saucers are still harder to find than cups. This phenomenon occurs in few patterns, and Patrician is one of them.

	Amber, Crystal	Pink	Green		Amber, Crystal	Pink	Green
Bowl, 4¾" Cream Soup	12.00	15.00	16.00	Plate, 6" Sherbet	7.00	5.00	6.00
Bowl, 5" Berry	8.00	9.50	9.00	Plate, 7½" Salad	10.00	12.50	10.00
Bowl, 6" Cereal	18.00	18.00	20.00	Plate, 9" Luncheon	8.00	6.50	8.00
Bowl, 8½" Large Berry	35.00	20.00	22.00	Plate, 10½" Dinner	5.50	20.00	27.50
Bowl, 10" Oval Vegetable	22.00	15.00	20.00	Plate, 10½" Grill	10.00	9.50	10.00
Butter Dish and Cover	75.00	195.00	95.00	Platter, 11½" Oval	22.00	17.00	17.00
Butter Dish Bottom	52.50	150.00	50.00	Salt and Pepper, Pr.	45.00	70.00	50.00
Butter Dish Top	22.50	45.00	45.00	Saucer	6.50	5.00	5.00
Cookie Jar and Cover	67.50		325.00	Sherbet	9.00	9.00	10.00
Creamer, Footed	7.00	8.50	9.50	Sugar	6.50	7.00	7.00
Cup	6.50	7.50	8.00	Sugar Cover	35.00	40.00	42.50
Jam Dish	20.00	20.00	25.00	Tumbler, 4", 5 oz.	24.00	22.00	25.00
Pitcher, 8", 75 oz. Moulded				Tumbler, 4¼", 9 oz.	21.00	18.50	20.00
Handle	90.00	85.00	90.00	Tumbler, 5½", 14 oz.	28.00	22.00	30.00
Pitcher, 8¼", 75 oz., Applied				Tumbler, 5¼", 8 oz. Ftd	35.00		40.00
Handle	110.00	90.00	110.00				

"PATRICK", LANCASTER GLASS COMPANY, EARLY 1930's

Colors: Yellow and pink.

Patrick collectors have told me that I made a mistake exposing this pattern to collectors. It was already hard enough to find! I have to agree that it is harder to find than its sister pattern, Jubilee. Many collectors of Jubilee have turned their attention to Patrick as a companion set. There is not enough Patrick for everyone who wants a set, and the price is beginning to reflect the strong demand! Even the prices for commonly found luncheon items are rising!

As in Jubilee, serving dishes are few and far between. I have never seen the three footed candy shown in the catalogues. For some reason, I keep finding cups without saucers in this pattern. If anyone knows why the saucers are not turning up, let me know.

Pink Patrick seems to be in short supply. I have seen a few pieces in my travels, but most of these were already in collections and not for sale. You may have to settle for some pieces to "go-with" this pattern. There are several floral patterns made by Lancaster with the same shapes of Patrick that can be blended into sets if you get stymied in finding serving pieces.

	Yellow, Pink		Yellow, Pink
Bowl, 9", Handled Fruit	35.00	Mayonnaise, 3-Piece	75.00
Bowl, 11", Console	40.00	Plate, 7" Sherbet	5.00
Candlesticks, Pr.	40.00	Plate, 7½" Salad	8.50
Candy Dish, 3-Footed	42.50	Plate, 8" Luncheon	12.00
Cheese & Cracker Set	45.00	Saucer	2.00
Creamer	17.50	Sherbet, 4¾"	20.00
Cup	12.00	Sugar	17.50
Goblet, 4" Cocktail	20.00	Tray, 11", 2-Handled	27.50
Goblet, 4¾", 6 oz. Juice	22.50	Tray, 11", Center-Handled	30.00
Goblet, 6", 10 oz. Water	27.50		

"PEACOCK REVERSE", LINE 412 PADEN CITY GLASS COMPANY, 1930's

Colors: Cobalt blue, red, amber, yellow, green, black and crystal.

Peacock Reverse has three new listings below! A center-handled server, a comport and a console bowl have all been found with this design. A pink 10" bud vase is shown in my *Very Rare Glassware of the Depression Era.* Another of these vases was found in pink and another was reported in amber.

Paden City's Line #412 (commonly called "Crow's Foot" by collectors) and Line #991 (which is Penny Line) make up the blanks on which Peacock Reverse has been seen. Pieces in green, amber and crystal have been found since the last book.

	All Colors		All Colors
Bowl, 4⅞" Square	22.00	Plate, 8½" Luncheon	25.00
Bowl, 8¾" Square	50.00	Plate 10⅜", 2-Handled	35.00
Bowl, 8¾" Square with handles	60.00	Saucer	12.50
Bowl, 11¾" Console	50.00	Sherbet, 4⅝" Tall, 3⅜" Diameter	35.00
Candlesticks, 5¾" Square Base, pr.	75.00	Sherbet, 4⅞" Tall, 3⅝" Diameter	35.00
Candy Dish, 6½" Square	65.00	Server, Center-Handled	40.00
Comport, 6¼" High, 3¼" Wide	37.50	Sugar, 2¾" Flat	50.00
Creamer, 2¾" Flat	50.00	Tumbler, 4", 10 oz. Flat	45.00
Cup	40.00	Vase, 10"	75.00
Plate, 5¾" Sherbet	17.50	Vase, 10", Bud	95.00

"PEACOCK & WILD ROSE", PADEN CITY GLASS COMPANY, LINE #1300, 1930's

Colors: Pink, green, cobalt blue, black, crystal and red.

A pink, 5" tall pitcher has been reported in Peacock & Wild Rose. That is very small for a pitcher. It might be the bottom for a tumble up. Hopefully, I will get a picture to go along with the information.

Vases are the most commonly found piece in this pattern. There are two styles of 10" vases. The bulbous-bottomed vase is pictured, but there is a more straight-sided one that can be found in black.

Although there are several "bird" designs in Paden City patterns, there is more recognition for the peacock patterns than for any other. Of course, there are more pieces of the peacock patterns seen than the other harder to find "bird" patterns.

	All Colors
Bowl, 8½", Flat	30.00
Bowl, 8½", Fruit, Oval, Footed	50.00
Bowl, 8¾", Footed	35.00
Bowl, 9½", Center-Handled	35.00
Bowl, 9½", Footed	40.00
Bowl, 10½", Center-Handled	40.00
Bowl, 10½", Footed	40.00
Bowl, 10½", Fruit	37.50
Bowl, 11", Console	35.00
Bowl, 14", Console	45.00
Candlestick, 5", Pr.	60.00
Candy Dish w/Cover, 7"	75.00
Cheese and Cracker Set	55.00
Comport, 6¼"	25.00
Ice Bucket, 6"	75.00
Ice Tub, 4¾"	65.00
Pitcher, 5" High	75.00
Plate, Cake, Low Foot	35.00
Relish, 3-Part	32.50
Vase, 10", Two Styles	75.00

Please refer to Foreword for pricing information

PETALWARE MacBETH-EVANS GLASS COMPANY, 1930-1940

Colors: Monax, Cremax, pink, crystal, cobalt and fired-on red, blue, green and yellow.

The red trimmed floral pattern that was shown on the cover of the eighth edition and in the top photograph on page 153 is not **Florette. Florette** is shown in the bottom photograph by the creamer and sugar with red flowers. The basic difference is that Florette does not have a red trim and is not as colorful. If you collect the red trimmed floral pattern and order by mail, you will have to explain that you want items with red trim and not **Florette**. As far as beauty goes, there is no comparison. The 9" berry bowl is the piece that most collectors of the red-trimmed floral are not finding.

Most of the fruit-decorated Petalware come in sets of eight. One such set consists of plates showing: cherry, apple, orange, plum, strawberry, blueberry, pear and grape. You may find other sets with different fruits. Some sets have the fruits named and others do not.

Monax and Cremax are terms given these colors by MacBeth-Evans. Cremax refers to the beige-colored Petalware shown in the lower photograph on the left and in the top photo with gold trim. The pastel-banded Cremax is the most collected. This is shown on the plate at the lower left. Monax is the white color that is most commonly found and decorated.

Cremax will show green under a black light, but white does not.

Pink Petalware sells very well in my shop. My biggest problem has been in finding enough to keep up with the demand. Pink is relatively inexpensive, and that is what seems to attract new collectors. But inexpensive can also be used to describe the price for undecorated Monax and undecorated Cremax.

Lamp shades like the larger one shown in the lower photograph do not sell very well; but if you want a **cheap** shade to go with this pattern, you should have little trouble finding one.

The cobalt mustard needs a metal lid, but is pictured the way you will most often find it. This is Petalware!

	Pink, Crystal	Plain	Cremax, Monax Florette, Fired-On Decorations	Red Trim Floral
Bowl, 4½" Cream Soup	4.00	7.50	8.50	
Bowl, 5¾" Cereal	3.50	4.50	6.50	20.00
Bowl, 7" Soup		40.00		
* Bowl, 9" Large Berry	7.50	12.50	15.00	45.00
Cup	2.50	4.50	6.00	12.00
** Creamer, Footed	2.50	4.50	8.00	15.00
Lamp Shade (many sizes) $8.00 to $15.00				
Mustard with Metal Cover in Cobalt Blue Only, $8.00				
Pitcher, 80 oz. (Crystal Decorated Bands)	22.00			
Plate, 6" Sherbet	1.50	2.00	4.00	
Plate, 8" Salad	1.75	3.00	6.00	10.00
Plate, 9" Dinner	3.50	5.00	8.00	
Plate, 11" Salver	4.00	6.50	12.00	
Plate, 12" Salver		6.50	15.00	22.50
Platter, 13" Oval	7.50	12.00	15.00	
Saucer	1.00	1.50	2.50	3.00
Saucer, Cream Soup Liner		10.00		
Sherbet, 4" Low Footed		20.00		
** Sherbet, 4½" Low Footed	3.00	4.50	7.50	20.00
** Sugar, Footed	2.50	4.50	7.50	15.00
Tidbit Servers or Lazy Susans, Several Styles 12.00 to 17.50				
***Tumblers (Crystal Decorated Bands) 2.50 to 7.50				

* Also in cobalt at $40.00

** Also in cobalt at $25.00

*** Several Sizes

"PRETZEL", No. 622 INDIANA GLASS COMPANY, 1930's-1970's

Colors: Crystal and teal.

Pretzel is another of Indiana's numbered patterns which is better known by its common collectors' name. The pitcher and tumblers are found rarely. There are three sizes of tumblers, but all are equally hard to locate. These, along with the pitcher, are shown in the insert below.

Also pictured is the only piece of teal Pretzel that I have ever seen even though it is "only" a cup. That is how one collector described it after seeing teal for the first time!

Be careful buying the celery dishes! Indiana is up to their old tricks by making them again! They can be found in crystal, amber, blue, and avocado green for $.89 in the local five and dime store.

The 4½" fruit cup has been found on a plate that has a 1¼" tab handle. Unfortunately the reader who reported this did not mention the size of the plate that has this tab handle. Be on the lookout for this.

Pretzel pieces that have embossed fruit in the center is selling about the same as the plain centered pieces. I have seen it priced higher, but it is **selling** at nearly the same price.

	Crystal
Bowl, 4½" Fruit Cup	2.50
Bowl, 7½" Soup	7.50
Bowl, 9⅜" Berry	12.00
Celery, 10¼" Tray	1.00
Creamer	4.50
* Cup	3.50
Olive, 7", Leaf Shape	2.50
Pickle, 8½", 2-Handled	3.00
Pitcher, 39 oz.	125.00
Plate, 6"	1.50
Plate, 7¼" Square, Indent	6.00
Plate, 7¼" Square, Indent 3-Part	6.00
Plate, 8⅜" Salad	3.00
Plate, 9⅜" Dinner	4.00
Plate, 11½" Sandwich	7.00
Saucer	1.00
Sugar	3.50
Tumbler, 5 oz., 3½"	14.00
Tumbler, 9 oz., 4½"	16.00
Tumbler, 12 oz., 5½"	20.00

* Teal - $15.00

PRIMO, "PANELLED ASTER" U.S. G.LASS COMPANY, EARLY 1930's

Colors: Green and yellow.

Primo is another of the obscure patterns of which there is little known as far as catalogue listings go. I continue to add new pieces to the listing as they are found. Recently, I had a report of a three-footed round console bowl in Primo. I have no photograph and was sent no measurements; so, I will only report it as a possibility. If you have this piece in your collection then send me some confirmation, please!

The coaster/ash tray combinations do not have the pattern on them. Evidently, they were made by U.S. Glass to go with other patterns besides Primo, since no pieces of Primo have been found in the pink or black to go with those colored coasters shown. Notice how exactly the tumbler fits the coaster! These coasters have been found in boxed Primo sets.

The berry bowls and cake plate seem to be the hardest to find pieces. Mould seam roughness is the norm for this pattern; so if you are finicky, look for another pattern to collect.

	Yellow, Green		Yellow, Green
Bowl, 4½"	6.50	Plate, 10" Dinner	10.00
Bowl, 7¾"	15.00	Plate, 10" Grill	7.50
Cake Plate, 10", 3-Footed	15.00	Saucer	2.00
Coaster/Ash Tray	6.50	Sherbet	7.50
Creamer	7.50	Sugar	7.50
Cup	6.50	Tumbler, 5¾", 9 oz.	12.00
Plate, 7½"	5.00		

Please refer to Foreword for pricing information

PRINCESS HOCKING GLASS COMPANY, 1931-1935

Colors: Green, Topaz yellow, apricot yellow, pink and blue.

Princess collectors are having a tough time finding tumblers and bowls in all colors. Green Princess collectors have to search long and hard for footed iced teas, cereal and berry bowls, undivided relishes and the elusive footed pitcher and tumblers to match.

Pink Princess collectors have problems finding the coasters, footed iced teas and the footed pitcher and matching tumblers.

Yellow Princess collectors say a lot of prayers. It is almost easier to list the commonly found pieces than it is to list the hard to find ones. The hardest to find pieces include the butter dish, juice pitcher, footed iced tea, undivided relish, coasters and ash trays. Collectors of yellow have even a greater handicap. "Topaz" is the official color listed by Hocking, and it is a pretty shade of yellow. However, some yellow is almost amber and has been called "apricot" by collectors. Most prefer the "Topaz" which makes the darker, amber shade difficult to sell.

Blue Princess collectors are out of luck! There have been only a few different pieces found in this pattern. They are all marked with an asterisk in the listing below. There are still reports of blue sets being seen in Texas. I can confirm the existence of one set, since I have a photograph of it! The pitcher found with this set is damaged; however, it is not Princess. It is blue Florentine like the one shown in my second book in 1975. That Florentine pitcher had been bought in Mexico City. This one is not far from Mexico, so it still leads one to believe that sometimes light blue Depression glass was distributed in that area. Yes, I would like to purchase this set, but have never been able to talk or communicate with the owner. It has always been through a third party! Maybe, some day I can show it to you.

The undivided relish is called a soup bowl by some dealers, so you need to be aware of that. It is so shallow, I wouldn't want to eat my soup out of it. It's what my grandmother would call a "polite" soup bowl (you eat just enough to "be polite").

	Green	Pink	Topaz, Apricot		Green	Pink	Topaz, Apricot
Ash Tray, 4½"	60.00	57.50	75.00	** Plate, 9" Grill	10.00	7.00	5.00
Bowl, 4½" Berry	18.00	13.00	35.00	Plate, 10½" Grill, Closed			
Bowl, 5" Cereal or Oatmeal	22.00	18.00	24.00	Handles	8.00	5.00	5.00
Bowl, 9" Octagonal Salad	27.00	20.00	75.00	Plate, 11" Handled Sandwich	10.00	7.50	20.00
Bowl, 9½" Hat-Shaped	30.00	18.00	90.00	Platter, 12" Closed Handles	15.00	12.00	40.00
Bowl, 10" Oval Vegetable	18.00	15.00	40.00	Relish, 7½" Divided	20.00	14.00	52.50
Butter Dish and Cover	70.00	70.00	500.00	Relish, 7½" Plain	70.00		125.00
Butter Dish Bottom	20.00	20.00	200.00	Salt and Pepper, 4½" Pr.	40.00	33.00	47.50
Butter Dish Top	50.00	50.00	300.00	Spice Shakers, 5½" Pr.	35.00		
Cake Stand, 10"	15.00	12.00		***Saucer (Same as Sherbet			
Candy Dish and Cover	37.50	37.50		Plate)	6.00	3.50	3.00
Coaster	25.00	55.00	75.00	Sherbet, Footed	15.00	11.00	27.50
* Cookie Jar and Cover	35.00	40.00		Sugar	8.50	6.50	10.00
Creamer, Oval	10.00	9.00	10.00	Sugar Cover	14.00	12.00	13.50
** Cup	9.00	6.50	7.50	Tumbler, 3", 5 oz. Juice	22.00	17.00	22.00
Pitcher 6", 37 oz.	35.00	35.00	500.00	Tumbler, 4", 9 oz. Water	20.00	14.00	18.00
Pitcher, 7⅜", 24 oz. Footed	500.00	425.00		Tumbler, 5¼", 13 oz. Iced Tea	27.50	16.50	20.00
Pitcher, 8", 60 oz.	37.50	35.00	65.00	Tumbler, 4¾", 9 oz. Sq. Ftd	55.00	45.00	
***Plate, 5½" Sherbet	5.50	3.50	3.00	Tumbler, 5¼", 10 oz. Footed	24.00	17.00	16.00
Plate, 8" Salad	9.50	7.00	9.00	Tumbler, 6½", 12½ oz. Ftd.	65.00	40.00	100.00
Plate, 9" Dinner	20.00	13.00	12.50	Vase, 8"	24.00	18.00	

* Blue-$550.00
** Blue-$95.00
*** Blue-$50.00

QUEEN MARY (PRISMATIC LINE), "VERTICAL RIBBED" HOCKING GLASS

COMPANY, 1936-1949

Colors: Pink, crystal and some Royal Ruby.

Queen Mary collectors are starting to unearth some interesting prices. See the new items in the listing below!

Footed pink tumblers and dinner plates have always been hard to find, but I am hearing reports that the flat tumblers are also becoming scarce. That actually surprises me! I will have to keep my eyes open after I finish this book and start the summer Depression glass show circuit. Queen Mary is a pattern that dealers did not use to carry to shows, but there has been such a collecting demand that many dealers are even beginning to add crystal Queen Mary to their stock.

The cereal bowl has the same shape as the butter bottom. Butter dishes were also called preserve dishes. These are difficult to find in pink. In Marietta, Georgia, last year there were three pink butters in three different booths! Each of these sold at that one show. I had never seen more than one at a show in the last ten years. It is funny how that happens. Several dealers find a piece of glass that each has not had for a while, and they all show up at the same show with the identical hard to find item.

There are two sizes of cups. The smaller cup sits on the saucer with cup ring. The larger cup sits on the combination saucer/ sherbet plate.

Only two collectors have commented on the footed creamer and sugar that is shown on the left side of the picture. They "look like" Queen Mary, but I have not found any confirmation on it.

Several pieces of Queen Mary were made in Royal Ruby including the candlesticks and large bowl. In the 1950's, the 3½" ash tray was made in Forest Green and Royal Ruby.

The 2" x 3¾" ash tray and 2" x 3¾" oval cigarette jar have been found labeled "Ace Hi Bridge Smoking Set."

	Pink	Crystal		Pink	Crystal
Ash Tray, 2" x 3¾" Oval	3.50	2.00	Creamer, Footed	15.00	
* Ash Tray, 3½" Round		2.00	Creamer, Oval	5.00	4.00
Bowl, 4" One Handle or None	3.00	2.50	Cup (2 sizes)	5.00	4.50
Bowl, 5" Berry	5.00	3.00	Plate, 6" and 6⅝"	2.50	2.50
Bowl, 5½", Two Handles	5.00	4.00	Plate, 8¾" Salad		4.00
Bowl, 6" Cereal	16.00	5.00	Plate, 9¾" Dinner	27.50	10.00
Bowl, 7" Small	9.00	6.00	Plate, 12" Sandwich	10.00	7.00
Bowl, 8¾" Large Berry	10.00	8.00	Plate, 14" Serving Tray	12.00	10.00
Butter Dish or Preserve and Cover	85.00	20.00	Relish tray, 12", 3-part	10.00	8.00
Butter Dish Bottom	20.00	4.00	Relish tray, 14", 4-Part	12.00	10.00
Butter Dish Top	65.00	16.00	Salt and Pepper, Pr.		16.00
Candy Dish and Cover	25.00	15.00	Saucer	1.50	1.50
** Candlesticks, 4½" Double Branch, Pr.		12.00	Sherbet, Footed	4.50	3.50
Celery or Pickle Dish, 5" x 10"	15.00	7.00	Sugar, Footed	15.00	
Cigarette Jar, 2" x 3" Oval	5.50	3.50	Sugar, Oval	4.50	4.00
Coaster, 3½"	2.50	2.00	Tumbler, 3½", 5 oz. Juice	7.50	3.00
Coaster/Ash Tray, 4¼" Square	4.50	4.50	Tumbler, 4", 9 oz. Water	8.50	4.00
Comport, 5¾"	7.50	5.00	Tumbler, 5", 10 oz. Footed	30.00	15.00

* Ruby Red-$5.00; Forest Green-$3.00

** Ruby Red-$30.00

RAINDROPS, "OPTIC DESIGN" FEDERAL GLASS COMPANY 1929-1933

Colors: Green and crystal.

Raindrops has little new to report. Collectors, I did change the cup and saucer to show the right pattern this time. Thank you readers who caught that problem. Mr. Shaker still has not found a mate! No one has written to tell me that they have another one of these little guys.

Raindrops makes a nice little luncheon set. It even has serving bowls to go with it that many of the smaller sets do not. Notice that the design has rounded bumps and not elongated ones as there are in Pear Optic or Thumbprint.

	Green		Green
Bowl, 4½" Fruit	3.00	Sherbet	5.00
Bowl, 6" Cereal	4.00	Sugar	5.00
Bowl, 7½" Berry	30.00	Sugar Cover	30.00
Cup	4.00	Tumbler, 3", 4 oz.	3.00
Creamer	5.00	Tumbler, 2⅛", 2 oz.	3.00
Plate, 6" Sherbet	1.50	Tumbler, 3⅞", 5 oz.	5.00
Plate, 8" Luncheon	3.50	Tumbler, 4⅛", 9 ½ oz.	7.50
Salt and Pepper, Pr.	150.00	Tumbler, 5", 10 oz.	7.50
Saucer	1.00	Whiskey, 1⅞", 1 oz.	4.00

RADIANCE NEW MARTINSVILLE GLASS COMPANY, 1936-1939

Colors: Red, cobalt and ice blue, amber, crystal and emerald green.

Radiance is a pattern that gains more respect from "antique" dealers than many other Depression glass patterns. Of course, it is better made glassware than those mass-produced wares. Radiance really belongs in my *Elegant Glassware of the Depression Era*, but it has been considered Depression glass for so long that it is hard to move patterns from book to book without drawing the ire of "die-hard" collectors. There are some changes coming!

Red and the ice blue are the most desired colors. There were only a few pieces made in cobalt blue; a set can not be accumulated in that color. The 6" ruffled candlestick, shown in blue in the lower picture, was omitted from the listing in the last book. So was the cordial although it was shown in two colors!

Several emerald green punch bowls have been found, but these have a plain crystal ladle. The expensive one listed looks like a long-handled punch cup. The punch bowl is round and looks like a bowling ball with the top cut off. I have one to show you in the next book in case you have never seen one.

Rarely found pieces in this pattern include the butter dish, pitcher, handled decanter and the five-piece condiment set. The vase has been found made into a lamp. I do not believe this was a factory project, but it could have been.

There are several different decorated designs in gold and platinum. The major problem with these is finding matching decorated pieces.

	Ice Blue, Red	Amber		Ice Blue, Red	Amber
Bowl, 5", Nut 2-Handled	12.00	7.50	Condiment Set, 4-piece w/Tray	200.00	125.00
Bowl, 6", Bonbon	13.00	8.50	Creamer	15.00	10.00
Bowl, 6", Bonbon, Footed	15.00	9.00	Cruet, Indiv.	45.00	30.00
Bowl, 6", Bonbon w/cover	40.00	25.00	Cup	12.00	10.00
Bowl, 7", Relish, 2-Part	15.00	10.00	Cup, Punch	10.00	5.00
Bowl, 7", Pickle	15.00	10.00	* Decanter w/Stopper, Handled	125.00	75.00
Bowl, 8", Relish, 3-Part	22.50	15.00	Goblet, 1 oz., Cordial	25.00	20.00
Bowl, 10", Celery	15.00	10.00	Ladle for Punch Bowl	100.00	75.00
Bowl, 10", Crimped	30.00	15.00	Lamp, 12"	80.00	50.00
Bowl, 10", Flared	27.50	17.50	Mayonnaise, 3 Piece, Set	35.00	18.00
Bowl, 12", Crimped	35.00	22.50	** Pitcher, 64 oz.	175.00	125.00
Bowl, 12", Flared	30.00	20.00	Plate, 8", Luncheon	12.00	7.50
Bowl, Punch	150.00	75.00	*** Plate, 14", Punch Bowl Liner	50.00	25.00
Butter Dish	350.00	150.00	Salt & Pepper, Pr.	60.00	37.50
Candlestick 6" Ruffled Pr.	95.00	60.00	Saucer	5.00	3.50
Candlestick 8" Pr.	50.00	30.00	Sugar	14.00	9.00
Candlestick 2-lite, Pr.	75.00	50.00	Tray, Oval	25.00	20.00
Cheese/Cracker, (11" Plate) Set	40.00	22.00	**** Tumbler, 9 oz.	20.00	12.50
Comport, 5"	17.50	12.00	Vase, 10", Flared	40.00	22.50
Comport, 6"	22.50	15.00			

* Cobalt blue $185.00
** Cobalt blue $350.00
*** Emerald green $25.00
**** Cobalt blue $28.00

"RIBBON" HAZEL ATLAS GLASS COMPANY, Early 1930's

Colors: Green; some black, crystal and pink.

Bowls are the elusive pieces in Ribbon! Until recently, I did not know there was a 5" cereal in this pattern! It is pictured on the left in a plate holder. The black bowl has been turned over to show the pattern which is on the outside.

Only pink shakers have been seen. No other pieces in pink have surfaced that have been reported to me. If you have any other pieces, let me know.

The candy dish is the most commonly seen piece of Ribbon. That fact and the economical price make it a perfect gift for non-collectors. It is also practical!

You may notice that the Ribbon shapes are the same as Cloverleaf and Ovide which are two other Hazel Atlas patterns. Either some glass designer really liked those shapes or the company reworked moulds to make the new patterns.

Collecting the lesser known and smaller patterns such as Ribbon is a fairly common practice among young collectors. They do not have to pawn the family's jewels because the price is still reasonable; and it is unlikely they will find more than five or six pieces at any one time. Plus, they get the invaluable experience and fun of participating in collecting Depression glass!

	Green	Black		Green	Black
Bowl, 4" Berry	7.00		Plate, 8" Luncheon	3.00	10.00
Bowl, 5" Cereal	12.00		Salt and Pepper, Pr.	20.00	35.00
Bowl, 8" Large Berry	18.00	25.00	Saucer	1.50	
Candy dish and Cover	30.00		Sherbet, Footed	4.00	
Creamer, Footed	9.00		Sugar, Footed	8.50	
Cup	3.50		Tumbler, 6", 10 oz.	17.50	
Plate, 6¼" Sherbet	1.50				

RING, "BANDED RINGS" HOCKING GLASS COMPANY 1927-1933

Colors: Crystal, crystal w/pink, red, blue, orange, yellow, black, silver, etc. rings; green, some pink, "Mayfair" blue and red.

Ring collectors usually start by collecting one particular color "scheme." Colored rings in a particular order on crystal is what I am calling a "scheme." Some collectors have been known to call it other things. Printable words include headache and "pain in the butt." There is a predominant "scheme" involving black, yellow, red and orange colored rings in that order. There are many others, also. It is the others which drives perfectionists *crazy*!

Crystal with platinum bands is another widely collected form of this pattern. Worn borders bedevil collectors in this decoration.

Green Ring can be collected, but not as easily as the crystal or decorated crystal. A reader tells me that for subscribing to *Country Gentleman* in the 1930's, you received a green berry bowl set consisting of an 8" berry and six 5" berry bowls.

Pink seems to be found only in pitcher and tumbler sets. A Wisconsin collector reports that the pink pitchers are very common in his part of the country. Tumblers were not mentioned in that letter; so, perhaps, only the pitchers were premium items.

	Crystal	Crystal Decor., Green		Crystal	Crystal Decor., Green
Bowl, 5" Berry	2.50	3.50	***Salt and Pepper, Pr., 3"	15.00	27.50
Bowl, 7" Soup	7.50	10.00	Sandwich Server, Center Handle	12.00	20.00
Bowl, 5¼", Divided	8.50		Saucer	1.25	1.50
Bowl, 8" Large Berry	5.00	7.50	Sherbet, Low (for 6½" Plate)	4.00	10.00
Butter Tub or Ice Tub	12.50	20.00	Sherbet, 4¾" Footed	4.00	7.50
Cocktail Shaker	12.50	20.00	Sugar, Footed	3.00	4.00
** Cup	3.00	3.50	Tumbler, 3½", 5 oz.	2.50	5.00
Creamer, Footed	3.50	4.50	Tumbler, 4¼", 9 oz.	3.50	6.00
Decanter and Stopper	19.50	27.50	* Tumbler, 4¾", 10 oz	7.00	
Goblet, 7¼", 9 oz.	6.00	12.50	Tumbler, 5⅛", 12 oz.	4.00	7.00
Ice Bucket	12.00	17.50	Tumbler, 3½" Footed Juice	4.00	6.00
Pitcher, 8", 60 oz.	12.00	17.50	Tumbler, 5½" Footed Water	4.00	7.00
* Pitcher, 8½", 80 oz.	15.00	22.50	Tumbler, 6½", Footed Iced Tea	5.00	10.00
Plate, 6¼" Sherbet	1.25	1.50	Vase, 8"	12.50	17.50
Plate, 6½", Off-Center ring	1.50	4.50	Whiskey, 2", 1½ oz.	3.50	5.50
** Plate, 8" Luncheon	1.50	3.00			

* Also found in Pink. Priced as Green.   ** Red-$17.50. Blue-$27.50   ***Green-$55.00

ROCK CRYSTAL, "EARLY AMERICAN ROCK CRYSTAL" McKEE GLASS COMPANY, 1920's and 1930's in colors

Colors: Four shades of green, aquamarine, vaseline, yellow, amber, pink and frosted pink, red slag, dark red, red, amberina red, crystal, frosted crystal, crystal with goofus decoration, crystal with gold decoration, amethyst, milk glass, blue frosted or "Jap" blue and cobalt blue.

Collecting Rock Crystal, as we have for fifteen years, continues to add excitement to our lives. The punch bowl shown here was the latest example. We received a call from a collector of Rock Crystal that we had met in Florida. Cathy had mentioned to him that we did not have a punch bowl, and he was calling to tell her about one he knew of for sale (without a base). Since she had seen a base at a recent show, she bought the bowl and called the dealer who had displayed the base and bought that also. Finally, both pieces arrived, and did we get a shock! The base and the bowl matched in size exactly so that the bowl could not fit on the base. Never before had anyone even considered that there were two different punch bases! We now have found the correct base for our bowl. In order to save any other collectors from this experience, I can give you the particulars on the bases of the punch bowls and if anyone needs our extra to fit your bowl, drop me a line. The proper base to our bowl is 5" across and stands 6¹⁄₁₆" tall. This base fits a punch bowl that is 4³⁄₁₆" across the bottom. The other style stand (that we do not need) is only 4⅛" wide and also stands 6¹⁄₁₆" tall. The bowl to fit this base must be around 3½" across the bottom, but I am only guessing as we do not have a punch bowl to fit it. There should be ¾" difference to make the base fit.

We re-photographed our set of crystal Rock Crystal with many new pieces. Unfortunately, the studio "misplaced" the pictures. Sorry!

Red, crystal and amber sets can be gathered with patience. I know of no other colors can that can be collected in complete sets!

There are many Rock Crystal pieces that collectors of other patterns buy to use as accessory items. Vases, cruets and a multitude of serving pieces are those pieces usually garnered for use.

	Crystal	All Other Colors	Red
* Bon Bon, 7½" S.E.	17.50	25.00	45.00
Bowl, 4" S.E.	9.00	12.00	20.00
Bowl, 4½" S.E.	10.00	12.00	22.50
Bowl, 5" S.E.	12.00	15.00	25.00
** Bowl, 5" Finger Bowl with 7" Plate, P.E.	18.00	25.00	45.00
Bowl, 7" Pickle or Spoon tray	120.00	25.00	47.50
Bowl, 7" Salad S.E.	17.50	22.50	40.00
Bowl, 8" Salad S.E.	20.00	22.00	55.00
Bowl, 9" Salad S.E.	20.00	23.00	60.00
Bowl, 10½" Salad S.E.	20.00	25.00	65.00
Bowl, 11½" 2-Part Relish	27.00	30.00	55.00
Bowl, 12" Oblong Celery	20.00	30.00	50.00
***Bowl, 12½" Footed Center Bowl	45.00	75.00	210.00
Bowl, 13" Roll Tray	25.00	40.00	85.00
Bowl, 14" 6-Part Relish	30.00	45.00	
Butter Dish and Cover	250.00		
Butter Dish Bottom	140.00		
Butter Dish Top	110.00		
****Candelabra, 2-Lite Pr.	35.00	70.00	175.00
Candelabra, 3-Lite Pr.	40.00	75.00	200.00
Candlestick, Flat, Stemmed Pr.	30.00	40.00	67.50
Candlestick, 5½" Low Pr.	27.50	45.00	100.00
Candlestick, 8" Tall Pr.	60.00	75.00	250.00
Candy and Cover, Round	30.00	60.00	125.00
Cake Stand, 11", 2¾" High, Footed	25.00	40.00	85.00

* S.E. McKee designation for scalloped edge

** P.E. McKee designation for plain edge

*** Red Slag-$350.00 Cobalt-$165.00

**** Cobalt-$85.00

Please refer to Foreword for pricing information

ROCK CRYSTAL, "EARLY AMERICAN ROCK CRYSTAL" (Con't.)

	Crystal	All Other Colors	Red
Comport, 7"	27.50	37.50	55.00
Creamer, Flat S.E.	20.00		
Creamer, 9 oz. Footed	15.00	25.00	50.00
Cruet and Stopper, 6 oz. Oil	65.00		
Cup, 7 oz.	12.00	20.00	55.00
Goblet, 7½ oz., 8 oz. Low Footed	13.50	22.50	45.00
Goblet, 11 oz. Low Footed Iced Tea	15.00	22.00	55.00
Jelly, 5" Footed S.E.	13.50	20.00	37.50
Lamp, Electric	95.00	200.00	380.00
Parfait, 3½ oz. Low Footed	9.00	30.00	60.00
Pitcher, qt. S.E.	75.00	150.00	
Pitcher, ½ gal., 7½" High	85.00	165.00	
Pitcher, 9" Large Covered	125.00	250.00	550.00
Pitcher, Fancy Tankard	140.00	400.00	650.00
Plate, 6" Bread and Butter S.E.	4.50	6.50	12.50
Plate, 7½" P.E. & S.E.	6.50	9.00	17.50
Plate, 8½" P.E. & S.E.	7.50	9.50	25.00
Plate, 9" S.E.	12.50	17.50	35.00
Plate, 10½" S.E.	13.50	18.50	40.00
Plate, 10½" Dinner S.E. (Large Center Design)	40.00	55.00	125.00
Plate, 11½" S.E.	14.50	20.00	45.00
Punch Bowl and Stand, 14" (2 Styles)	350.00		
Punch Bowl Stand Only (2 Styles)	100.00		
Salt and Pepper (2 Styles) Pr.	60.00	100.00	
Salt Dip	30.00		
Sandwich Server, Center-handled	20.00	35.00	85.00
Saucer	6.00	7.00	15.00
Sherbet or Egg, 3½ oz. Footed	14.00	20.00	50.00
Spooner	27.50		
Stemware, 1 oz. Footed Cordial	15.00	35.00	50.00
Stemware, 2 oz. Wine	16.00	23.00	45.00
Stemware, 3 oz. Wine	16.00	25.00	45.00
Stemware, 3½ oz. Footed Cocktail	12.00	17.50	30.00
Stemware, 6 oz. Footed Champagne	12.50	17.50	28.00
Stemware, 8 oz. Large Footed Goblet	13.50	22.50	45.00
Sundae, 6 oz. Low Footed	9.50	15.00	28.00
Sugar, 10 oz. Open	11.00	18.00	30.00
Sugar, Lid	25.00	35.00	65.00
Syrup with Lid	95.00		
Tray, 5⅜" x 7⅜", ⅞" high	50.00		
Tumbler, 2½ oz. Whiskey	12.50	17.50	40.00
Tumbler, 5 oz. Juice	12.00	20.00	40.00
Tumbler, 5 oz. Old Fashioned	12.00	20.00	40.00
Tumbler, 9 oz. Concave or Straight	15.00	22.00	40.00
Tumbler, 12 oz. Concave or Straight	20.00	30.00	50.00
Vase, Cornucopia	55.00	75.00	
Vase, 11" Footed	40.00	75.00	125.00

ROSE CAMEO BELMONT TUMBLER COMPANY, 1931

Colors: Green.

Rose Cameo is not confusing new collectors as it once did. Cameo, with its dancing girl, and this cameo encircled rose were often mixed up. It worked to my advantage about fifteen years ago when I reported that I had ordered an ice tub for Rose Cameo and would show it in the next book. It turned out to be Cameo. I did lose a new listing, but it was worth it.

Still no confirmation as to what company really made this pattern. Belmont Tumbler Company had a 1931 patent on this pattern, but glass shards of Rose Cameo have been found at the factory site of Hazel Atlas. Maybe time will unravel this mystery. Of course, a yellow Cloverleaf shaker was dug up at the site of Akro Agate's factory and we know that Akro did not make Cloverleaf. (Did you know some glass collectors dabble in archaeology in pursuit of glass?)

Remember that there are two styles of tumblers. The difference in these is noted by the flaring of the rims.

	Green
Bowl, 4½" Berry	4.50
Bowl, 5" Cereal	8.00
Bowl, 6" Straight Sides	12.00
Plate, 7" Salad	5.50
Sherbet	8.00
Tumbler, 5" Footed (2 Styles)	12.00

ROSEMARY, "DUTCH ROSE" FEDERAL GLASS COMPANY 1935-1937

Colors: Amber, green, pink; some iridized.

You can read the story of Rosemary's transformation from Federal's Mayfair pattern on page 116. Needless to say, Rosemary's existence came about because of another glass company, Anchor Hocking.

Rosemary cereal bowls and tumblers are the desirable pieces to own in all colors. These are especially tough to find in pink. Pink is the challenging set to put together with amber being the easiest. However, a full complement of amber cereals, cream soups, tumblers and grill plates will take you **some** time to find.

The iridized salad plate shown in the last book now has a painted friend! This newly reported 7" plate is decorated with blue flowers with yellow centers and red roses with green leaves. I do not know if this was a special ordered set or someone was exercising artistic creativity. If you find additional pieces to match this description, let me know.

You will find Rosemary an intriguing pattern whether you are a beginning collector or a collector looking for a new set to challenge your collecting abilities.

	Amber	Green	Pink
Bowl, 5" Berry	4.00	6.00	8.50
Bowl, 5" Cream Soup	10.00	15.00	18.00
Bowl, 6" Cereal	20.00	22.00	25.00
Bowl, 10" Oval Vegetable	10.00	20.00	22.00
Creamer, Footed	6.50	9.50	12.50
Cup	4.00	7.00	7.50
Plate, 6¾" Salad	4.00	6.00	5.50
Plate, Dinner	5.50	10.00	12.00
Plate, Grill	6.00	10.00	15.00
Platter, 12" Oval	10.00	15.00	22.50
Saucer	2.00	2.50	3.00
Sugar, Footed	6.50	9.50	12.50
Tumbler, 4¼", 9 oz.	22.50	25.00	37.50

ROULETTE, "MANY WINDOWS" HOCKING GLASS COMPANY, 1935-1939

Colors: Green, pink and crystal.

Roulette is a surprising pattern. You can find plenty of green basic pieces: cups, saucers, sherbets and luncheon plates. The sandwich plate and fruit bowl are available. After that, you will spend a lot of time looking for the six different tumblers!

Pink is only a pitcher and tumbler set. There are at least five sizes of pink tumblers. These tumblers are easier to find than in green, but I have never seen the footed tumbler in pink. Have you?

Crystal tumbler and pitcher sets are found infrequently, but there is so little demand for them that their rarity is completely overlooked. Some of these crystal sets are decorated with colored stripes. In fact, this colored stripe effect makes an "Art Deco" look. So far, even this "look" has not caught on with collectors.

Green Roulette tumbler demand is phenomenal. Have you seen an "old fashioned" tumbler for sale recently? I just paid $35.00 to have one to photograph for the next book! Other green tumbler prices are skyrocketing, also. Pink tumbler prices are on the rise, but not as dramatically.

The name, "Many Windows" was given this pattern before Roulette was found to be the real pattern name. I assume that was from the windowed effect the design makes as it encircles the tumbler. I mention this since I heard the term for the first time last week in a shop in Ohio. A lady asked the proprietor if he had any pieces of "Many Windows" in green. He shook his head and said that he did not. I am positive he had no idea what she was talking about because I saw a green Roulette pitcher near the rear of the shop before I left. The lady had already left when I spotted the pitcher. I asked the man if he knew what the pattern on the pitcher was and he said it was "Just green Depression glass, but I could have it for $45.00." He still owns it!

	Crystal	Pink, Green
Bowl, 9" Fruit	8.50	10.00
Cup	34.50	4.25
Pitcher, 8", 65 oz.	22.50	25.00
Plate, 6" Sherbet	2.00	2.25
Plate, 8½" Luncheon	4.00	4.00
Plate, 12" Sandwich	9.00	9.00
Saucer	1.25	2.25
Sherbet	3.00	4.50
Tumbler, 3¼", 5 oz. Juice	6.50	12.50
Tumbler, 3¼", 7½ oz. Old Fashioned	22.50	35.00
Tumbler, 4⅛", 9 oz. Water	11.00	15.00
Tumbler, 5⅛", 12 oz. Iced Tea	12.00	19.50
Tumbler, 5½", 10 oz. Footed	11.00	17.50
Whiskey, 2½", 1½ oz.	6.50	12.50

"ROUND ROBIN" MANUFACTURER UNKNOWN, Probably early 1930's

Colors: Green, iridescent and crystal.

Round Robin's manufacturer remains anonymous. The domino tray is the important piece in this small pattern. It has only been found in green. For new readers, the domino tray held the creamer in the center ring with sugar cubes surrounding it. Sugar cubes were made by a famous sugar company, and the tray became synonymous with this name.

Sherbets are the hardest pieces to find outside the domino tray. These are particularly hard to find in green.

Very few pieces are found in crystal. Crystal has to have been made to have iridescent pieces in the pattern. Crystal is sprayed with the iridescent color and put back into the furnace and baked. Obviously, not all the crystal was sprayed; and thus, some crystal is found today.

Luncheon sets can be found in the iridized color. I have met few collectors of iridized Round Robin. I have never seen an iridescent sandwich plate. If you have one, I'd like to know.

The Round Robin cup is footed. Not many mass produced Depression glass patterns had a footed cup.

	Green	Iridescent
Bowl, 4" Berry	4.25	4.00
Cup, Footed	4.50	5.00
Creamer, Footed	6.00	5.50
Domino Tray	25.00	
Plate, 6" Sherbet	1.50	1.50
Plate, 8" Luncheon	2.50	3.00
Plate, 12" Sandwich	6.00	6.00
Saucer	1.50	1.50
Sherbet	4.50	5.00
Sugar	5.00	5.00

ROXANA HAZEL ATLAS GLASS COMPANY, 1932

Colors: Yellow, crystal and some white.

Roxana was only listed in catalogues for one year. It is a rare pattern when compared to thousands of pieces made over the years in many other patterns. Unfortunately, there are so few pieces available that some collectors avoid it. The common denominator of many collectors of this pattern is the name. Only one Roxana I have met at shows did not collect it. At the time I autographed her book, she was just starting and had not selected a pattern.

So far, only the 4½" bowl has been found in white. Yellow tumblers and the 4½" bowl are difficult to find. The gold decorated plate was bought in hopes it would "show off" the pattern a little better in the photograph. This delicate pattern is difficult to capture on film since the light shade of yellow has a tendency to disappear under bright lights.

Note that the sherbet is footed, but not stemmed. I have asked readers for nearly twenty years to please contact me if you find an additional piece in this little pattern. It looks as if these seven pieces are going to be all there is. I still wonder why there is no cup for the saucer!

	Yellow	White
Bowl, 4½" x 2⅜"	6.00	10.00
Bowl, 5" Berry	4.00	
Bowl, 6" Cereal	7.50	
Plate, 6" Sherbet	2.50	
Saucer	2.50	
Sherbet, Footed	4.50	
Tumbler, 4¼", 9 oz.	10.00	

ROYAL LACE HAZEL ATLAS GLASS COMPANY, 1934-1941

Colors: Cobalt blue, crystal, green, pink; some amethyst.

Royal Lace continues to be a fast selling pattern in the four major colors. I have bought two collections of all four colors, and can make the following observations.

There are five different pitchers made in Royal Lace: 1) 48 oz. straight side; 2) 64 oz., 8", no ice lip; 3) 68 oz., 8", w/ice lip; 4) 86 oz., 8", no ice lip; 5) 96 oz., 8½", w/ice lip. The ten ounce difference is caused by the spout on the pitcher without lip dipping below the top edge of the pitcher. This causes the liquid to run out before you get to the top.

Crystal and pink pitchers can be found in all five styles. Green can only be found in four styles. (There is no 68 oz. with ice lip in green). There are only three styles found in blue which are all shown on page 175. (There have been no blue 86 oz. without ice lip or 68 oz. with ice lip pitchers found.)

Water tumblers (9 oz.) can be found in two styles. Some of these are panelled.

Over the years there has been some confusion over the cobalt blue console bowl styles because of the price discrepancies. All three bowls are shown. The straight edge bowl (which is commonly found) is in the center of the top picture. In the bottom picture the ruffled edge bowl is on the left and the rolled edge is on the right behind the creamer and sugar. Candlesticks that match each bowl are shown in the same pictures.

The straight edge candlestick, behind and to the right of the cup in the top photograph, can be found without the candle holder in the center. This is called a nut cup by collectors, but was probably a manufacturing mistake. In any case, these are in demand by some collectors who have collected large sets and did not know about this piece until recently!

The 4⅞",10 oz. tumblers are still the most difficult tumbler to find. It would be even worse if all collectors sought all four sizes of tumblers. Many only purchase the water tumblers and the straight sided pitcher. Since so many of this style pitcher and water tumblers were made, demand is obviously what continues to drive up the price!

I hope you enjoy this expanded selection of six photographs of Royal Lace from these collections!

	Crystal	Pink	Green	Blue
Bowl, 4¾" Cream soup	8.50	14.00	22.50	25.00
Bowl, 5" Berry	10.00	20.00	22.00	32.00
Bowl, 10" Round Berry	12.00	18.00	22.50	42.50
Bowl, 10", 3-Legged Straight Edge	13.50	20.00	30.00	42.50
Bowl, 10", 3-Legged Rolled Edge	95.00	27.50	60.00	235.00
Bowl, 10", 3-Legged Ruffled Edge	17.50	25.00	50.00	300.00
Bowl, 11" Oval Vegetable	13.00	18.00	22.00	37.50
Butter Dish and Cover	55.00	120.00	225.00	435.00
Butter Dish Bottom	35.00	80.00	150.00	300.00
Butter Dish Top	20.00	40.00	75.00	135.00
Candlestick, Straight Edge Pr.	20.00	27.50	45.00	75.00
Candlestick, Rolled Edge Pr.	37.50	37.50	55.00	115.00
Candlestick Ruffled Edge Pr.	22.50	35.00	50.00	110.00
Cookie Jar and Cover	25.00	37.50	52.50	250.00
Cream, Footed	8.00	11.00	17.50	30.00
Cup	5.50	9.50	14.00	23.50
Nut Bowl	75.00	145.00	135.00	250.00

	Crystal	Pink	Green	Blue
Pitcher, 48 oz., Straight Sides	32.00	42.00	80.00	85.00
Pitcher, 64 oz., 8", w/o/L	35.00	55.00	85.00	125.00
Pitcher, 8", 68 oz., w/Lip	40.00	49.50		
Pitcher, 8", 86 oz., w/o/L	42.50	55.00	100.00	
Pitcher, 8½", 96 oz., w/Lip	45.00	62.50	120.00	175.00
Plate, 6", Sherbet	2.50	3.50	6.00	9.00
Plate, 8½" Luncheon	5.00	8.00	10.00	22.50
Plate, 9⅞" Diner	9.00	14.00	18.00	28.00
Plate, 9" Grill	6.00	9.50	15.00	25.00
Platter, 13" Oval	12.50	17.50	25.00	42.00
Salt and Pepper, Pr.	35.00	45.00	100.00	205.00
Saucer	2.50	3.50	5.00	6.50
Sherbet, Footed	7.00	12.00	18.00	35.00
* Sherbet in Metal Holder	3.50			22.00
Sugar	7.00	9.00	15.00	20.00
Sugar Lid	13.00	25.00	30.00	110.00
Tumbler, 3½", 5 oz.	12.00	15.00	22.00	32.50
Tumbler, 4⅛", 9 oz.	8.50	12.00	20.00	30.00
Tumbler, 4⅞", 10 oz.	17.00	30.00	32.50	60.00
Tumbler, 5⅜", 12 oz.	17.50	30.00	35.00	50.00
** Toddy or Cider Set: Includes Cookie Jar Metal Lid, Metal tray, 8 Roly-Poly Cups and Ladle				135.00

* Amethyst $35.00
**Amethyst $125.00

Please refer to Foreword for pricing information

ROYAL RUBY ANCHOR HOCKING GLASS COMPANY, 1938-1960's; 1977

Colors: Ruby red.

Royal Ruby is the Anchor Hocking name for their red color. The Royal Ruby sticker appeared on all pieces of red no matter what the pattern may have been. Red Bubble or Sandwich did not mean anything but Royal Ruby to the factory. So, if you find a red piece that seems to be another of Hocking's patterns, do not be surprised by the sticker. **Only Anchor Hocking's red can be called Royal Ruby**. It is a patented name which can only be used by them!

There are conflicting reports on the "card holder" I have shown on the right of the photo. This has a Royal Ruby top on a divided crystal base. Some collectors have reported this as a cigarette pack holder. That is possible; but we collecting non-smokers prefer the card holder label!

Both style sherbets are shown in front. The stemmed is on the right and the footed is on the left. Oval vegetable bowls are still in short supply. These are one of the toughest to find pieces in this pattern. Other items in short supply (besides the card holder) are the 3 quart upright pitcher, punch bowl base, deep popcorn bowl and the salad bowl with 13¾" underliner.

I get lots of letters on Royal Ruby beer bottles. There were six or seven sizes of these made for a national beer company in the late 1940's and early 1950's. I do not consider them dinnerware items, although some collectors might disagree.

Remember that the square shaped Royal Ruby items were made in the 1950's and that the round dinnerware items are products of the early promotions from the late 1930's.

I finally discovered why so many slotted sugar lids do not fit the sugar bowls. (The lids for the sugars are all slotted for a spoon.) Not all these lids were made for Royal Ruby sugars; some were made for a crystal sugar which is slightly smaller in diameter making its lid unusable on anything else.

	Red		Red		Red
Ash Tray, 4½" Square	2.50	Pitcher, 3 qt. Tilted	25.00	Tumbler, 2½ oz. Footed	
Bowl, 4¼" Berry	4.00	Pitcher, 3 qt. Upright	32.50	Wine	11.00
Bowl, 5¼", Popcorn	9.00	Plate, 6½" Sherbet	2.00	Tumbler, 3½ oz. Cocktail	7.50
Bowl, 7½" Soup	9.50	Plate, 7" Salad	3.50	Tumbler, 12 oz., 6" Footed	
Bowl, 8" Oval Vegetable	30.00	Plate, 7¾" Luncheon	4.00	Tea	12.00
Bowl, 8½" Large Berry	13.00	Plate, 9" or 9¼" Dinner	8.00	Tumbler, 5 oz. Juice,	
Bowl, 10" Deep, Popcorn	22.00	Plate, 13¾"	15.00	2 Styles	5.00
Bowl, 11½" Salad	22.00	Punch Bowl	15.00	Tumbler, 9 oz. Water	5.00
Card Holder/Cigarette Box	40.00	Punch Bowl Base	17.50	Tumbler, 10 oz. Water	5.00
Creamer, Flat	6.00	Punch Cup	2.00	Tumbler, 13 oz. Iced Tea	10.00
Creamer, Footed	7.50	Saucer (Round or Square)	1.50	Vase, 4" Ball-Shaped	4.50
Cup (Round or Square)	3.50	Sherbet, Stemmed	6.00	Vase, 6½" Bulbous, Tall	7.50
Goblet, Ball Stem	7.50	Sherbet, Footed	7.50	Vases, Several Styles	
Lamp	20.00	Sugar, Flat	6.00	(Small)	5.00
Pitcher, 22 oz. Tilted or		Sugar, Footed	5.00	Vases, Several Styles	
Upright	20.00	Sugar, Lid	8.00	(Large)	10.00

"S" PATTERN, "STIPPLED ROSE BAND" MacBETH-EVANS GLASS COMPANY, 1930-1933

Colors: Crystal; crystal w/trims of silver, blue, green, amber; pink; some amber, green, fired-on red, Monax, and light yellow.

"S" Pattern collectors seem to buy more of the platinum trimmed and pastel banded crystal than they do the plain crystal. The only problem with that is there is not enough of the decorated to meet the demand! Some collectors refuse to mix the decorated with plain crystal and are being stifled in their collecting. Those who have been willing to combine plain and decorated pieces are managing to pick up a piece here and there. They will have sets first!

Color variances in the amber make some of it more yellow than amber. This makes the amber difficult to match consistently. The differences are almost as distinct as they are in Hocking's Princess.

A pink or green pitcher and tumbler set still turns up occasionally, but the demand for these has dwindled considerably. Years ago, there were a large group of pitcher collectors; rare pitchers sold fast. Today, there are few pitcher collectors and most of these collectors already own the hard to find pitchers. A rare piece of glass has to have someone who wishes to own it before it will sell. No matter how rare an item is, it takes demand to make it sell. Is is simple economics; no demand means no sale, and rarity be hanged!

	Crystal	Yellow, Amber, Crystal With Trims		Crystal	Yellow, Amber, Crystal With Trims
			Plate, 11¾" Heavy Cake	30.00	35.00
* Bowl, 5½" Cereal	2.50	3.50	***Plate, 13" Heavy Cake	47.50	60.00
Bowl, 8½" Large Berry	7.50	12.50	Saucer	1.00	1.50
* Creamer, Thick or Thin	4.00	5.50	Sherbet, Low Footed	3.50	6.00
* Cup, Thick or Thin	2.50	3.50	* Sugar, Thick and Thin	4.00	5.50
Pitcher, 80 oz. (Like "Dogwood")			Tumbler, 3½", 5 oz.	2.50	4.50
(Green or Pink 500.00)	37.50	85.00	Tumbler, 4", 9 oz. (Green or Pink 50.00)	3.50	5.50
Pitcher, 80 oz. (Like "American			Tumbler, 4¾, 10 oz.	3.50	6.00
Sweetheart")	45.00		Tumbler, 5", 12 oz.	7.50	10.00
Plate, 6" Sherbet (Monax 8.00)	1.50	2.00			
** Plate, 8¼" Luncheon	2.00	2.50	* Fired-on red items will run approximately twice price of amber		
Plate, 9¼" Dinner	3.50	4.50	** Red-$40.00; Monax-$10.00		
Plate, Grill	5.00	6.50	***Amber-$77.50		

178

SANDWICH HOCKING GLASS COMPANY, 1939-1964; 1977

Colors: Crystal 1950's-1960's   Pink 1939-1940 Forest Green 1950's-1960's

Amber 1960's   Royal Ruby 1939-1940 White/Ivory (opaque) 1950's-1960's

Hocking's Sandwich collecting continues to prosper while Indiana's Sandwich does not! Hocking has gone to some trouble to preserve the collectability of their older glassware; however, Indiana did not. Therein lies the difference. Crystal collectors continue to increase the price of this popular pattern. In fact, this may be the most collected crystal pattern in this book. I can not think of any other that I sell better!

Remember that Hocking re-introduced a crystal cookie jar that was much larger than the old. For a comparison of these cookie jars I am enclosing measurements.

	NEW	OLD
Height	10¼"	9¼"
Opening Width	5½"	4⅞"
Diameter/Largest Part	22"	19"

Those pieces that are in short supply continue to be found, but demand keeps absorbing the supply. I always seem to have a large supply of cups, saucers and 8" plates. These were premiums for buying $3.00 (about ten gallons) of gas at a Marathon station in 1964. We had quite a few of these free dishes when we married twenty-five years ago. The promotion took four weeks for cup and saucers and the next four weeks for the plates. For only $2.89 you could buy the Ivory with gold trim punch bowl set with an oil change and lubrication.

Other pieces in crystal which are shy about showing themselves include the little ruffled custard shown on the hard to find liner, the cereal bowl and 9" salad bowl which uses the 12" plate as an underliner. Dinner plates and footed tumblers can be found, but it sometimes takes a lot of searching.

Notice the difference in the small red bowls. Some of these have smooth edges and some have scalloped. The smooth edge measures 4⅞" while the scalloped is 5¼". The smooth edge bowl is more difficult to find, but collectors prefer the scalloped edge to go with the other two scalloped edge bowls. This is another case where demand determines price!

There is little demand for pink, but the amber is beginning to acquire more devotees. The footed amber tumbler is nearly impossible to find! The one in the photograph is the only one I have ever seen. Maybe you are having better luck with them than I am.

Green is still THE color in demand. For some reason, the green draws rave reviews even with new collectors. Maybe the Forest Green with a pattern seems more desirable than the plain Forest Green. Dinner plates at $52.50 do not seem to discourage anyone. I have noticed a lack of saucers recently. There seems to be five cups for every four saucers. You might remember I mentioned that if you see a stack of saucers priced cheaply. Prices for green have risen due to scarcity and demand!

For new collectors, I need to add that those five cheaply priced pieces of green were packed in Mother's oats. Everyone ate oats; so there are literally thousands of those pieces available today. All other pieces of Forest Green sandwich are in short supply.

	Crystal	Desert Gold	Ruby Red	Forest Green	Pink		Crystal	Desert Gold	Forest Green
Bowl, 4⁵⁄₁₆", Smooth	4.00			2.00		Pitcher, 6" Juice	45.00		95.00
Bowl, 4⅞", Ruffled	9.50					Pitcher, ½ gal. Ice Lip	50.00		195.00
Bowl, 4⅞" Smooth	4.00	3.00	12.00		3.50	Plate, 7" Dessert	8.00	8.00	
Bowl, 5¼" Scalloped	6.00		15.00			Plate, 8"	3.00		
Bowl, 6½" Cereal	20.00	9.00				Plate, 9" Dinner	12.00	7.00	52.50
Bowl, 6½" Smooth	7.00	6.00				Plate, 9" Indent For			
Bowl, 6½" Scalloped	6.00		20.00	30.00		Punch Cup	3.00		
Bowl, 7" Salad	6.50			45.00		Plate, 12" Sandwich	9.00	10.00	
Bowl, 8" Scalloped	6.50		30.00	50.00	13.00	Punch Bowl, 9¾"	15.00		
Bowl, 8¼" Oval	6.00					Punch Bowl Stand	17.50		
Bowl, 9" Salad	20.00	22.50				Punch Cup	2.00		
Butter Dish, Low	32.50					Saucer	1.00	3.00	6.00
Butter Dish Bottom	17.50					Sherbet, Footed	6.00		
Butter Dish Top	15.00					Sugar and Cover	12.50		*17.00
Cookie Jar and Cover	30.00	30.00		16.00		Tumbler, 3⅜" 3 oz.			
Creamer	4.00			20.00		Juice	10.00		
Cup, Tea or Coffee	1.50	3.50		13.00		Tumbler, 3⁹⁄₁₆" 5 oz.			
Custard Cup	3.50			1.50		Juice	5.00		2.75
Custard Cup, Ruffled	10.00					Tumbler, 9 oz. Water	6.50		3.25
Custard Cup Liner	8.00			1.50		Tumbler, 9 oz. Footed	17.50	45.00	

Please refer to Foreword for pricing information

SANDWICH INDIANA GLASS COMPANY, 1920's-1980's

Colors:

Crystal Late 1920's-**Today**	Pink Late 1920's-Early 1930's	Teal Blue 1950's-**1980's**
Amber Late 1920's-**1980's**	Red 1933-**1970's**	Lt. Green 1930's-**1980's**

Every time I sit down to write about this pattern I wonder why. I considered dropping it out, and then wonder if that would be fair to collectors. The big news is that Indiana has made a full set in light green. I made the date bold in the dates above so some antique dealers could see it. I have been to two antique shows recently (Florida and Ohio) where a whole set has been displayed as old, rare, Indiana glass. It is not old! It is not rare! It is Indiana! One out of three is not too good. I highly recommend that you avoid **this** Sandwich pattern. If you already have a set, fine. I hope you like it a lot as you may be looking at it for some time.

The mould for the old wine broke and a new one was designed. All the wines made in the last few years are fatter than the earlier ones which were shaped like Iris wines. The newer are shaped more like the cocktail in Iris, only taller. (See page 99 for this comparison. The cocktail is behind the painted red Iris sherbet and the wine is behind the right side of the blue shade.)

I will repeat what I have said in the past, but it palls to do so!

The big "news" is that Indiana made a butter dish for Tiara which is extremely close to the old teal color made in the 1950's. It was available as a hostess gift item for selling a certain amount of Tiara glass. Because of the new Sandwich being made today by Indiana, I'm dropping crystal from my listing. It's become a **collector's pariah!** The list is too long to examine each piece to tell the difference between old and new. In many cases, there is little difference since the same moulds are being used. Hopefully, somebody at Indiana will wise up and stop making the old colors as I was told they would do after the "pink Avocado" fiasco in 1974. Instead of trying to entice collectors to new wares, they are stuck on trying to destroy the market for the old glassware which has been collectible for years but which may never be again. Perhaps you could start collecting Hocking Sandwich, if you like the pattern. They remade a cookie jar, but they carefully made it different from the old which showed their awareness of collectors in the field! For those of you who have collected the crystal Indiana Sandwich or the teal butter dish and have a sizable investment involved, I can only say that time will tell as to the future collectability of this pattern. At present, it doesn't look too promising. The really maddening thing is that all this "new" Sandwich is being touted to prospective buyers as glass that's going to be worth a great deal in the future based on its past history—and the company is steadily destroying those very properties they're using to sell the new glass! Supreme irony!

I can vouch for six items in red Sandwich dating from 1933, i.e. cups, saucers, luncheon plates, water goblets, creamers and sugars. However, in 1969, Tiara Home Products produced red pitchers, 9 oz. goblets, cups, saucers, wines, wine decanters, 13" serving trays, creamers, sugars and salad and dinner plates. Now, if your dishes glow yellow under a black light or if you KNOW that your Aunt Sophie held her red dishes in her lap while fording the swollen stream in a buggy, then I'd say your red Sandwich pieces are old. Other than that, I know of no way to tell if they are or not. NO, I WON'T EVEN SAY THAT OLD RED GLASS GLOWS UNDER BLACK LIGHT. I KNOW some of it does because of a certain type ore they used then. However, I've seen some newer glass glow; but Tiara's 1969 red Sandwich glass does not. Presently, the only color remotely worth having is pink. I used to say "pink and green," but now the company has made the green!

	Pink	Teal Blue	Red		Pink	Teal Blue	Red
Ash Tray Set (Club, Spade, Heart, Diamond Shapes)				Goblet, 9 oz.	15.00		40.00
$3.00 each crystal	15.00			Pitcher, 68 oz.	100.00		
Bowl, 4¼" Berry	3.00			Plate, 6" Sherbet	2.50	4.50	
Bowl, 6"	3.50			Plate, 7" Bread and Butter	3.50		
Bowl, 6" 6 Sides		7.50		Plate, 8" Oval, Indent for Sherbet	5.00	7.50	
Bowl, 8¼"	10.00			Plate, 8⅜" Luncheon	4.50		15.00
Bowl, 9" Console	15.00			Plate, 10½" Dinner	12.50		
Bowl, 10" Console	18.00			Plate, 13" Sandwich	12.50		
* Butter Dish and Cover, Domed	157.50	150.00		Sandwich Server, Center Handle	27.50		
Butter Dish Bottom	47.50	40.00		Saucer	2.50	3.50	5.00
Butter Dish Top	110.00	110.00		Sherbet, 3¼"	5.00	6.00	
Candlesticks, 3½" Pr.	15.00			Sugar, Large Open	8.50		40.00
Candlesticks 7" Pr.	37.50			Tumbler, 3 oz. Footed Cocktail	15.00		
Creamer	6.50		40.00	Tumbler, 8 oz. Footed Water	12.50		
Creamer and Sugar on Diamond Shaped Tray		27.50		Tumbler, 12 oz. Footed Iced Tea	22.50		
Cruet, 6½ oz. and Stopper		127.50					
Cup	4.50	4.50	25.00	** Wine, 3", 4 oz.	17.50		
** Decanter and Stopper	85.00						

* Beware new Teal   ** Beware new Green

SHARON, "CABBAGE ROSE" FEDERAL GLASS COMPANY, 1935-1939

Colors: Pink, green, amber; some crystal. *(See Reproduction Section)*

Sharon has recovered from all the reproductions and is briskly being collected once again. It is not that people stopped collecting as much as new collectors did not start. Without new collectors, basic pieces do not sell; and dealers have to stop buying them. It becomes a vicious cycle with only the rare, unusual and under priced pieces finding new homes. **Now** every dealer who stopped buying, is crying that he can't find enough inventory to meet the demand!

A rising market is a great sign, unless you are an author trying to keep up with the rising prices! It is a **good** problem for me that has not been a major concern in the last few books.

Pink Sharon has several pieces in short supply including cheese dishes, thick iced teas and jam dishes. The jam dish is like the butter bottom, but it has no indentation for the top. It differs from the 2" deep soup bowl by standing only 1½" tall. The cheese dish can be seen in the amber picture next to the butter. The butter is on the outside of the cheese. Notice how the butter is much taller, although the butter base is only 1½" tall. The tops are the same; but the cheese bottom is like a salad plate with a raised band on top of it. The lid fits inside this raised band!

You can easily see the difference in the thick and thin tumblers in either picture! The heavy tumblers are easier to find in green; and the price reflects that. In amber, as in pink, the heavy iced teas are more rarely seen.

Amber footed teas are the most scarce of all Sharon tumblers. There are fewer collectors of amber and the price indicates that for now. (More collectors of amber would raise this price drastically).

Having purchased six piece place settings in all three Sharon colors, I can relate that the thirty amber tumblers were the first ones to be completely sold. It was a close race between the amber footed teas and the thick, flat iced teas in pink as to which sold out first; they both sold on the first day of an ad placed in the *Daze.*(see page 222)

The footed tumbler below was made to be converted into an oil lamp by screwing on a burner. Only one of these has ever been found. Maybe you will find the next one!

	Amber	Pink	Green
Bowl, 5" Berry	6.00	7.50	9.00
Bowl, 5" Cream Soup	20.00	30.00	35.00
Bowl, 6" Cereal	13.00	16.00	18.00
Bowl, 7½" Flat Soup, 2" Deep	35.00	30.00	
Bowl, 8½" Large Berry	4.50	16.00	23.00
Bowl, 9½" Oval Vegetable	13.00	16.00	20.00
Bowl, 10½" Fruit	19.00	25.00	25.00
Butter Dish and Cover	40.00	37.50	70.00
Butter Dish Bottom	20.00	17.50	30.00
Butter Dish Top	20.00	20.00	40.00
* Cake Plate, 11½" Footed	16.00	25.00	45.00
Candy Jar and Cover	35.00	37.50	145.00
Cheese Dish and Cover	165.00	625.00	
Creamer, Footed	11.00	12.50	16.00
Cup	8.00	10.00	14.00
Jam Dish, 7½"	27.50	105.00	35.00
Pitcher, 80 oz. with Ice Lip	115.00	100.00	300.00
Pitcher, 80 oz. without Ice Lip	110.00	95.00	325.00
Plate, 6" Bread and Butter	3.00	3.50	4.50
** Plate, 7½" Salad	11.00	16.50	15.00
Plate, 9½" Dinner	10.00	12.00	13.00
Platter, 12½" Oval	12.00	13.50	16.00
Salt and Pepper, Pr.	35.00	35.00	57.50
Saucer	4.00	6.00	6.00
Sherbet, Footed	9.00	10.00	25.00
Sugar	7.00	7.50	10.00
Sugar Lid	17.50	17.50	30.00
Tumbler, 4⅛", 9 oz. Thick	22.00	25.00	50.00
Tumbler, 4⅛", 9 oz. Thin	22.00	25.00	55.00
Tumbler, 5¼", 12 oz. Thin	50.00	33.00	85.00
Tumbler, 5¼", 12 oz. Thick	40.00	60.00	80.00
***Tumbler, 6½", 15 oz. Footed	75.00	34.00	

* Crystal-$5.00

** Crystal-$13.50

***Crystal-$15.00

"SHIPS" or "SAILBOAT" also known as "SPORTSMAN SERIES" HAZEL

ATLAS GLASS COMPANY, LATE 1930's

Color: Cobalt blue w/white, yellow and red decoration.

"Ships" shot glasses for $100.00? Those little jewels have gone up in price ever since one was shown on the rare page in my first book. I can say that I never envisioned any tumbler in Depression bringing that much money, let alone a shot glass!

I decided to show some of the different styles and accessory pieces that can be collected to go with this pattern that has its basic beginnings on the Moderntone blank. None of these are in the Hazel Atlas listing below; so I will put prices in parentheses as I mention them.

The tray ($20.00) was bought years ago with a pitcher and tumbler set on it. These accessory items are fun to look for and you never know what will pop up. The ash tray ($20.00) and the three sectional box ($35.00) behind the tray may be manufactured by the same company since the designs are very similar. The ash tray with the metal ship ($45.00) is more than likely Hazel Atlas. There are several other metal objects that can be found on these trays.

Cathy likes to refer to the cocktail shaker and tumbler on the right as "fancy ships." These pieces and the rest of the picture are all Hazel Atlas varieties of the "Sportsman Series." The "Polo" series sells well in our "horse country" of Kentucky. People who collect Dutch related paraphernalia enjoy the "Windmills."

Whatever the sport - skiing, boating, fishing, golfing or horse riding - you can find a beverage set to your liking.

The "Ships" decorated Moderntone is not abundant. Be sure to look for unworn white, not beige, decorations on these pieces. Prices are for MINT pieces. Worn and discolored items should fetch much less if someone will even purchase them. We have one yellow "Ships" tumbler that is not a discoloration. It really is "raincoat" yellow rather than white. No, it is not attractive - merely odd!

	Blue/White		Blue/White
Cup (Plain) "Moderntone"	7.50	Saucer	13.00
Cocktail Mixer w/Stirrer	17.50	Tumbler, 2 oz., 2¼" Shot Glass	100.00
Cocktail Shaker	25.00	Tumbler, 5 oz., 3¾", Juice	8.00
Ice Bowl	25.00	Tumbler, 6 oz., Roly Poly	7.50
Pitcher w/o Lip, 82 oz.	40.00	Tumbler, 8 oz., 3⅜", Old Fashion	13.00
Pitcher w/Lip, 86 oz.	35.00	Tumbler, 9 oz., 3¾", Straight Water	11.00
Plate, 5⅞", Bread & Butter	16.00	Tumbler, 9 oz., 4⅝", Water	8.00
Plate, 8", Salad	18.00	Tumbler, 10½ oz., 4⅞", Iced Tea	10.00
Plate, 9", Dinner	22.00	Tumbler, 12 oz., Iced Tea	16.00

SIERRA, "PINWHEEL" JEANNETTE GLASS COMPANY, 1931-1933

Colors: Green, pink and some ultramarine.

Where did all the green Sierra pitchers, tumblers and oval vegetable bowls go? You can find these pieces in pink with diligent looking, but finding them in green is a major scavenger hunt. The pitcher and tumbler eluded me this time, but I do have an oval bowl for you to see.

I hope the ultramarine cup jumped out at you. I also have a photograph of a cereal in that color sent by a reader. I expect more pieces will be found. It may have been an experimental color run by Jeannette when they were making Doric and Pansy or Swirl. It may also be one of those "lunch box" pieces a factory worker made that you so often read about. Glass workers supposedly carried out thousands of pieces of glass in their lunch boxes. Of course, they only carried out the best colors and all the experimental pieces. HA HA !

It's possible, as only last week two employees of a nut house sold tons of almonds for $1.00 a pound before they got caught. They carried out a few pounds at a time. However, there was no ready market for this cheap glass in the 1930's.

Sugar bowls are harder to find than the lids. It is the pointed edges on the sugar bowl which chip so easily that make this bowl so hard to find in MINT condition.

You need to look carefully at all pink Sierra butter dishes. You might run into the Adam/Sierra combination. Be sure to read about this under Adam.

Look carefully at the cups. Sometimes the wrong cup is placed on Sierra saucers. You always have to be on your toes when you are buying!

	Pink	Green		Pink	Green
Bowl, 5½" Cereal	8.00	9.00	Platter, 11" Oval	27.50	35.00
Bowl, 8½" Large Berry	12.00	18.00	Salt and Pepper, Pr.	30.00	32.50
Bowl, 9¼" Oval Vegetable	30.00	75.00	Saucer	3.50	4.50
Butter Dish and Cover	45.00	50.00	Serving Tray, 10¼", 2 Handles	11.00	13.00
Creamer	12.00	16.00	Sugar	15.00	18.00
Cup	8.00	10.00	Sugar Cover	10.00	10.00
Pitcher, 6½", 32 oz.	50.00	85.00	Tumbler, 4½", 9 oz. Footed	35.00	55.00
Plate, 9" Dinner	11.00	14.00			

SPIRAL HOCKING GLASS COMPANY, 1928-1930

Colors: Green and pink.

Spiral pictures have always included a Twisted Optic piece for comparison to the Spiral. Can you spot it this time? Remember that Spiral swirls go to the left or clockwise while Twisted Optic spirals go to the right or counterclockwise.

The problem spiral designed patterns give collectors occurs with the placement of the spirals on the piece. Inside or outside affects the left or right handed spiraling. It makes a difference in the way you look at it!

Green Spiral is the most commonly found, but there is some pink available. Maybe that will tell you that the blue mayonnaise is the Twisted Optic example in this picture since Spiral is not found in blue.

The Spiral center-handled server has a solid handle and the Twisted Optic center-handled server has an open handle if you have trouble identifying these.

The Spiral platter is not commonly found. This makes a nice luncheon or bridge set that can be purchased rather economically.

	Pink, Green			Pink, Green
Bowl, 4¾" Berry	4.00		Platter 12"	15.00
Bowl, 7" Mixing	7.50		Preserve and Cover	22.00
Bowl, 8" Large Berry	9.00		Salt and Pepper, Pr.	17.50
Creamer, Flat or Footed	6.00		Sandwich Server, Center Handle	17.50
Cup	4.00		Saucer	1.00
Ice or Butter Tub	17.50		Sherbet	3.00
Pitcher, 7⅝", 58 oz.	22.00		Sugar, Flat or Footed	6.00
Plate,6" Sherbet	1.00		Tumbler, 3", 5 oz. Juice	3.00
Plate, 8" Luncheon	2.00		Tumbler, 5", 9 oz. Water	6.00

STARLIGHT HAZEL ATLAS GLASS COMPANY, 1938-1940

Colors: Crystal, pink; some white, cobalt.

Crystal Starlight collectors still have trouble finding sherbets and the large salad bowls. The 13" sandwich plate is also elusive. Many collectors use the salad bowl and the sandwich plate as a set.

I have often wondered why Starlight shakers are found with a one-holed shaker top. I have now found out! It is a top designed to keep the salt "moisture proof." Shakers with these tops are often found in Florida and other southern areas where the humid air has always plugged up shaker holes.

Generally speaking, Starlight is another one of the smaller sets that can be collected without loans having to be obtained. The only difficulty comes in finding it. The pink and blue bowls make nice accessory pieces that can be used alongside the crystal. There is not enough white found to make a set of it practical. If you love a challenge, you would be one of the few folks looking for the white. It is a wide open territory!

Sometimes the pink, closed-handled bowl can be found in a metal holder. This metal holder encircles the base and extends up and over the handles in a swirled fashion which holds a salad spoon and fork. Another form of salad set for this pattern gives you two ways to incorporate this pattern when serving guests.

	Crystal, White	Pink		Crystal, White	Pink
Bowl, 5½" Cereal	5.00	7.00	Plate, 9" Dinner	5.00	
* Bowl, 8½", Closed Handles	5.00	12.00	Plate, 13" Sandwich	10.00	12.00
Bowl, 11½" Salad	15.00		Relish Dish	10.00	
Bowl, 12", 2¾" deep	20.00		Salt and Pepper, Pr.	17.50	
Creamer, Oval	3.50		Saucer	1.00	
Cup	3.00		Sherbet	10.00	
Plate, 6" Bread and Butter	2.00		Sugar, Oval	3.50	
Plate, 8½" Luncheon	2.50				

* Cobalt-$25.00

Please refer to Foreword for pricing information

STRAWBERRY U.S. GLASS COMPANY, Early 1930's

Colors: Pink, green, crystal; some iridized.

Strawberry and Cherryberry have been split into two separate patterns for this book. See page 30 for the Cherryberry listing.

The iridescent Strawberry pitcher is quite a find! You will see few of those in your travels. I have seen three in all my years of searching. Crystal is priced the same as iridescent because it is so rare. There are few crystal Strawberry collectors; that is a good thing since so little of it is found! Strawberry sugar covers are another item that is missing from most collections as is the 2" deep bowl shown in the Cherryberry photograph. Some collectors have mistakenly called the sugar with missing lid a spooner. It is a sugar bowl without handles which is sometimes seen in Depression era glass.

You will have to remember that Strawberry is another of those patterns that has very rough mould seams. This occurs on the tumblers, pitchers and even the plates. If mould roughness offends your collecting sensibilities, then this pattern is not for you.

Strawberry is another of the U.S. Glass patterns with a plain butter dish bottom that is interchangeable with other U.S. Glass patterns. Strawberry, also, has no cup or saucer.

	Crystal, Iridescent	Pink, Green		Crystal, Iridescent	Pink, Green
Bowl, 4" Berry	5.00	7.00	Olive Dish, 5" One-Handled	6.50	10.00
Bowl, 6¼", 2" Deep	35.00	55.00	Pickle Dish, 8¼" Oval	7.00	10.00
Bowl, 6½" Deep Salad	10.00	15.00	Pitcher, 7¾"	150.00	130.00
Bowl, 7½" Deep Berry	12.00	16.00	Plate, 6" Sherbet	4.00	6.00
Butter Dish and Cover	125.00	127.50	Plate, 7½" Salad	7.00	11.00
Butter Dish Bottom	75.00	75.00	Sherbet	5.50	6.50
Butter Dish Top	50.00	52.50	Sugar, Small Open	10.00	12.50
Comport, 5¾"	9.00	15.00	Sugar Large	17.50	20.00
Creamer, Small	9.00	12.50	Sugar Cover	30.00	40.00
Creamer, 4⅝" Large	17.50	25.00	Tumbler, 3⅝", 8 oz.	15.00	22.50

SUNFLOWER JEANNETTE GLASS COMPANY, 1930's

Colors: Pink, green, some delphite; some opaques.

Sunflower cake plates still appear in numbers to stagger the mind. These were packed in twenty pound bags of flour for several years. Everyone bought flour in large quantities since baking was necessarily in vogue, then. This cake plate is the only commonly found green piece in Sunflower.

The 7" trivet shown in the center in pink still remains the only difficult to find piece although collector demand keeps prices increasing steadily. Green is found less often than pink; therefore, prices for green are outdistancing prices in pink.

Both colors make nice luncheon or bridge sets; however, serving bowls become a problem. One collector solved this problem by using Cherry Blossom bowls. She said the colors were comparable (both are made by Jeannette) and everyone complimented her beautiful "antique" dishes. No one even knew she used two different patterns. Believe me, there is a whole world of people who still do not know what Depression glass is - or that it comes in different "patterns."

The ultramarine ash tray is the only piece found in that color. Opaque colors seem to show up once in a while. A set in the Delphite blue would be great, but that creamer is all I have found. I have always called the odd creamer color "mustard" because my wife edits out the proper goose related color it really is. The sugar has been called "mayonnaise" for the same editing reason related to cow fertilizer! I have always tried to relate the facts as I see them.

	Pink	Green		Pink	Green
* Ash Tray, 5", Center Design Only	7.50	9.00	Saucer	4.00	6.00
Cake Plate, 10", 3 Legs	9.00	9.00	Sugar (Opaque 85.00)	12.00	15.00
** Creamer (Opaque 85.00)	12.50	15.00	Tumbler, 4¾", 8 oz. Footed	17.50	22.00
Cup (Opaque 75.00)	8.00	10.00	Trivet, 7", 3 Legs, Turned Up Edge	195.00	200.00
Plate, 9" Dinner	9.00	12.00			

* Found in ultramarine-$25.00
** Delphite-$75.00

Please refer to Foreword for pricing information

SWANKY SWIGS 1930's-1950's

Swanky Swigs originally came with a Kraft cheese product in them. The Swanky on the bottom right still contains "Old English Sharp" and has a twenty-seven cent price from 1954 on it. There are lots of new Swankys being found and you can keep up with these new discoveries through a monthly newspaper on Depression glass. (See page 222.) I will try to expand this section and show many more sizes with the next edition!

Top Photo					
Top Row	Band No.1		Red & Black	3⅜"	1.50-2.50
			Red & Blue	3⅜"	2.00-3.00
			Blue	3⅜"	2.50-3.50
	Band No.2		Red & Black	4¾"	3.00-4.00
			Red & Black	3⅜"	2.00-3.00
	Band No.3		Blue & White	3⅜"	2.00-3.00
	Circle & Dot:		Blue	4¾"	5.00-7.50
			Blue	3½"	4.00-5.00
			Red, Green	3½"	2.50-3.50
			Black	3½"	4.00-5.00
			Red	4¾"	5.00-7.50
	Dot		Black	4¾"	6.00-8.00
			Blue	3½"	4.00-5.00
2nd Row	Star:		Blue	4¾"	4.00-5.00
			Blue, Red, Green, Black	3½"	2.50-3.50
			Cobalt w/White Stars	4¾"	12.00-14.00
	Centennials:		W.Va. Cobalt	4¾"	14.00-16.00
			Texas Cobalt	4¾"	20.00-25.00
			Texas Blue, Black, Green	3½"	20.00-22.00
	Checkerboard		Blue, Red	3½"	17.50-20.00
3rd Row	Checkerboard		Green	3½"	20.00-25.00
	Sailboat		Blue	4½"	10.00-15.00
			Blue	3½"	8.00-10.00
			Red,Green	4½"	10.00-12.50
			Green, Lt. Green	3½"	8.00-10.00
	Tulip No.1		Blue, Red	4½"	10.00-12.00
			Blue, Red	3½"	2.50-3.50
4th Row	Tulip No.1		Green	4½"	10.00-12.00
			Green, Black	3½"	2.50-3.50
			Green w/Label	3½"	4.00-5.00
	*Tulip No.2		Red, Green, Black	3½"	18.00-20.00
	Carnival		Blue, Red	3½"	2.00-3.00
			Green, Yellow	3½"	4.00-6.00
	Tulip No. 3		Dk. Blue, Lt. Blue	3¾"	1.50-2.00
Second Photo					
1st Row	Tulip No. 3		Red, Yellow	3¾"	1.50-2.00
	Posey: Tulip		Red	4½"	12.00-15.00
			Red	3½"	2.00-3.00
			Red	3¼"	8.00-10.00
	Posey: Violet, Jonquil, Cornflower No.1			4½"	12.00-15.00
	Posey: Violet, Jonquil, Cornflower No.1			3½"	2.00-3.00
	Cornflower No. 2		Lt. Blue, Dk. Blue	3½"	2.00-3.00
2nd Row	Cornflower No. 2		Red, Yellow	3½"	2.00-3.00
	Forget-Me-Not		Dk. Blue, Blue, Red, Yellow	3½"	1.00-2.00
			Yellow w/Label	3½"	5.00-6.00
	Daisy		Red & White	3¾"	12.00-15.00
	Daisy		Red, White & Green	3¾"	1.50-2.00
	Bustling Betsy		Blue	3¾"	2.00-3.00
			Blue	3¼"	6.00-7.00
			Green, Orange	3¾"	2.00-3.00
3rd Row	Bustling Betsy		Yellow, Red, Brown	3¾"	2.00-3.00
	Antique Pattern:				
	Clock & Coal Scuttle		Brown	3¾"	2.00-3.00
	Lamp & Kettle		Blue	3¾"	2.00-3.00
	Coffee Grinder & Plate		Green	3¾"	2.00-3.00
	Spinning Wheel & Bellows		Red	3¾"	2.00-3.00
	Coffee Pot & Trivet		Black	3¾"	2.00-3.00
	Churn & Cradle		Orange	3¾"	3.00-4.00
4th Row	Kiddie Cup:				
	Squirrel & Deer		Brown	3¾"	2.00-3.00
	Bear & Pig		Blue	3¾"	2.00-3.00
	Cat & Rabbit		Green	3¾"	2.00-3.00
	Bird & Elephant		Red	3¾"	2.00-3.00
	Bird & Elephant w/Label			3¾"	5.00-6.00
	Duck & Horse		Black	3¾"	2.00-3.00
	Dog & Rooster		Orange	3¾	3.00-4.00
	Dog & Rooster w/Cheese				15.00-20.00

* West Coast lower in price

KRAFT
PIMENTO
CHEESE SPREAD
KRAFT
Olive
Pimento
KRAFT
Old
English
KRAFT
Old English

SWIRL, "PETAL SWIRL" JEANNETTE GLASS COMPANY, 1937-1938

Colors: Ultramarine, pink, Delphite; some amber and "ice" blue.

Several new Swirl pitchers have been reported in ultramarine, but so far there has not been a pink one seen. I say, so far, because many collectors of Swirl combine this pattern with Jeannette's "Jennyware" kitchenware line which does have a pink pitcher in it! Some people have confused the two patterns because they are similar in styles and made in the same colors. If you find mixing bowls, measuring cups or reamers, then you have crossed over into the kitchenware line and out of the Swirl dinnerware set. See my **Kitchen Glassware of the Depression Years** for complete "Jennyware" listings.

Swirl can be found in several experimental colors. Delphite blue can be collected in a small set. Vegetable bowls (9") seem to be the primary experimental piece. Notice the amber and "ice" blue in the photo. I also had a report of one in crystal but it was never confirmed. There are two styles of this bowl found. Notice how the ultramarine and pink bowls have a rimmed inside edge. Other 9" Swirl bowls can be found without this rimmed edge.

The pink coaster shown in the foreground is often found inside a small rubber tire. These were souvenir pieces distributed by tire companies. These small tires have become collectible advertising items. Those with the company name on the glass insert are more in demand; but those with a plain Swirl glass insert (such as this coaster) are collected if the miniature tire is embossed with the name of a tire company.

Almost all pieces of Swirl can be found with two different edges. Some pieces have ruffled edges and some are plain. The plate in the pattern shot has a ruffled edge. The pink saucer and plate with cereal sitting on it are plain while the ultramarine saucer is ruffled. This makes a difference to people who order merchandise by mail. Either style is acceptable to most collectors, but some will not mix styles in their collection. If you only want plain edged pieces, please tell the dealer before he ships your order. This is not a problem if you are shopping and see the merchandise. It is your responsibility to specify what you want if you place an order.

Candy and butter dish bottoms are more abundant than tops in this pattern. Remember that before you buy only the bottom.

As with other patterns that come in ultramarine, there are green tinted pieces as well as the regular color. This green tint is hard to match, and most collectors avoid this shade. Because of this avoidance, many times you can buy the green tint at a super bargain price!

	Pink	Ultra-marine	Delphite		Pink	Ultra-marine	Delphite
Bowl, 6¼" Cereal	7.00	10.00	9.50	Plate, 6½" Sherbet	2.50	3.50	3.00
Bowl, 9" Salad	9.50	15.00	22.00	Plate, 7¼"	5.00	8.00	
Bowl, 9" Salad, Rimmed	12.00	18.00		Plate, 8" Salad	5.00	9.50	5.00
Bowl, 10" Footed, Closed				Plate, 9¼" dinner	7.00	11.00	7.50
Handles		22.00		Plate, 10½"			12.00
Bowl, 10½" Footed Console	12.50	19.00		Plate, 12½" Sandwich	7.50	15.00	
Butter Dish	150.00	210.00		Platter, 12" Oval			22.50
Butter Dish Bottom	25.00	35.00		Salt and Pepper, Pr.		30.00	
Butter Dish Top	125.00	175.00		Saucer	1.50	2.00	2.00
Candle Holders, Double				Sherbet, Low Footed	6.00	11.00	
Branch Pr.		25.00		Soup, Tab Handles (Lug)	14.00	17.50	
Candle Holders, Single				Sugar, Footed	6.50	9.50	7.50
Branch Pr.			85.00	Tray, 10½", Two-Handled			17.50
Candy Dish, Open, 3 Legs	8.00	10.00		Tumbler, 4", 9 oz.	8.00	18.00	
Candy Dish with Cover	60.00	85.00		Tumbler, 4⅝", 9 oz.	11.00		
Coaster, 1" x 3¼"	5.50	7.50		Tumbler, 5⅛", 13 oz.	20.00	55.00	
Creamer, Footed	6.50	9.50	7.50	Tumbler, 9 oz. Footed	12.50	20.00	
Cup	4.75	9.00	6.00	Vase, 6½" Footed, Ruffled	11.50		
Pitcher, 48 oz. Footed		1,250.00		Vase, 8½" Footed, Two Styles		17.50	

TEA ROOM INDIANA GLASS COMPANY, 1926-1931

Colors: Pink, green, amber and some crystal.

Tea Room is still one of the hottest Depression glass collectibles. Green is collected more often than pink; and a few collectors are beginning to seek the crystal! Crystal pieces are bringing up to half these prices of the pink except for the commonly found 9½" ruffled vase and the pitcher (priced separately below).

For those who have had trouble distinguishing the two styles of banana splits, look at the picture of pink. The flat banana split is in front between the finger bowl and mustard. The footed banana split is to the left of the amber creamer and sugar in the bottom picture and behind the crystal mustard in the top picture. Both styles of banana splits are very desirable pieces to own in any color!

The small, green sugar with handles and cover in the front of the top picture has created some interesting comments. (There is also a pink one without lid and matching creamer in lower photo.) This creamer and sugar are of the same mould shape as another Indiana pattern known as "Cracked Ice." These are not "Cracked Ice" since the design shows parallel lines just as on Tea Room. In any case, this creamer and sugar are nice "look-alike" pieces if not the real thing.

There has been a club formed by Tea Room and Pyramid collectors. They have their own newsletter. I have been promised copies of all the newsletters that have been printed and would have listed the address of this club for those who may be interested. However, these newsletters haven't arrived yet. You may be able to ascertain information on your own if you are interested.

Amber pitcher and tumblers continue to be found in the Atlanta area. They may have been used in a Coca-Cola promotion as remembered by an octogenarian lady I met at a show in that area.

Some interesting lamps are showing up which used tumblers that had been frosted. The regular lamp (shown here in pink) is not as plentiful as it once was. It has been a while since I have seen one in green.

The flat sugar and the marmalade bottom are the same. The marmalade takes a notched lid; the sugar lid is not notched. Finding either of these is not an easy task!

As the name implies, Tea Room was intended to be used in the "tea rooms" and "ice cream" parlors of the day. That is why you find so many soda fountain type items in this pattern.

	Green	Pink		Green	Pink
Bowl, Finger	40.00	32.00	Salt and Pepper, Pr.	40.00	37.50
Bowl, 7½" Banana Split, Flat	65.00	70.00	* Saucer	20.00	20.00
Bowl, 7½" Banana Split, Footed	60.00	50.00	Sherbet, Low Footed	16.00	14.00
Bowl, 8½" Celery	25.00	20.00	Sherbet, Low Flared Edge	25.00	20.00
Bowl, 8¾" Deep Salad	65.00	50.00	Sherbet, Tall Footed	30.00	27.50
Bowl, 9½" Oval Vegetable	50.00	45.00	Sugar w/Lid, 3"	95.00	90.00
Candlestick, Low, Pr.	37.50	32.00	Sugar, 4"	12.50	10.00
Creamer, 3¼"	20.00	20.00	Sugar, 4½" Footed (Amber $60.00)	14.00	12.00
Creamer, 4"	12.50	10.00	Sugar, Rectangular	14.00	12.50
Creamer, 4½" Footed (Amber $60.00)	13.50	12.00	Sugar, Flat with Cover	165.00	125.00
Creamer, Rectangular	14.00	12.50	Sundae, Footed, Ruffled Top	75.00	60.00
Creamer & Sugar on Tray, 3½"	55.00	50.00	Tray, Center-Handled	155.00	115.00
* Cup	35.00	35.00	Tray, Rectangular Sugar & Creamer	40.00	30.00
Goblet, 9 oz.	60.00	50.00	Tumbler, 8½ oz., Flat	75.00	65.00
Ice Bucket	40.00	35.00	Tumbler, 6 oz. Footed	25.00	25.00
Lamp, 9" Electric	40.00	35.00	Tumbler, 9 oz. Footed (Amber $55.00)	22.00	20.00
Marmalade, Notched Lid	165.00	125.00	Tumbler, 11 oz. Footed	32.50	27.50
Mustard, Covered	115.00	100.00	Tumbler, 12 oz. Footed	40.00	35.00
Parfait	50.00	45.00	Vase, 6½" Ruffled Edge	90.00	75.00
** Pitcher, 64 oz. (Amber $400.00)	100.00	95.00	***Vase, 9½" Ruffled Edge	80.00	65.00
Plate, 6½" Sherbet	22.00	22.00	Vase, 9½" Straight	50.00	40.00
Plate, 8¼", Luncheon	25.00	22.50	Vase, 11" Ruffled Edge	150.00	175.00
Plate, 10½", 2-Handled	40.00	35.00	Vase, 11" Straight	80.00	75.00
Relish, Divided	16.00	13.00			

* Prices for absolutely mint pieces

** Crystal-$275.00

***Crystal-$12.50

Please refer to Foreword for pricing information

THISTLE MacBETH-EVANS, 1929-1930

Colors: Pink, green; some yellow and crystal.

Thistle continues to drive our photographer crazy! There is almost no way to get the pattern on film. The lights make the pattern do a disappearing act. That disappearance is sort of familiar to Thistle collectors. This pattern has been known to hide very well.

Green is generally more scarce than pink except for the large fruit bowl which is almost nonexistent in pink. The one in the picture is only one of two I have ever seen.

The mould shapes in this pattern are the same as Dogwood. In Thistle, however, there's only the thin style cup and saucer instead of the thicker style. Why a creamer and sugar was never made is beyond me!

The thick butter dish, pitcher, tumbler and other heavily moulded pieces with Thistle designs are new! They are being made by Mosser Glass Company in Cambridge, Ohio. They are not a part of this pattern, but copies of a much older pattern glass.

	Pink	Green
Bowl, 5½" Cereal	15.00	17.50
Bowl, 10¼" Large Fruit	200.00	135.00
Cup, Thin	15.00	17.50
Plate, 8" Luncheon	8.00	12.50
Plate, 10¼" Grill	12.50	15.00
Plate, 13" Heavy Cake	75.00	100.00
Saucer	7.50	7.50

"THUMBPRINT", PEAR OPTIC FEDERAL GLASS COMPANY, 1929-1930

Color: Green

"Thumbprint" is the common collector's name for a pattern called Pear Optic by Federal. Most companies had a "Thumbprint" type pattern; so, there are many pieces from other companies that are collected with this Federal pattern. Many of Federal's pieces have the **F** in a shield symbol used by the company to mark their glassware.

The picture shown here (taken by photographer Raymond Mills) is of a set owned by Imogene McKinney of Texas. I started to replace this photograph; but I have so little of this pattern in my stock, it seemed a shame to downgrade!

"Thumbprint" is often confused with Raindrops, but notice how the "bumps" on Thumbprint are elongated whereas the "bumps" on Raindrops are round.

	Green
Bowl, 4¾" Berry	2.50
Bowl, 5" Cereal	3.00
Bowl, 8" Large Berry	7.00
Creamer, Footed	10.00
Cup	2.50
Plate, 6" Sherbet	1.25
Plate, 8" Luncheon	2.00
Plate, 9¼" Dinner	4.50
Salt and Pepper, Pr.	20.00
Saucer	1.00
Sherbet	4.50
Sugar, Footed	10.00
Tumbler, 4", 5 oz.	3.50
Tumbler, 5", 10 oz.	4.00
Tumbler, 5½", 12 oz.	4.00
Whiskey, 2¼", 1 oz.	3.00

Please refer to Foreword for pricing information

TWISTED OPTIC IMPERIAL GLASS COMPANY, 1927-1930

Colors: Pink, green, amber; some blue and canary yellow.

No tricks in Twisted Optic! All the pieces shown belong to that pattern. You can see an additional blue piece under Spiral placed there to help in differentiating the two patterns which are often confused. If it is some color besides pink or green, then it is most likely Twisted Optic since Spiral only comes in pink or green.

Twisted Optic spirals to the right and Spiral's go to the left!

The major problem is not between these two patterns that spiral in opposite directions, but that many other companies made spiraling patterns, also.

Many collectors lump these spiralling patterns together in order to be able to have a bigger collection! Other collectors are purist and will not mix patterns. You, alone, have to make this decision.

	*All Colors		*All Colors
Bowl, 4¾" Cream Soup	9.00	Plate, 7½" x 9" Oval with Indent	4.00
Bowl, 5" Cereal	3.00	Plate, 8" Luncheon	2.00
Bowl, 7" Salad	6.00	Plate, 10", Sandwich	7.50
Candlesticks, 3" Pr.	10.00	Preserve (Same as Candy with Slotted Lid)	20.00
Candy Jar and Cover	20.00	Sandwich Server, Open Center Handle	17.50
Creamer	6.00	Sandwich Server, Two-Handled	9.50
Cup	3.00	Saucer	1.00
Mayonnaise	15.00	Sherbet	5.00
Pitcher, 64 oz.	22.50	Sugar	5.00
Plate, 6" Sherbet	1.50	Tumbler, 4½", 9 oz.	4.50
Plate, 7" Salad	2.00	Tumbler, 5¼", 12 oz.	6.50

* Blue, Canary Yellow 50% more

U.S. SWIRL U.S. GLASS COMPANY, Late 1920's

Colors: Pink, green and crystal.

U.S. Swirl has now been found in crystal, but not enough to know if a set can be collected. There is a new tumbler listing (3⅝") which corresponds with the only known size of Aunt Polly and Cherryberry/Strawberry tumblers.

I had a report of **iridized** U.S. Swirl a couple of years ago; but it was never confirmed. It seems likely, but you have to "show me" (and I am not from Missouri).

A green creamer still eludes me. If you have an extra one, let me hear from you! I seem to be seeing more pink than green in my travels. I suspect this pattern is so rare that many of you are only acquainted with it through this picture.

	Green	Pink		Green	Pink
Bowl, 4⅜", Berry	4.50	5.00	Pitcher, 8", 48 oz.	35.00	35.00
Bowl, 5½", 1 Handle	8.50	9.00	Plate, 6⅛", Sherbet	1.50	1.75
Bowl, 7⅞, Large Berry	11.00	12.00	Plate, 7⅞, Salad	4.50	5.00
Bowl, 8¼", Oval	20.00	20.00	Salt and Pepper, Pr.	35.00	35.00
Butter and Cover	52.50	67.50	Sherbet, 3¼"	3.50	4.00
Butter Bottom	42.50	52.50	Sugar w/Lid	25.00	25.00
Butter Top	10.00	15.00	Tumbler, 3⅝", 8 oz.	7.00	8.00
Candy w/Cover, 2-Handled	20.00	22.50	Tumbler, 4⅝", 12 oz.	9.00	10.00
Creamer	10.00	11.00	Vase, 6½"	12.50	13.50

Please refer to Foreword for pricing information

"VICTORY" DIAMOND GLASS-WARE COMPANY, 1929-1932

Colors: Amber, pink, green; some cobalt blue and black.

Victory collectors seek all colors; but the cobalt blue attracts collectors interested in the color more than the pattern. The same collecting concept occurs in this pattern with collectors of black glass, but not to the extent that it does with cobalt blue.

We took a six piece setting of cobalt blue to Sanford, Florida, for a Depression glass show last year. Several of the pieces were bought by collectors who had to be told what the pattern was. The gravy boat and platter drew ohs and ahs, but it was several shows later that a collector searching for that gravy boat got his wish!

I decided to show only the black and the blue Victory since there is more demand for these colors. You will be able to gather a set in amber, green or pink much faster than those colors shown, if you like this pattern.

The gravy boat and platter is the premier piece in any color. Finding goblets, cereal and soup bowls as well as the oval vegetable, will keep you searching long and hard, no matter which color you choose.

You will find several styles of decorations besides the gold trimmed pieces shown here. There are floral decorations and even a black decorated design that is very "Art Deco" looking. I have seen more decorated console sets (bowl and candlesticks) than anything, but I assume that whole sets can be found with gold trim. Complete sets of floral decorated ware may not be available, but if you should see a decorated set, send me a snapshot, please!

	Amber, Pink, Green	Black, Blue		Amber, Pink, Green	Black, Blue
Bon Bon, 7"	9.00	15.00	Goblet, 5", 7 oz.	17.50	
Bowl, 6½" Cereal	8.00	20.00	Gravy Boat and Platter	125.00	275.00
Bowl, 8½" Flat Soup	12.00	30.00	Mayonnaise Set: 3½" Tall, 5½" Across,		
Bowl, 9" Oval Vegetable	25.00	60.00	8½" Indented Plate, w/Ladle	35.00	85.00
Bowl, 11" Rolled Edge	20.00	35.00	Plate, 6" Bread and Butter	3.00	8.00
Bowl, 12" Console	27.50	55.00	Plate, 7" Salad	5.50	10.00
Bowl, 12½" Flat Edge	22.50	50.00	Plate, 8" Luncheon	5.00	12.50
Candlesticks, 3" Pr.	25.00	75.00	Plate, 9" Dinner	15.00	27.50
Cheese & Cracker Set, 12" Indented			Platter, 12"	17.50	50.00
Plate & Compote	35.00		Sandwich Server, Center Handle	20.00	45.00
Comport, 6" Tall, 6¾" Diameter	10.00		Saucer	2.00	6.00
Creamer	10.00	35.00	Sherbet, Footed	10.00	17.50
Cup	6.00	25.00	Sugar	10.00	35.00

VITROCK, "FLOWER RIM" HOCKING GLASS COMPANY, 1934-1937

Colors: White and white w/fired-on colors, usually red or green.

Vitrock was Hocking's answer to the "milk glass" craze. Only this "Flower Rim" pattern and Lake Como were made into dinnerware sets in this very durable line. Vitrock competed with Hazel Atlas "Platonite" and by all indications of what is available today, "Platonite" won.

Vitrock is known better for the kitchenware line of reamers, measuring cups and mixing bowls found in this white color. You can see more of this in my *Kitchen Glassware of the Depression Years*. Some collectors are gathering different patterns that can "cross-over" into other fields.

The fired-on colors can make decorative accessory pieces for special occasions. You can find fired-on blue as well as the three colors shown!

The platter and the cream soup are pieces that are few and far between!

	White		White
Bowl, 4" Berry	3.50	Plate, 7¼" Salad	1.50
Bowl, 5½" Cream Soup	12.00	Plate, 8¾" Luncheon	2.00
Bowl, 6" Fruit	4.00	Plate, 9" Soup	9.00
Bowl, 7½" Cereal	4.00	Plate, 10" Dinner	5.00
Bowl, 9½" Vegetable	8.00	Platter, 11½"	20.00
Creamer, Oval	3.00	Saucer	1.00
Cup	2.00	Sugar, Oval	3.00

Please refer to Foreword for pricing information

WATERFORD, "WAFFLE" HOCKING GLASS COMPANY, 1938-1944

Colors: Crystal, pink; some yellow, white; Forest Green 1950's.

Pink Waterford collectors are having difficulty finding any of the harder to find pieces at any price. Cereal bowls, pitchers and butter dishes are not even seen at shows. Of these three pieces, the cereal is the most elusive. It was even hard to find the cereals when they were priced at $1.50 when my first book was issued in 1972!

For neophytes, the items listed below with Miss America style in parentheses, are Waterford patterned pieces that have the same mould shapes as Miss America. You can see some of these pieces in my Seventh edition of this book or in the *Very Rare Glassware of the Depression Years*. It seems likely that the first designs for Waterford were patterned on the shapes of Miss America which had been discontinued the year before Waterford was introduced. For some unknown reason, a newly designed shape was chosen and the experimental (?) pieces have been found in small quantities. It is unlikely that a full set could be found, but one never knows what resides in the attics, basements and garages of the American people!

There is a "look-alike" footed cup that is sometimes sold as a Waterford punch cup. This cup and the larger lamps that are sometimes displayed as Waterford are only similar to Waterford. Waterford has a flattened, not rounded, "diamond" shape on each section of the design. There is a large pitcher with a indented circular design in each diamond that is not Waterford. This pitcher was made by Hocking, but has more of a "bullseye" look. These only sell in the $20.00 range, so do not pay Waterford prices for it!

The yellow and amber goblets shown below are compliments of Anchor Hocking's photography from pieces stored in their morgue.

Crystal Waterford collectors can still complete sets, but there are some pieces in crystal that are hard to find. Cereal bowls are toughest to find, but goblets are also disappearing. Check the inside rims for roughness on this pattern. A little roughness is normal; so don't let that keep you from owning a hard to find piece. Minor chips is another matter that you will have to decide about on each piece.

You will find a few pieces in white and some that are fired-on green and pink as shown in Oyster and Pearl. ("Dusty Rose" and "Springtime Green" are the names for these colors usually found on ash trays and selling for the same price as the crystal ones). Forest Green 13 ¾" plates were made in the 1950's promotion; these are usually found in the $10.00 range. Some crystal has also been found trimmed in red, but not much.

Advertising ash trays such as the "Post Cereals" shown below are now selling for $8.00 to $12.00 depending upon the desirability of the advertising on the piece!

	Crystal	Pink		Crystal	Pink
* Ash Tray, 4"	6.00		Pitcher, 80 oz. Tilted Ice Lip	25.00	110.00
Bowl, 4¾" Berry	5.00	8.50	Plate, 6" Sherbet	1.50	3.50
Bowl, 5½" Cereal	12.00	18.00	Plate, 7⅛" Salad	2.50	4.50
Bowl, 8¼" Large Berry	7.50	12.50	Plate, 9⅝" Dinner	5.00	12.00
Butter Dish and Cover	23.00	185.00	Plate, 10¼" Handled Cake	5.00	9.50
Butter Dish Bottom	5.00	25.00	Plate, 13¾" Sandwich	5.00	20.00
Butter Dish Top	18.00	160.00	Relish, 13¾", 5-Part	13.00	
Coaster, 4"	2.50		Salt and Pepper, 2 Types	7.50	
Creamer, Oval	2.50	7.50	Saucer	1.00	3.50
Creamer (Miss America Style)	22.50		Sherbet, Footed	3.50	9.50
Cup	4.00	10.00	Sherbet, Footed, Scalloped Base	3.25	
Cup (Miss America Style)		20.00	Sugar	2.50	6.50
Goblets, 5¼", 5⅝"	12.00		Sugar Cover, Oval	2.50	17.50
Goblet, 5½" (Miss America Style)	25.00	65.00	Sugar (Miss America Style)	22.50	
Lamp, 4" Spherical Base	22.50		Tumbler, 3½", 5 oz. Juice (Miss America Style)		50.00
Pitcher, 42 oz. Tilted Juice	17.50		Tumbler, 4⅞", 10 oz. Footed	8.50	14.00

* With Ads $10.00

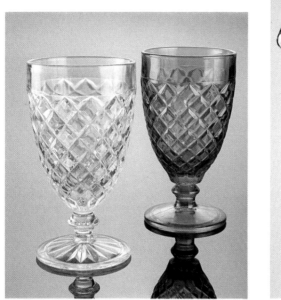

Please refer to Foreword for pricing information

WINDSOR, "WINDSOR DIAMOND" JEANNETTE GLASS COMPANY, 1936-1946

Colors: Pink, green, crystal; some Delphite, amberina red and ice blue.

Windsor is the last pattern in this book, but I did not write it last this time. I have been accused of being tired when I get to Windsor and not treating it equally. I have had enough of this "pattern discrimination"!

There have been some new discoveries in Windsor! A yellow (vaseline) powder jar which has a Cube top and Windsor bottom is shown in my ***Very Rare Glassware of the Depression Years*** and a pink powder jar with Windsor top and Cube bottom has also been reported.

A new style pink ash tray has been found and, also, a pink boat-shaped bowl with handles! The handles make this bowl easier to use, but they surely look strange!

Notice the two different styles of butters in the lower photograph. One is similar to the shape of Holiday! There are also two styles of sugar and lids. In the lower photograph, the crystal sugar bowl has no lip for the lid to rest against (shaped like Holiday); in the upper shot, the pink sugar shows the style with lip. The pink sugar and lid without the lip are hard to find.

The relish trays can be found with or without tab handles. The tab handled style can be seen in pink in the top photograph and the trays without handles can be seen in crystal in the bottom picture. Pink trays without handles are much in demand!

Green Windsor tumblers are elusive. Even the water tumbler (which is commonly found in pink), is in short supply. The 13⅝" plate that the creamer, sugar and butter dish are sitting on in the top picture, is often found as a beverage set with a pitcher and six water tumblers. That may have been a heavily promoted or premium item since so many pitcher and water tumblers are available today.

The crystal 10½" pointed edge bowl which, along with the comport, makes up a punch bowl and stand is hard to find in pink. The comport fits up inside the base of this bowl to keep it from sliding off the base. In recent years, there have been newly made comports in crystal and sprayed-on multi-colored ones which have a beaded edge. The crystal will not work as a punch stand because of this beaded edge.

	Crystal	Pink	Green		Crystal	Pink	Green
* Ash Tray, 5¾"	11.50	30.00	40.00	Plate, 6" Sherbet	1.50	2.50	3.50
Bowl, 4¾" Berry	2.50	5.00	7.00	Plate, 7" Salad	3.00	9.50	13.50
Bowl, 5" Pointed Edge	3.00	8.00		** Plate, 9" Dinner	3.50	9.50	13.50
Bowl, 5" Cream Soup	4.50	15.00	20.00	Plate, 10¼" Handled Sandwich	4.00	9.00	10.00
Bowl, 5⅛, 5⅜" Cereals	7.00	12.00	15.00	Plate, 13⅝" Chop	7.50	30.00	30.00
Bowl, 7⅛", Three Legs	6.00	15.00		Platter, 11½" Oval	4.50	10.00	12.00
Bowl, 8" Pointed Edge	8.00	25.00		****Powder Jar		45.00	
Bowl, 8", 2-Handled	4.50	11.00	15.00	Relish Platter, 11½" Divided	9.50	175.00	
Bowl, 8½" Large Berry	4.50	10.00	12.00	Salt and Pepper, Pr.	12.50	30.00	40.00
Bowl, 9½" Oval Vegetable	5.00	12.00	17.50	Saucer (Ice Blue $15.00)	1.50	2.50	3.00
Bowl, 10½" Salad	6.00			Sherbet, Footed	2.50	8.00	10.00
Bowl, 10½" Pointed Edge	20.00	85.00		Sugar and Cover	4.50	17.50	22.00
Bowl, 12½" Fruit Console	20.00	75.00		Sugar and Cover (Like "Holiday")	4.00	75.00	
Bowl, 7" x 11¾" Boat Shape	12.00	20.00	25.00	Tray, 4", Square, w/Handles	2.50	6.00	8.00
Butter Dish (Two Styles)	22.50	37.50	70.00	Tray, 4", Square, wo/Handles	5.00	30.00	
Cake Plate, 10¾" Footed	6.00	11.50	13.00	Tray, 4⅛" x 9", w/Handles	3.00	6.50	12.00
Candlesticks, 3" Pr.	15.00	65.00		Tray, 4⅛" x 9", wo/Handles	8.50	45.00	
Candy Jar and Cover	15.00			Tray, 8½" x 9¾", w/Handles	5.00	18.50	25.00
Coaster, 3¼"	2.50	8.00	15.00	Tray, 8½" x 9¾", wo/Handles	12.50	75.00	35.00
Comport	8.00			** Tumbler, 3¼", 5 oz.	6.00	15.00	25.00
** Creamer	3.00	7.50	8.00	** Tumbler, 4", 9 oz. (Red 50.00)	5.00	10.00	22.00
Creamer (Shaped as "Holiday")	4.00			Tumbler, 5", 12 oz.	7.50	20.00	37.50
** Cup	2.50	6.00	7.00	Tumbler, 4" Footed	6.00		
Pitcher, 4½", 16 oz.	17.50	95.00		Tumbler, 7¼" Footed	10.00		
***Pitcher, 6¾", 52 oz.	11.00	18.50	40.00				

   * Delphite-$40.00

  ** Blue-$55.00

 *** Red-$400.00

**** Yellow-$150.00

Please refer to Foreword for pricing information

206

REPRODUCTIONS

NEW "ADAM" PRIVATELY PRODUCED OUT OF KOREA THROUGH ST. LOUIS IMPORTING COMPANY

ONLY THE ADAM BUTTER DISH HAS BEEN REPRODUCED!
The new Adam butter is being offered at $6.50 wholesale. Identification of the new is easy.
Top: Notice the veins in the leaves.
New: Large leaf veins do not join or touch in center of leaf.
Old: Large leaf veins all touch or join center vein on the old.
A further note in the original Adam butterdish: the veins of all the leaves at the center of the design are very clear cut and precisely moulded: in the new, these center leaf veins are very indistinct -- and almost invisible in one leaf of the center design.
Bottom: Place butter dish bottom upside down for observation
New: Four (4) "Arrowhead-like" points line up in northwest, northeast, southeast and southwest directions of compass. There are very bad mould lines and a very glossy light pink color on the butter dishes I have examined; but these could be improved.
Old: Four (4) "Arrowhead-like" points line up in north, east, south and west directions of compass.

NEW "AVOCADO" INDIANA GLASS COMPANY Tiara Exclusives Line, 1974 . . .
Colors: Pink, frosted pink, yellow, blue, red, amethyst and green.

In 1979 a green Avocado pitcher was produced. It is darker than the original green and was a limited hostess gift item. Yellow pieces that are beginning to show up are all new! Yellow was never made originally!

The pink Indiana made was described under the pattern. It tends to be more orange than the original color. The other colors shown pose little threat since these colors were not made originally.

I understand that Tiara sales counselors tell potential clientele that their newly made glass is collectible because it is made from old moulds. I don't share this view. I feel it's like saying that since you were married in your grandmother's wedding dress, you will have the same happy marriage for the fifty-seven years she did. All you can truly say is that you were married in her dress. I think all you can say about the new Avocado is that it was made from the old moulds. TIME, SCARCITY and PEOPLE'S WHIMS determine collectability in so far as I'm able to determine it. It's taken nearly fifty years or more for people to turn to collecting Depression Glass—and that's done, in part, because EVERYONE "remembers" it; they had some in their home at one time or another; it has universal appeal. Who is to say what will be collectible in the next hundred years. If we all knew, we could all get rich!

If you like the new Tiara products, then by all means buy them; but don't do so DEPENDING upon their being collectible just because they are made in the image of the old! You have an equal chance, I feel, of going to Las Vegas and DEPENDING upon getting rich at the blackjack table.

REPRODUCTIONS (Continued)

NEW "CAMEO"

Colors: Green, pink, cobalt blue (shakers); yellow, green and pink (child's dishes).

Although the photographer I left this shaker with opted to shoot the side without the dancing girl, I trust you can still see how very weak the pattern is on this reproduction made by Mosser of the Cameo shaker. Also, you can see how much glass remains in the bottom of the shaker; and, of course, the new tops all make this easy to spot at the market. These were to be bought wholesale at around $6.00; but did not sell well. A new IMPORTER is making shakers in pink, cobalt blue and a terrible green color. These, too, are weakly patterned! They were never originally made in the blue, but **beware of PINK**!

The children's dishes pose no problem to collectors since they were never made originally. The sugar and creamer are a shade over 1½" tall and the butter dish is just 3¾" from handle to handle. There are now more than thirty children's pieces made in miniature from original pieces. These are "scale models" of the larger size. This type of production I have no quarrel with as they aren't planned to "dupe" anyone.

NEW "CHERRY BLOSSOM" (Continued on next page)

Colors: Pink, green, blue, delphite, cobalt, red and iridized colors.

Please use information provided only for the piece described. Do not apply information on tumbler for pitcher, etc.

Several different people have gotten into the act of making reproduction Cherry Blossom. We've even enjoyed some reproductions of reproductions **and now reproductions of those reproductions!** All the items pictured on the next pages are extremely easy to spot as reproductions once you know what to look for with the possible exception of the 13" divided platter pictured at the back. It's too heavy, weighing 2¾ pounds, and has a thick, ⅜" of glass in the bottom; but the design isn't too bad! The edges of the leaves aren't smooth; but neither are they serrated like old leaves.

I could write a book on the differences between old and new scalloped bottom, AOP Cherry pitchers. The easiest way to tell the difference is to turn the pitcher over. My old Cherry pitcher has nine cherries on the bottom. The new one only has seven. Further, the branch crossing the bottom of my old Cherry pitchers **LOOKS** like a branch. It's knobby and gnarled and has several leaves and cherry stems directly attached to it. The new pitcher just has a bald strip of glass cutting the bottom of the pitcher in half. Further, the old Cherry pitchers have a plain glass background for the cherries and leaves in the bottom of the pitcher. In the new pitchers, there's a rough, filled in, straw-like background. You see no plain glass. (My new Cherry pitcher just cracked sitting in a box by my typing stand—another tendency which I understand is common to the new)!

As for the new tumblers, the easiest way to tell old from new is to look at the ring dividing the patterned portion of the glass from the plain glass lip. The old tumblers have three indented rings dividing the pattern from the plain glass rim. The new has only one. (Further, as in the pitcher, the arching encircling the cherry blossoms on the new tumblers is very sharply ridged. On the old tumblers, that arching is so smooth you can barely feel it. Again, the pattern at the bottom of the new tumblers is brief and practically nonexistent in the center curve of the glass bottom. This was sharply defined on most of the old tumblers. You can see how far toward the edge the pattern came on the green Cherry tumbler pictured with the pattern. The pattern, what there is, on the new tumblers mostly hugs the center of the foot.

Now for a quick run down of the various items.

2 handled tray - old; 1⅞ lbs; ³⁄₁₆" glass in bottom; leaves and cherries east/west from north/south handles; leaves have real spine and serrated edges; cherry stems end in triangle of glass. **new:** 2⅛ lbs; ¼" glass in bottom; leaves and cherries north/south with the handles; canal type leaves (but uneven edges; cherry stem ends before cup shaped line).

cake plate - new: color too light pink, leaves have too many parallel veins which give them a "feathery" look; arches at plate edge don't line up with lines on inside of the rim to which the feet are attached.

8½" bowl - new: crude leaves with smooth edges; veins in parallel lines.

cereal bowl - new: wrong shape, looks like 8½" bowl, small 2" center. **old:** large center, 2½" inside ring, nearly 3½" if you count the outer rim before the sides turn up.

plate - new: center shown close up; smooth edged leaves, fish spine type center leaf portion; weighs 1 pound plus; feels thicker at edge with mould offset lines clearly visible. (See next page). **old:** center leaves look like real leaves with spines, veins and serrated edges; weighs ¾ pound; clean edges; no mould offset.

cup - new: area in bottom left free of design; canal leaves; smooth, thick top to cup handle (old has triangle grasp point).

saucer - new: off set mould line edge; canal leaf center.

NEW CHERRY BLOSSOM (Continued)

First of all, notice the cup bottom and the close up of the center design on the reproduction plate. Once you learn to recognize these "fake" leaves, you'll be able to spot 95 percent of the reproduction Cherry Blossom. These new leaves look like orderly docking stations at the local marina with a straight canal going down the center. Old Cherry Blossom dishes have real looking leaves, complete with main stem, delicate veins branching from that stem, and serrated edges. Notice the smooth edges of the reproduction leaves.

The Cherry child's dishes were first made in 1973.

First to appear was a child's Cherry cup (with a slightly lop-sided handle) having the cherries hanging upside down when the cup was held in the right hand. (This defiance of gravity was due to the inversion of the design when the mould, taken from an original cup, was inverted to create the outside of the "new" cup). After I reported this error, it was quickly corrected by re-inverting the inverted mould. These later cups were thus improved in design but slightly off color. The saucers tended to have slightly off center designs, too. Next came the "child's butter dish" which was never made by Jeannette. It was essentially the child's cup without a handle turned upside down over the saucer and having a little glob of glass added as a knob for lifting purposes. You could get this item in pink, green, light blue, cobalt, gray-green, and iridescent carnival colors. A blue one is pictured on the preceding page.

Pictured are many of the colors of butter dishes made so far. Shakers were begun in 1977. Some shakers were dated '77 on the bottom and were marketed at the ridiculous price of $27.95, a whopping profit margin! Shortly afterward, the non dated variety appeared. How can you tell new shakers from old -- should you get the one in a million chance to do so?

First, look at the tops. New tops COULD indicate new shakers. Next, notice the protruding ledges beneath the tops. In the new they are squared off juts rather than the nicely rounded scallops on the old (which are pictured under Cherry Blossom pattern). The design on the newer shakers is often weak in spots. Finally, notice how far up inside the shakers the solid glass (next to the foot) remains. The newer shakers have almost twice as much glass in that area. They appear to be ¼ full of glass before you ever add the salt!

Now, IN 1989, A NEW DISTRIBUTOR IN GEORGIA IS AT WORK! He is making shakers in cobalt blue, pink, and an ugly green, that is no problem to spot! These shakers are similar in quality to those made before, but the present pink color is **good;** yet the quality and design of each batch could vary greatly. Realize that **only two original pair of pink shakers were ever found** and those were found before any reproductions were made in 1976!

Butter dishes are naturally more deceptive in pink and green since those were the only original colors. The major flaw in the new butter is that there is ONE band encircling the bottom edge of the butter top; there are TWO bands very close together along the skirt of the old top. Using your tactile sense, the new has a sharply defined design up inside; the old was glazed and is smooth to touch. The knob on the new is more sharply defined than the smoothly formed knob on the old butter top. Today, with thousands of newly-made butters on the market, tactile sense is not as good an indication as it once was.

NEW "MADRID" CALLED "RECOLLECTION" Currently being made.

I hope you have already read about Recollection Madrid on page 112. The current rage of Indiana Glass is to make Madrid in **blue, pink and crystal.** These colors are being sold through all kinds of outlets ranging from better department stores to discount catalogues. In the past few months we have received several ads stating that this is genuine Depression glass made from old moulds. None of this is made from old glass moulds unless you consider 1976 old. Most of the pieces are from moulds that were never made originally.

The blue is becoming a big seller for Indiana according to reports I am receiving around the country. It is a brighter, more florescent blue than the originally found color.

Look at the top picture! None of these items were ever made in the old pattern Madrid. The new grill plate has one division splitting the plate in half, but the old had three sections. A goblet or vase was never made. The vase is sold with a candle making it a "hurricane lamp." The heavy tumbler was placed on top of a candlestick to make this vase/hurricane lamp. That candlestick gets a workout. It was attached to a plate to make a pedestaled cake stand and to a butter dish to make a preserve stand. That's a clever idea, actually.

The shakers are short and heavy and you can see both original styles pictured on page 113. The latest item I have seen is a heavy 11 oz. flat tumbler being sold for $7.99 in a set of four or six called "On the Rocks." The biggest giveaway to this newer glass is the pale, washed out color. (It really looks washed out in the bottom photograph here. This is a little over done, but all the new is almost that bad.)

The bottom picture shows items that were originally made. The only concern in these pieces are the cups, saucers and oval vegetable bowl. These three pieces were made in pink in the 1930's. None of the others shown were ever made in the 1930's in pink; so realize that when you see the butter dish, dinner plate, soup bowl, or sugar and creamer. These are new items! Once you have learned what this washed-out pink looks like by seeing these items out for sale, the color will let know when you see other pieces. My suggestion is to avoid pink Madrid except for the pitcher and tumblers.

The most difficult piece for new collectors to tell new from old is the candlestick. The new ones all have raised ridges inside to hold the candle more firmly. All old ones do not have these ridges. You may even find new candlesticks in black.

NEW "MAYFAIR" (Continued on next page)
Colors: cobalt blue, pink and green (odd shade).

Mayfair Shaker
The corner ridges on the old shaker rise ½ way to the top and then smooth out. The new shaker corner ridges rise to the top and are quite pronounced. The measurement differences are listed below, but the **diameter of the opening is the critical and easiest way to tell old from new!**

	OLD	NEW
Diameter of opening	¾"	⅝"
Diameter of lid	⅞"	¾"
Height	4¹⁄₁₆"	4"

REPRODUCTIONS (Continued)

NEW "MAYFAIR"

Colors: Pink, green, blue, cobalt (shot glasses), 1977 up. Pink, green, amethyst, cobalt blue (cookie jars), 1982 to present.

Only the pink shot glass need cause any concern to collectors because the glass wasn't made in those other colors originally. At first glance the color of the newer shots is often too-light pink or too orange. Dead giveaway is the stem of the flower design, however. In the old, that stem branched to form a "A" shape; in the new, you have a single stem. Further, in the new design, the leaf is hollow with the veins moulded in. In the old, the leaf is moulded in and the veining is left hollow. In the center of the flower on the old, dots (anther) cluster entirely to one side and are rather distinct. Nothing like that occurs in the new design.

As for the cookie jars, at cursory glance the base of the cookie jar has a very indistinct design. It will feel smooth to the touch because it's so faint. In the old cookie jars, there's a distinct pattern which feels like raised embossing to the touch. Next, turn the bottom upside down. The new bottom is perfectly smooth. The old bottom contains a 1¾" mould circle rim that is raised enough to catch your fingernail in it. There are other distinctions as well; but that is the quickest way to tell old from new.

On the Mayfair cookie jar lid, the new design (parallel to the straight side of the lid) at the edge curves gracefully toward the center "V" shape (rather like bird wings in flight); in the old, that edge is a flat straight line going into the "V" (like airplane wings sticking straight out from the side of the plane as you face it head on).

The green color of the cookie jar, as you can see from the picture, is not the pretty, yellow/green color of true green Mayfair. It also doesn't "glow" under black light as the old green does.

So, you see, none of these reproductions give us any trouble; they're all easily spotted by those of us now "in the know"!

NEW "MISS AMERICA"

Colors: Crystal, green, pink, ice blue, red amberina and cobalt blue.

The new butter dish in "Miss America" design is probably the best of the newer products; yet there are three distinct differences to be found between the original butter top and the newly made one. Since the value of the butter dish lies in the top, it seems more profitable to examine it. **There is a new importer who is making reproductions of the reproductions.** Unfortunately, these newer models vary greatly from one batch to the next. The only noticeable thing I have seen on these butters is how the top knob sticks up away from the butter caused by a longer than usual stem on the knob. All the other characteristics still hold true, but the paragraph in bold below is the best way to tell old from new!

In the new butter dishes pictured, notice that the panels reaching the edge of the butter bottom tend to have a pronounced curving, skirt-like edge. In the original dish, there is much less curving at the edge of these panels.

Second, pick up the top of the new dish and feel up inside it. If the butter top knob is filled with glass so that it is convex (curved outward), the dish is new; the old inside knob area is concave (curved inward).

Finally, from the underside, look through the top toward the knob. In the original butter dish you would see a perfectly formed multi-sided star; in the newer version, you see distorted rays with no visible points.

Shakers have been made in green, pink, cobalt blue and crystal. The latest batch of **shakers are becoming more difficult to distinguish from the old!** The new distributor's copies are creating havoc with new collectors and dealers alike. The measurements given below for shakers **do not all** hold true for the latest reproductions. It is impossible to know which generation of shaker reproductions that you will find, so you have to be careful on these! Know your dealer and **if the price is too good to be true,** there is likely a good reason! **It's NEW!**

The shakers will have new tops; but since some old shakers have been given new tops, that isn't conclusive at all. Unscrew the lid. Old shakers have a very neatly formed ridge of glass on which to screw the lid. It overlaps a little and has neatly rounded-off ends. Old shakers stand 3⅜" tall without the lid. **Most new** ones stand 3¼" tall. Old shakers have almost a forefinger's depth inside (female finger) or a fraction shy of 2½". **Most new** shakers have an inside depth of 2", about the second digit bend of a female's finger. (I'm doing finger depths since most of you will have those with you at the flea market, rather than a tape measure.) In men, the old shaker's depth covers my knuckle; the new shakers leaves my knuckle exposed. Most new shakers simply have more glass on the inside of the shaker—something you can spot from twelve feet away! The hobs are more rounded on the newer shaker, particularly near the stem and seams; in the old shaker these areas remained pointedly sharp!

New Miss America tumblers have ½" of glass in the bottom, have a smooth edge on the bottom of the glass with no mould rim and show only two distinct mould marks on the sides of the glass. Old tumblers have only ¼" of glass in the bottom, have a distinct mould line rimming the bottom of the tumbler and have four distinct mould marks up the sides of the tumbler. The new green tumbler doesn't "glow" under black light as did the old.

New Miss America pitchers (without ice lip only) are all perfectly smooth rimmed at the top edge above the handle. All old pitchers that I have seen have a "hump" in the top rim of the glass above the handle area, rather like a camel's hump. The very bottom diamonds next to the foot in the new pitchers "squash" into elongated diamonds. In the old pitchers, these get noticeably smaller, but they retain their diamond shape.

REPRODUCTIONS   (Continued)

NEW SANDWICH (Indiana) INDIANA GLASS COMPANY
Tiara Exclusive Line, 1969 . . .

Colors: Amber, blue, red, crystal and green.

    The smoky blue (made in 1976) and amber shown here are representative of Tiara's line of Sandwich which is presently available in crystal, amber and green. The green has been made in full sets. The original green was a yellow-green that glows under a black light. I have been told the new does not, but have not tested it myself!

    The bad news is that the crystal has been made now and there are only minute differences in this new and the old. I will list the pieces made in crystal and you can make yourself aware of these re-issues if you collect the crystal Sandwich.

Ash Tray Set
Basket, Handles, 10½"
Bowl, 4" Berry
Bowl, 8"
Butter Dish & Cover
Candlesticks, 8½"
Cup, 9 oz.
Cup (Fits Indent in 6 oz. Oval Sandwich Plate)
Decanter & Stopper, 10"
Goblet, 5¼", 8 oz.

Pitcher, 8" Tall, 68 oz. Fluted Rim
Plate, 10" Dinner
Plate, 8" Salad
Plate, 8½" x 6¾" Oval Sandwich
Sandwich Tray, Handled
Saucer, 6"
Sherbet
Tray, 10" (Underliner for Wine Decanter & Goblets)
Tumbler, 6½" High, 12 oz.

NEW "SHARON" Privately Produced 1976 . . .

Colors: Blue, dark green, light green, pink and burnt umber.

    A blue Sharon butter turned up in 1976 and turned my phone line to a liquid fire! The color is Mayfair blue—a fluke and dead giveaway as far as real Sharon is concerned.

    When found in similar colors to the old, pink and green, you can immediately tell that the new version has more glass in the top where it changes from pattern to clear glass, a thick, defined ring of glass as opposed to a thin, barely defined ring of glass in the old. The knob of the new dish tends to stick up more. In the old butter dish there's barely room to fit your finger to grasp the knob. The new butter dish has a sharply defined ridge of glass in the bottom around which the top sits. The old butter has such a slight rim that the top easily scoots off the bottom.

    In 1977 a "cheese dish" appeared having the same top as the butter and having all the flaws inherent in that top which were discussed in detail above. However, the bottom of this dish was all wrong. It's about half way between a flat plate and a butter dish bottom, bowl shaped; and it is over thick, giving it an awkward appearance. The real cheese bottom was a salad plate with a rim for holding the top. These "round bottom cheese dishes" are but a parody of the old and are easily spotted. We removed the top from one in the picture so you could see its heaviness and its bowl shape.

NEW "SHARON" (Continued)

Some of the latest reproductions in Sharon are a too-light pink creamer and sugar with lid. They are pictured with the "Made in Taiwan" label. These sell for around $15.00 for the pair and are also easy to spot as reproductions. I'll just mention the most obvious differences. Turn the creamer so you are looking directly at the spout. In the old creamer the mould line runs dead center of that spout; in the new, the mould line runs decidedly to the left of center spout.

On the sugar, the leaves and roses are "off" but not enough to DESCRIBE it to new collectors. Therefore, look at the center design, both sides, at the stars located at the very bottom of the motif. A thin leaf stem should run directly from that center star upward on BOTH sides. In this new sugar, the stem only runs from one; it stops way short of the star on one side; OR look inside the sugar bowl at where the handle attaches to the bottom of the bowl; in the new bowl, this attachment looks like a perfect circle; in the old, its an upside down "v" shaped tear drop.

As for the sugar lid, the knob of the new lid is perfectly smooth as you grasp its edges. The old knob has a mould seam running mid circumference. You could tell these two lids apart blind folded!

While there is a hair's difference between the height, mouth opening diameter, and inside depth of the old Sharon shakers and those newly produced, I won't attempt to upset you with those sixteenth and thirty seconds of a degree of difference. Suffice it to say that in physical shape, they are very close. However, as concerns design, they're miles apart.

The old shakers have true appearing roses. The flowers really LOOK like roses. On the new shakers, they look like poorly drawn circles with wobbly concentric rings. The leaves are not as clearly defined on the new shakers as the old. However, forgetting all that, in the old shakers, the first design you see below the lid is a ROSE BUD. It's angled like a rocket shooting off into outer space with three leaves at the base of the bud (where the rocket fuel would burn out). In the new shakers, this "bud" has become four paddles of a windmill. It's the difference between this 🌾 and this 🦋 .

Candy dishes have been made in pink and green. These candy jars are among the easiest items to discern old from new. Pick up the lid and look from the bottom side. On the old there is a 2" circle knob ring; on the new the ring is only ½". This shows from the top also but it is difficult to measure with the knob in the center. There are other major differences but this one will not be mould corrected easily. The bottoms are also simple to distinguish. The base diameter of the old is 3¼" and the new only 3". Quality of the new is rough, poorly shaped and moulded on the example I have, but I do not know if that is true of all reproductions of the candy. I sure hope so!

221

A Publication I recommend:

DEPRESSION GLASS DAZE

THE ORIGINAL NATIONAL DEPRESSION GLASS NEWSPAPER

Depression Glass Daze, the Original, National monthly newpaper dedicated to the buying, selling and collecting of colored glassware of the 20's and 30's. We average 60 pages each month, filled with feature articles by top-notch columnists, readers' "finds", club happenings, show news, a china corner, a current listing of new glass issues to beware of and a multitude of ads! You can find it in the **DAZE**! Keep up with what's happening in the dee gee world with a subscription to the **DAZE**. Buy, sell or trade from the convenience of your easy chair.

Name_____ Street_____

City_____ State_____ Zip_____

☐ 1 Year - $15.00   ☐ Check Enclosed   ☐ Please bill me

☐ Mastercard   ☐ Visa   (Foreign subscribers - Please add $1.00 per year)

Card No._____ Exp. Date_____

Signature _____

Order to D.G.D., Box 57GF, Otisville, MI 48463-0008 - Please allow 30 days

Books By Gene Florence

Kitchen Glassware of the Depression Years, 4th Edition $19.95

Pocket Guide to Depression Glass $9.95

Collector's Encyclopedia of Occupied Japan I $14.95

Collector's Encyclopedia of Occupied Japan II $14.95

Collector's Encyclopedia of Occupied Japan III $19.95

Elegant Glassware of the Depression Era $19.95

Very Rare Glassware of the Depression Years $24.95

The Standard Baseball Card Price Guide, 2nd Edition $9.95

Add $2.00 postage for the first book,
45¢ for each additional book.

Copies of these books may be ordered from:

Gene Florence
P.O. Box 22186
Lexington, KY 40522

or

Collector Books
P.O. Box 3009
Paducah, KY 42002-3009

Schroeder's Antiques Price Guide

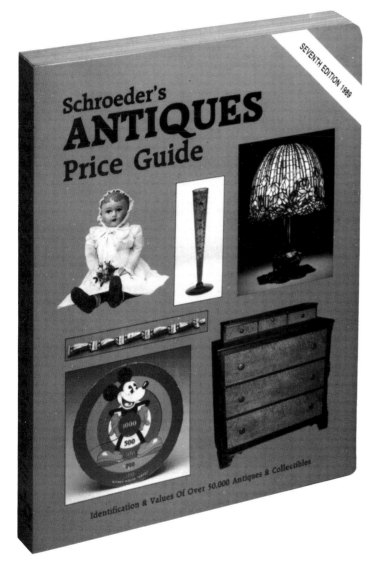

Schroeder's Antiques Price Guide has climbed its way to the top in a field already supplied with several well-established publications! The word is out, *Schroeder's Price Guide* is the best buy at any price. Over 500 categories are covered, with more than 50,000 listings. But it's not volume alone that makes Schroeder's the unique guide it is recognized to be. From ABC Plates to Zsolnay, if it merits the interest of today's collector, you'll find it in Schroeder's. Each subject is represented with histories and background information. In addition, hundreds of sharp original photos are used each year to illustrate not only the rare and the unusual, but the everyday "fun-type" collectibles as well -- not postage stamp pictures, but large close-up shots that show important details clearly.

Each edition is completely re-typeset from all new sources. We have not and will not simply change prices in each new edition. All new copy and all new illustrations make Schroeder's THE price guide on antiques and collectibles.

The writing and researching team behind this giant is proportionately large. It is backed by a staff of more than seventy of Collector Books' finest authors, as well as a board of advisors made up of well-known antique authorities and the country's top dealers, all specialists in their fields. Accuracy is their primary aim. Prices are gathered over the entire year previous to publication, from ads and personal contacts. Then each category is thoroughly checked to spot inconsistencies, listings that may not be entirely reflective of actual market dealings, and lines too vague to be of merit.

Only the best of the lot remains for publication. You'll find *Schroeder's Antiques Price Guide* the one to buy for factual information and quality.

No dealer, collector or investor can afford not to own this book. It is available from your favorite bookseller or antiques dealer at the low price of $12.95. If you are unable to find this price guide in your area, it's available from Collector Books, P. O. Box 3009, Paducah, KY 42001 at $12.95 plus $2.00 for postage and handling.

8½ x 11, 608 Pages $12.95

COLLECTOR BOOKS
A Division of Schroeder Publishing Co., Inc.